About Island Press

Since 1984, the nonprofit organization Island Press has been stimulating, shaping, and communicating ideas that are essential for solving environmental problems worldwide. With more than 1,000 titles in print and some 30 new releases each year, we are the nation's leading publisher on environmental issues. We identify innovative thinkers and emerging trends in the environmental field. We work with world-renowned experts and authors to develop cross-disciplinary solutions to environmental challenges.

Island Press designs and executes educational campaigns in conjunction with our authors to communicate their critical messages in print, in person, and online using the latest technologies, innovative programs, and the media. Our goal is to reach targeted audiences—scientists, policymakers, environmental advocates, urban planners, the media, and concerned citizens—with information that can be used to create the framework for long-term ecological health and human well-being.

Island Press gratefully acknowledges major support of our work by The Agua Fund, The Andrew W. Mellon Foundation, The Bobolink Foundation, The Curtis and Edith Munson Foundation, Forrest C. and Frances H. Lattner Foundation, The JPB Foundation, The Kresge Foundation, The Oram Foundation, Inc., The Overbrook Foundation, The S.D. Bechtel, Jr. Foundation, The Summit Charitable Foundation, Inc., and many other generous supporters.

The opinions expressed in this book are those of the author(s) and do not necessarily reflect the views of our supporters.

BEYOND MOBILITY

BEYOND MOBILITY

Planning Cities for People and Places

Robert Cervero, Erick Guerra, and Stefan Al

Washington | Covelo | London

Island Press is a trademark of The Center for Resource Economics.

Keywords: Autonomous vehicles, climate change, driverless cars, edge city, environmental mitigation, the global south, just city, lifestyle preferences, placemaking, public health, public transit, road contraction, shared mobility, social capital, suburban retrofits, sustainable city, transit-oriented development (TOD), urban amenities, urban economics, urban recalibration, walkability

Library of Congress Control Number: 2017940670

All Island Press books are printed on environmentally responsible materials.

Manufactured in the United States of America
10 9 8 7 6 5 4 3 2 1

CONTENTS

PREFACE

That changes are needed in the planning and design of cities—for the sake of the planet, social equality, and a host of other reasons—is understood and accepted by most urban planners and designers. As planner–academics who have researched and worked in the urban transportation field to varying degrees, we maintain as the core premise of this book that improving mobility (i.e., the efficiency of motorized travel) has overly dominated past planning practices. This notion is not new. However, in our view, going beyond the rhetoric of postmobility planning and laying out a systematic framework for reordering priorities and meaningfully reforming policies and practices has received less attention than deserved.

Many commentaries on urban reforms are framed from the perspective of spatial planning, that is changing the design, layouts, and geographic arrangements of cities and their surroundings. Less is said about the pace of structural change. Shifting from sprawl to more compact development is often treated in binary terms, going from one form of urbanism to an entirely different one. Instead, we advance the idea of urban recalibration, the process of changing the accumulated rules, standards, regulations, and codes that govern the planning and design of our cityscapes and tend to directly or indirectly promote mobility, whether for cars, buses, or fire trucks, at the expense of other considerations. *Beyond Mobility* is about recalibrating how we plan, design, and build cities in ways that shift the focus from motorized movement to the needs and aspirations of people and the places they want to go.

Some of the ideas for this work germinated when the three of us discussed and debated these topics during a roughly 4-year period when our coordinates aligned at the University of California at Berkeley in the late 2000s and early 2010s. With Berkeley once the academic home of such urban planning luminaries as Donald Appleyard, Allan Jacobs, and Peter Hall, it's perhaps no surprise that debating ways of reining in the excesses of car-oriented living occupied a good amount of time among folks in the transportation and urban design fields, us included. Contrary to what some might think or assume upon reading this book's title, we're not out to remove cars from city streets. Like most people living in America, we use and drive cars and plan to continue doing so, whether autonomous or steered by humans. However, we hope that the ideas put forward in this book will contribute to nudging us and others in the direction of walking, biking, and using buses and trains for a larger share of our personal travel-pies in years to come. If this helps with cleansing the air, building social capital, and shedding a few pounds, all the better.

Although this book was a collaborative undertaking, as in any work involving three busy academics, there was necessarily a division of labor. This division largely aligned with our respective interests, past and present. Robert Cervero was the principal author of chapters 1, 3, 4, 6, 7, 8, and 11 and contributed to other chapters as well, particularly chapters 5 and 9. Erick Guerra prepared most of chapters 9 and 10 and also contributed to chapters 1 and 11 and the three chapters in part one of the book. Stefan Al authored chapters 2 and 5 and helped with other aspects of the book, including the introduction.

Although we accept full responsibility for what is presented in this volume, we would be remiss if we didn't acknowledge a number of people who contributed to this work. We thank Heather Boyer of Island Press for her support throughout the project and due diligence in seeing the manuscript through to completion. Elizabeth Theocharides, a graduate student in city planning and transportation engineering at Berkeley, was of tremendous help with many parts of this book, including background literature reviews, statistical analyses, preparation of maps and figures, and help with organizing artwork. Meiqing Li, a master's planning student at the University of Pennsylvania, helped with preparing several maps and the background research on transit-oriented development in China. Elisabeth Machielse, Sean McKay, and Thomas Orgren, architecture and city planning students at the University of Pennsylvania, contributed with background research and literature reviews for chapters 2 and 5. Brenna Raffe of Island Press also deserves our thanks for her help with organizing some of this book's images and manuscript preparation. We owe a debt of gratitude to many others who at various stages helped us with some part of this book, including Reena Tiwari, Ian Carleton, Felipe Targa, John Renne, Peter Calthorpe, Megan Gibb, Bernie Suchicital, Bert Gregory, Chang-Deok Kang, Steve Yui, Charles Kooshian, Larry Orman, Xavier Iglesias, Lu Nadal, Tom Radak, Gilles Duranton, Salvador Herrera, Paavo Monkkonen, Camilo Caudillo, Jorge Montejano, and John Taylor, among others. And outside our professional lives, we thank those who provided a different kind of support during this undertaking, emotionally and in other ways, notably Sophia, Chris, and Kristen Cervero, Alexandria Wyllie, Amaliris Gonzalez, the Guerra family, Rebecca Jin, Vera Al, and Janneke van Kuijzen.

Putting together a case-focused book that examines experiences in many corners of the world would not have been possible without funding support. Although there was no one main sponsor of the work, we did receive much-appreciated funding from multiple sources. The Friesen endowment provided research support to Robert Cervero during a 6-year period when he was the Carmel P. Friesen Chair in Urban Studies at Berkeley. Some of the work reported in this book would not have been possible without the generous support of Candy and Howard Friesen. Research presented in this book was also made possible through funding support from the University of California Transportation Center, the Technologies for Safe and Efficient Transportation University Transportation Center, the Volvo Research and Education Foundation, the World Bank, UN Habitat, the Transit Cooperative Research Program of the U.S. Department of Transportation, Hong Kong's MTR Corporation, the Organisation for Economic Co-operation and Development, the Brookings Institution, the University of Pennsylvania's University Research Foundation, the Lincoln Institute of Land Policy, and the city of Los Angeles.

A closing comment on this book's narrative arc is in order. Although we begin on a somewhat pessimistic note—citing the tons of excess carbon emitted, the millions of lives lost annually to collisions and local pollution, and the public dollars wasted as a result of a mobility-focused approach to planning and designing cities—we conclude on an optimistic one. The waste and harm of our current system, coupled with the growing body of examples and evidence of alternative planning approaches, are leading to gradual but visible reforms in the rules, regulations, and investments that shape cities. We are hopeful that new technologies and shifting demographic and social trends will reinforce and strengthen the momentum to move *Beyond Mobility* and create the kinds of great, diverse, and economically productive places where we, our friends, and family aspire to live, work, learn, and play.

1

Urban Recalibration

Beyond Mobility is about reordering priorities. In the planning and design of cities, far more attention must go toward serving the needs and aspirations of people and the creation of great places as opposed to expediting movement. Historically it has been the opposite. In the United States and increasingly elsewhere, investments in motorways and underground rail systems have been first and foremost about moving people between point A and point B as quickly and safely as possible. On the surface, of course, this is desirable. However, the cumulative consequences of this nearly singular focus on expeditious movement have revealed themselves with passage of time, measured in smoggy air basins, sprawling suburbs, and—despite hundreds of billions of dollars in investments—a failure to stem traffic congestion, to name a few. An urban recalibration is in order, we argue, one that follows a more people- and place-focused approach to city building.

Recalibration is a term found in handbooks for precision instruments and flight manuals. It has resonance in city planning circles as well. The roads, subdivisions, and utility corridors that give shape to cities were calibrated from engineering and design manuals with noble aims, such as minimizing accident risks and accommodating the turning radii of eight-wheel fire trucks, but with little attention to unintended consequences. Mobility and public safety are important, but so are clean air and walkable streets. Moreover, traffic engineers have long gauged performance in terms of throughputs of motorized vehicles, not people. The consequence: a vicious cycle of road expansions to accommodate car traffic rather than channeling more resources into modes that are efficient users of road space, such as public transit and cycling. Over the twentieth century, street widths and parking standards continually increased, taking up the majority of public space to accommodate cars.[1] In some cities, parking lots alone account for more than a third of the metropolitan footprint.[2] The approaches, metrics, and standards used to design cities, we believe, are in serious need of recalibration—not necessarily a seismic shift but rather a rebalancing of priorities that gives at least as much urban planning and community design attention to serving people and places as to mobility. *Beyond Mobility* charts a pathway for doing so.

The call for urban recalibration and reframing the role of mobility in cities finds its roots in the derived nature of most travel. People drive cars and take trains to go places. It is the makeup and quality of these places and the social and economic interactions they spawn that we value most, more so than the physical act of getting there. As Amory Lovins has said of the energy sector, people don't care about kilowatts; they care about hot showers, cold beer, and lit rooms. Similarly, people travel to reach jobs, friends, sports arenas, and the like. They seek social and economic interaction, not movement. To the degree that distance is a barrier to interaction, time spent moving over space is time that can often be better spent doing other things (socializing with friends, reading a magazine at the local café, or even logging in more hours—and presumably making more money— at the workplace). Transportation, then, is a means to an end, a vehicle for achieving something else. It is mostly secondary to a larger purpose.

An apt analogy on getting the priorities right is the design of a house. Think of "place" as the house and "transportation" as its utilities. In conceptualizing and planning a house, prospective homeowners dwell on what matters most to them: the layout, floor-plan, architectural styles, kitchen designs, views, and so on. They don't initially focus on the utilities of a house—the plumbing, wiring, conduits, and pipes—and then design the house around them. The same should hold when scaling up to a neighborhood or city. Recalibrating the planning and design of cities, then, is about lifting the priority given to place vis-à-vis mobility.

In emphasizing mobility, twentieth-century transportation infrastructure has often had harmful effects on people and places. Dangerous and difficult-to-cross intersections and multilane roads have hindered people's ability to move freely and children's opportunities to play. Although transportation investments have connected people on a regional level, they have also uprooted communities and lowered home values, epitomized by highways cutting through American neighborhoods in the 1950s and 1960s. In 1953, local residents fiercely protested Robert Moses's planned six-lane Cross Bronx Expressway, calling it the "Heartbreak Highway," but to no avail. Moses's plan was approved and built quickly, bulldozing homes in densely populated neighborhoods in the Bronx, lowering property values, and severing neighborhoods. The Cross Bronx Expressway was but one of the many destructive urban highways built over the ensuing two decades, often with the federal government footing 90 percent of the bill.

Giving stronger priority to place is another way of saying cities should be highly accessible. Accessibility is about the ease of reaching places where people want to go. Cities
can become more accessible by increasing mobility (the speed of getting between point A
and B), proximity (bringing point A and B closer together), or some combination thereof.
Focusing on accessibility and, relatedly, places leads to an entirely different framework for
planning and designing cities and their transportation infrastructure. Rather than laying
more and more asphalt to connect people with places, activities (e.g., homes, businesses,
and shops) might instead be sited closer to each other. A vast body of research shows that
the resulting mixed land use patterns can shorten distances and invite more leisurely
paced, pollution-free travel. It's been said that planning for the automobile city focuses
on saving time. Planning for the accessible city focuses on time well spent.

As discussed in this book's second chapter, walkable, mixed-use neighborhoods also
build social capital and instill a sense of safety through natural surveillance. For more and
more urban dwellers, such neighborhood attributes are every bit as, if not more, important than travel speeds. A principal aim of *Beyond Mobility*, then, is to provide a framework
for designing cities and siting activities so that urban places become more accessible and,
as a result, allow more interaction of all types. Such transformative places include regen-
erated former industrial sites (chapter 5), business parks converted to mixed-use activity
centers (chapter 6), walkable neighborhoods huddled around transit stops (chapter 7),
and former traffic arteries that now accommodate pedestrians, cyclists, and an active
street life (chapter 8).

The book's cover portrays the kinds of physical transformations that are possible by
redesigning cityscapes and moving beyond mobility. The cover photo shows an electric tram in Rio de Janeiro's Porto Maravilha area, sharing a street with pedestrians and
flanked by a bright mural that adds color and art to what was once a blank and monotonous warehouse wall. Porto Maravilha is a product of the city's decision to tear down an
imposing viaduct that separated downtown Rio from its waterfront, replaced by a tramway, pedestrian plaza, streetscape improvements, and museum, all in time for the 2016
Summer Olympics. Before-and-after images depict the transformation of this valuable yet
long-neglected coastal real estate, from a conduit for swiftly moving trucks and cars to
a people-oriented place served by a tram, with a strong accent on aesthetics, amenities,
and place-making (figure 1-1). Income from increases in permissible commercial densities
and land price appreciations helped finance the project, although it, like other high-ticket
Olympic-driven public expenditures in a city with high poverty rates, sparked massive
public protests for being pro-rich and anti-poor. Recalibrating cities to focus more on
people and places must weigh social consequences. Actions must be socially inclusive,
a significant challenge in light of the price increases that typically result from creating

Figure 1-1. Urban recalibration in Rio de Janeiro: Porto Maravilha project. *(top)* A former elevated freeway hugging Rio's waterfront was replaced by *(bottom)* a tramway, pedestrian plaza, and contemporary museum. (Photos by Companhia de Desenvolvimento Urbano da Região do Porto do Rio de Janeiro [Cdurp].)

higher-quality urban spaces. Strategies for overcoming such challenges are discussed in this book's concluding chapter.

Another example of urban recalibration is London's congestion pricing scheme, in this case reflecting a shift in policy (i.e., software) more than, as in the case of Rio, a physical (i.e., hardware) transformation. London introduced congestion charges in early 2003, building on Singapore's success with charging motorist fees for entering a cordoned central-city area in peak periods. The first 5 years of congestion charging were matched by, as proponents promised, faster driving speeds for those willing to pay tolls. By late 2008, however, speeds began to fall to their precongestion pricing levels. This creep back was due in part to the taking of some 20 percent of central London's road space for buses, pedestrians, and cyclists. In her study of London's charging scheme, Andrea Broaddus notes, "Traffic engineers had whittled away at the road capacity released by congestion charging until it amounted to a significant 'capacity grab' of road space and travel time savings away from drivers and toward bus riders, pedestrians, and cyclists."[3] Yet the populace continued to accept congestion charges. Londoners conceded private car mobility in return for what many perceived to be a better living environment: cleaner air, fewer accidents, more space for pedestrians, and a more bike-friendly urban milieu. Central London's reordering of priorities is evident even at the microscopic intersection level. Besides space, another constrained resource in the urban transportation sector, traffic signal times, was reallocated to nonmotorists. "Reduced waiting time for pedestrians," Broaddus writes, "meant longer waiting times for motorized traffic, in effect a redistribution of time away from motorized traffic toward pedestrians."[4] In London's case, the core of the city was recalibrated, reflected by reassignment of road space and reallotments of signal timings, to focus more on people and places and less on private vehicle movements.

Challenges to Creating Sustainable and Just Cities

Cities are the social, cultural, and economic hubs of human activity—"our greatest achievement" in the words of Ed Glaeser in the *Triumph of the City*.[5] They have been fundamental to nearly all human advances in historical memory, from the birth of modern philosophy in Athens and the Renaissance in Florence to the automotive industry in Detroit and the digital revolution in Silicon Valley.[6] Thus cities create wealth. Today, the world's 600 largest cities, representing a fifth of the world's population, generate 60 percent of global gross domestic product (GDP).[7] Cities are also home to the majority of the world's population and ground zero of global population growth. The United Nations estimates that the planet will add another 1.5 billion urban residents to cities over the next 20 years.[8] That is the equivalent to adding eight megacities (i.e., eight Jakartas, Lagoses, or Rio de Janeiros) every year over the next two decades, a daunting challenge to say the least. How these cities grow will be fundamental to human health, wealth, and happiness.

If well designed, cities are also the greenest places on Earth. Manhattanites consume carbon at the level that the rest of the United States did in the 1920s.[9] Many walk or take transit to get about Manhattan and its surroundings, consuming one-tenth the petroleum of the typical American. However, not all cities are well designed, and indeed few are as transit and pedestrian friendly as New York. Consequently, the world's cities have oversized, disproportionate environmental footprints. With more than 50 percent of the world's population, cities account for 60 to 80 percent of the world's energy consumption and generate as much as 70 percent of the human-induced greenhouse gas emissions, primarily through the consumption of fossil fuels for energy supply and transportation.[10] Cities are also highly vulnerable to the ill effects of climate change, especially coastal cities of the Global South that risk inundation from rising sea levels.

Cities unfortunately also suffer from extreme poverty and deprivation. Some 900 million people—a third of the world's urban population—today live in slums.[11] In sub-Saharan Africa, slum dwellers make up nearly three-quarters of the urban population.[12] The World Bank estimated that, in 2002, three-quarters of a billion city dwellers lived on less than US$2 per day worldwide, a number that has surely grown.[13] Moreover, today some 250 million urban dwellers have no electricity.[14] And every year, more than 800,000 deaths occur worldwide due to poor sanitation, with the share in cities rising as urban growth outpaces the corresponding expansion of sewage and piped water facilities.[15] All this underscores the importance of ensuring that the rewards from recalibrating the planning and design of cities do not accrue just to well-off classes. To gain legitimacy, not to mention political traction and social acceptance, actions must be pro-poor, at some level helping to alleviate urban poverty and improve living conditions.

It is difficult to overstate the importance of accessibility in making urban living more affordable and socially just. Across the globe, urban residents typically spend more on housing and transportation than all other goods combined.[16] Poor access drains the few resources the poor have at their disposal. In Mexico City, the poorest fifth of households spend about a quarter of their income on public transit.[17] Those on the periphery face daunting commutes that last an average of 1 hour and 20 minutes in each direction. In the United States, where transit supply is sparse in most neighborhoods, limited accessibility prevents many low-income people from finding work, reaching medical services, or shopping at well-stocked supermarkets.

From a fiscal perspective, governments pour substantial resources into transportation investments and foot a big portion of the bill for mobility-oriented planning practices, particularly sprawl and the public health impacts of pollution and traffic collisions. In the United States, at the close of the twentieth century, the cost of providing infrastructure and services in sprawling, car-oriented developments—excluding external social costs—was nearly $30,000 more per housing unit than in compact developments.[18] Added to this are the less visible yet prevalent costs of auto-oriented living, including physical inactivity, traffic fatalities, and deteriorating air quality, costs that at some level the public sector has to spend resources to try to offset.[19]

Despite the importance of cities and their inhabitants, too often the form, shape, and even culture of cities have become the unintended consequence of policies and investments to improve mobility. Truly transportation has become the tail that wags the dog. Putting people and place back at the center of how and why we invest in urban transportation is essential to improving humanity's overall social, environmental, and economic well-being in the twenty-first century.

The Case for Moving Beyond Mobility

As outline above, the costs of designing cities around movement are becoming ever more apparent. So too are the opportunities to shift our dominant transportation paradigm to focus investments on creating vibrant and livable cities with neighborhoods that cater to their residents, not just their residents' movement. In making this case, we draw on experiences and statistics from a range of cities and countries in Europe, North America, Asia, and to a lesser extent Africa throughout the book. Some of the figures—though well known in the fields of public health and transportation planning—are shocking. Every year our current transportation paradigm generates more than 1.25 million fatalities directly through traffic collisions and contributes to billions of lost years of life from local pollution. Worldwide, 3.2 million people died prematurely in 2010 because of air pollution, four times as many as a decade earlier.[20]

The reordering of transportation planning priorities is but part of the motivation behind *Beyond Mobility*. A stronger focus on accessibility and place, we believe, creates better communities, environments, and economies.[21] This is the focus of Part 1.

What do we mean by better communities, environments, and economies? Better communities are safe, walkable, healthy places that promote sustainable and equitable access to a wealth of destinations by multiple modes and strengthen interpersonal connections and community interactions. This stands in stark contrast with twentieth-century modernism's emphasis on segregated land uses, fast movement, and disconnected tower blocks—particularly as envisioned by architect Le Corbusier. Instead, we argue for the kinds of smaller, human-scaled blocks, shared spaces, and complete streets promoted by acclaimed scholars and practitioners such as Donald Appleyard, Jane Jacobs, William Whyte, and Lewis Mumford. As Mumford put it so eloquently in *The Highway and the City*, "The right to have access to every building in the city by private motorcar in an age when everyone possesses such a vehicle is actually the right to destroy the city."[22] Across the globe, the rise and popularity of reclaiming public space from private vehicles, calming traffic, and creating great, walkable neighborhoods are all manifestations of this desire to create better, more people-oriented communities.

Although the concept of better communities is somewhat normative and elusive, better environments are clear, measurable, and directly attributable to the shape of cities and the design of transportation networks. Car-dependent cities and countries consume substantially more land, fossil fuels, and natural habitat than more compact and multimodal places. They also produce substantially more local and global pollution. As climate change harms and threatens the planet and its inhabitants, urban environments designed around oversized single-occupant vehicles powered by fossil fuels look increasingly out of touch. Furthermore, a growing body of evidence suggests that moving away from car dependency can have important environmental and public health benefits—not just from lower pollution but also from increasing walking, biking, and other physical activity. Examples around the world demonstrate that income and auto-mobility need not move hand in hand. Wealthy cities such as Zurich, Copenhagen, Tokyo, and Amsterdam rely on a mix of cycling paths, tramways, underground railways, buses, and pedestrian paths that are well integrated and designed into the urban fabric. Increasingly, the world's wealthiest and most economically productive cities are leaders in redesigning transportation infrastructure to promote safer, healthier, and more pleasant neighborhoods.

In fact, moving beyond mobility can improve economic performance—not just through reduced collisions, fatalities, pollution, and infrastructure expenditures but also by bringing people closer together and creating the types of places that are most attractive to the most productive and mobile workers. The production benefits of locating people and firms in close proximity are well established and at the heart of what make cities the drivers of global economic growth. Cities are not just important places of production but increasingly compete with each other as important spaces of consumption.[23] Walkable, transit-accessible neighborhoods with well-designed urban environments are desirable and fetch a price premium. Real estate companies have started to report metrics on walkability alongside more traditional information such as size, number of bedrooms, school district, and proximity to major roads and transit lines. At the metropolitan scale, lower vehicle travel per capita is often associated with higher GDP per capita.[24] Nevertheless, car ownership and car use—not to mention road-based freight delivery—are important components of urban life. The goal of *Beyond Mobility* is not to wage a war on the car but to put it in its proper place as one of many tools to improve cities for their residents.

Contexts for Urban Recalibration

Urban recalibration—elevating the importance of people and places vis-à-vis mobility in the planning and design of cities—occurs at a variety of scales and contexts (box 1-1). Sometimes with great success. Other times with substantial challenges. Across the globe, communities are working to create a seamless fit between transit and surrounding land use, retrofit car-oriented suburban environments, reclaim surplus or dangerous roadway for other uses, and make use of neglected urban spaces such as abandoned railways in urban centers.

Urban recalibration occurs in core cities through the reuse and revitalization of underused land, for instance in abandoned industrial parks and freight corridors. The High

Box 1-1

Urban Recalibration at Multiple Scales

Urban recalibration can occur at multiple geographic scales: microdesigns (e.g., parklets), corridors (e.g., road dieting), and city-regions (e.g., urban growth boundary that halts the spread of auto-oriented sprawl and preserves ag-land).

Box Figure 1-1. *(top left)* Parklet in Lafayette, California (conversion of a parking space to a micropark along the city's main boulevard, Mount Diablo Boulevard); *(top right)* Road diet (taking of motor lane and reassignment to cyclists as a dedicated cycle track in Montreal); *(bottom)* Urban growth boundary in Portland, Oregon, delimiting what's urban and what's rural. (Photos by *[top left]* Robert Cervero; *[top right]* Dan Malouff, BeyondDC.com; *[bottom]* Google Earth.)

Line in New York City is emblematic of this type of transformation. Once a mere conduit to move goods around, today it is a thriving park, an engine for densification and revitalization of the entire Chelsea district, and one of the city's most popular destinations for tourism and recreation. London's Docklands and Rotterdam's Kop van Zuid are examples of how cities can reuse declining industrial ports to spark economic growth and reconnect cities to their waterfronts. In each of these and other cases presented throughout the book, cities have taken advantage of land that became redundant or underused because of shifts in transportation technology and the urban economy. New technologies, such as self-driving cars and buses, will probably provide substantial new opportunities for this type of urban revitalization.

Transit-oriented development (TOD)—the close coupling of public transport investments and urban development—is one of the most celebrated forms of urban development. By concentrating jobs and residences around well-designed and walkable transit stations, successful TODs provide livable and accessible communities at far lower social, economic, and environmental costs than sprawling car-oriented developments. The premium that residents and businesses will pay to be in high-quality TODs testifies to their popularity with the general public as well as socially or environmentally minded planners and bureaucrats. Although the process of developing new housing developments and offices around transit stations is as old as transit, the contemporary focus on creating more sustainable built environments around transit is more recent. From the San Francisco Bay to the Pearl River Delta, new developments around high-quality transit are helping cities reshape urban growth and expand economically while minimizing the harm to the environment and human health. However, for all its promise TOD cannot by itself overcome weak real estate markets or thrive when poorly planned or designed. Nor can limited or low-quality transit service provide much of an incentive for reducing car use, particularly when surrounded by seas of parking. For each successful TOD case study, there is another that failed to materialize or meet its full potential. We explore a range of cases to identify not only where TOD has been successful or fallen short but where it has met specific objectives such as financially supporting the transit system, providing opportunities and residences for children, or sparking the adaptive reuse of older buildings.

Suburban transformations—particularly in places with limited or no transit service—offer one of the greatest challenges and opportunities for urban recalibration. In the United States, many urban areas have grown entirely around the automobile and lack the density or form that is suitable for sustainable modes of transportation. Ongoing efforts to add housing and create a sense of place around suburban office parks and struggling shopping centers have produced positive local results but have not succeeded in changing the overall suburban landscape or substantially reducing car dependency. Suburban retrofits nevertheless provide a model for moving beyond mobility in the far-flung suburbs that account for so much of the American urban landscape. In the Global South, by contrast, suburbs are generally dense, poor, and transit reliant but lack adequate connections to major employment centers and other urban amenities. The challenge here is to provide residents with adequate infrastructure and secure property rights while improving transit and road connections to the rest of city. Steep topography, limited financial resources, and other competing priorities add to the challenge of suburban transformation in the world's many suburban slums.

In both suburban and urban locations, there has been a recent push for projects and programs to reclaim or redesign car-oriented roadways to make spaces safer, less disruptive, and more people oriented. We refer to projects—from small-scale, local traffic calming to the replacement of freeways with boulevards or greenways—as road contractions. Cities such as San Francisco and Seoul have become leaders in scaling back from the auto-oriented highway designs of the 1960s and 1970s to create healthier, economically vibrant, and pleasant new spaces. Major freeway conversions such as San Francisco's Embarcadero and Seoul's Cheong Gye Cheon have not only created more pleasant and safer urban environments but also increased local property values with little or no measurable effect on traffic congestion. Across the globe, reclaiming roadway for residents and visitors—whether temporarily through street closures or permanently through roadway redesigns—has contributed to cities' increasing popularity, livability, and attractiveness. Although it took a devastating earthquake to lead San Francisco to downgrade the Embarcadero, few if any residents would choose to destroy the current boulevard for the sake of a freeway. Although freeway conversions are contentious, once accomplished they have been wildly popular.

Emerging Opportunities and Challenges

In the final chapters of the book, we change gears to discuss technological and social changes that will strongly influence the balance between mobility and place in the twenty-first century. Principal among these is the gravitational shift in where people reside and which cities are growing most quickly. Since the closure of San Francisco's Embarcadero Freeway in 1989, the number of people living in Chinese cities has increased by nearly half a billion. As cities of the Global South add an estimated 1.5 billion residents over the next two decades, how can recalibrating cityscapes and moving beyond mobility best contribute to a more prosperous and humane future? If these cities and countries follow the mistakes of designing cities around transportation networks, they will miss an opportunity to create more livable, economically productive, safe, and healthy environments. Local pollution levels and traffic fatality rates are already catastrophic in many Indian and Chinese cities. Global greenhouse gas emissions continue to rise at a dangerous rate. Whereas many local and national governments have chosen to replicate the post–World

War II design practices of American cities, others are forging a new path by integrating city building with public transportation services, bicycle networks, and pedestrian paths. As cities and countries in the Global South become wealthier, the most successful will be the ones that are most attractive to human capital. Clear skies, safe streets, and convenient access to the city will be essential.

Technology will also play a predominant role in how cities and transportation systems evolve in the coming years. Already, car-sharing companies (e.g., Zipcar and Car2Go) and smart-phone technologies (e.g., Uber and Lyft) are changing the way people travel. Companies are starting to deliver packages by drones, and improvements in video conferencing may finally start to match the quality of face-to-face meetings. How might a realignment of priorities away from mobility work in a world of rapid technological change? Self-driving vehicles, in particular, may fundamentally alter the balance and relationship between mobility and place. Not only might they reduce collisions and congestion, they could disconnect parking from destinations—a form of ubiquitous valet parking—and facilitate a movement to reclaim more urban space for pedestrians, shops, and housing. On the other hand, driverless cars threaten to substantially increase the speed and efficiency of vehicular movements, presaging a world of hypermobility. Ultimately, whether driverless cars reduce or increase how much people drive will depend on a host of factors, in particular whether people continue to own private vehicles or shift to a model where people rent mobility by the mile in shared cars, minivans, and minibuses. In this regard, socially and environmentally responsible public policies, such as real-time congestion pricing that passes on true charges to motorists, will be more important than ever. The potential benefits of new technologies are greatest in the Global South, where a leapfrog technology such as automated minivans could radically improve the quantity and quality of transit—much as cell phones did for telephony.

The book ends by reflecting on opportunities and challenges posed by the combination of powerful megatrends, such as aging societies and collaborative consumption, and technological advances, discussed previously, in charting sustainable urban futures. The role of public policies in nudging these unfolding trends in ways that create not only environmentally sustainable but also inclusive, socially just cities is highlighted. Accusations of "social engineering" are sometimes leveled against such efforts. Some might argue that the lifestyles of Americans are engineered to the point where many are compelled to drive to almost anywhere and everywhere. Ultimately what will bring about the kinds of urban recalibrations chronicled in this book are increases in market choices: choices on where to live, work, learn, shop, and play, and how to move about the city. More livable, connected places stand the best chance of emerging if market forces and consumer preferences—aided by government actions that remove distortions, advance forward-looking urban planning, embrace resourcefulness in the design of communities, and ensure inclusivity and access to all—are allowed to work their magic.

Close

The call to return to a more people-oriented form of building cities and designing transportation networks is not new. It exists in a variety of movements including New Urbanism, Urban Acupuncture, Livable Cities, Smart Growth, and Complete Streets. This book seeks to build on past work through a synthesis of the contemporary practices involving some level of urban recalibration at multiple scales and on the global stage. Where possible, we discuss dividends, whether in terms of real estate market performance, residential satisfaction, or other indicators of community well-being. There are limits, of course, to gauging the benefits of moving beyond mobility, or more broadly place-making. Often, case experiences and images communicate experiences as well as metrics and statistics.

Many definitions of place-making can be found in the literature, associating it with "public spaces that promote health, happiness, and well-being," "economically vibrant, aesthetically attractive, pedestrian-friendly places," and "distinctive, memorable, and livable communities."[25] For us, the simpler idea, in keeping with the themes of this book, is the creation of more places where people want to *be*, not just pass through. Noted urban designer Jan Gehl has a similar take: "Place-making is turning a neighborhood, town or city from a place you can't wait to get through to one you never want to leave."[26] Implicit in all these statement is the need to strike a better balance in the planning for mobility and places.

We need to emphasize that this book is not anti-car. The private automobile is one of the world's great inventions, providing unprecedented levels of personal mobility. It allows people to move effortlessly about the city, on demand, whenever desired. The car is also the most sensible means of travel for many trips, such as hauling bags of groceries and weekend excursions to the countryside. Nor are we arguing against future road building. Being stuck in traffic hardly contributes to good urbanism and livable communities. Hours wasted in traffic queues is but another form of pollution, what John Whitelegg called "time pollution."[27] Although many people have a hard time coming up with a suitable definition of what makes a place livable, one thing it is not is extremely congested. Indeed, when people are asked what they most dislike about city living, public opinion polls routinely cite traffic congestion as one of the top urban ills.

Although urban recalibration does not mean jettisoning cars, halting road construction, or eliminating traffic engineering departments, it does mean reining in the car's outsized presence in cities and suburbs. Throughout this book, we argue for the planning and design of cities and the pricing and management of transportation resources in ways that reduce the excessive reliance and sometimes seemingly indiscriminate use of private cars to go anywhere and everywhere. This overdependence is exacerbated by the car often being idle and, when used, grossly oversized and overpowered for many trips that are made. The typical car sits on asphalt 23 hours per day. When used, three out of four seats are often empty. Relying on a 2-ton steel cage to shuttle a 150-pound person around a neighborhood is unforgivably wasteful in an era of increasingly turbulent weather patterns and steadily rising sea levels, fueled by carbon emissions. The idea of balancing is to design cities in ways that reduce wasteful travel and encourage judicious auto-mobility. It does not mean ceasing future road construction or ignoring the need for efficient freight logistics in industrial corridors. We believe compact, mixed-use, walkable communities that focus on place-making and quality of environment are wholly compatible with building and maintaining functional and efficient networks for motorized travel. We are most likely to do so by striking a better balance between mobility and place in the future planning and design of cities.

Throughout this book, we emphasize the harm that a mobility-focused approach to city planning has wrought on the environment, economy, and public health. Our aim here is less polemical and more normative. Notably, we hope at some level this work influences practices in rapidly modernizing and motorizing parts of the world where course corrections can have big impacts and are not too late. Ultimately, this book provides a tour of the challenges and opportunities that cities face in reordering community priorities to deemphasize movement and focus more on the needs of people and places. In making our case, we tend to emphasize places where one or more us have lived, worked, or conducted research. This adds not only the richness of personal experience but also access to data and the confidence to describe some of the opportunities and challenges in better balancing mobility and place. As a result, we may miss some policies or cities that are leading exemplars of one or more of the many movements to create more human-focused cities and mobility choices. It would not be possible to fit a detailed description of every practice of urban recalibration in a single book. In this sense, the work is more illustrative (and we hope inspirational at some level) than encyclopedic. Such shortcomings notwithstanding, we celebrate the growing demand for a shift in global thinking about the role of transportation in creating better communities, environments, and economies.

PART I

Making the Case

The next three chapters make the case for a reordering of transportation planning priorities beyond mobility. Worldwide, the costs of designing cities around movement are becoming ever more apparent, including more than 1.25 million annual fatalities from traffic collisions and 3.2 million premature deaths from air pollution. Fortunately, also becoming increasingly evident are the opportunities to shift our dominant transportation paradigm to focus investments on creating vibrant and livable places that cater to their residents, not just their residents' movement. In part one of this book, we argue that this urban recalibration from mobility to place-making creates better communities, environments, and economies.

Better communities are safe, walkable, healthy places that promote sustainable and equitable access to a wealth of destinations by multiple modes and strengthen interpersonal connections and community interactions. This stands in stark contrast with twentieth-century modernism's emphasis on segregated land uses, expeditious movement, and disconnected tower blocks, particularly as envisioned by the likes of architect Le Corbusier. Instead, we argue for the kinds of smaller, human-scaled blocks, shared spaces, and complete streets promoted by acclaimed scholars and practitioners such as Jane Jacob. Streets are not just Le Corbusier's "traffic machines" but serve many functions, such as opportunities for people to chat, children to play, shoppers to browse storefronts, and sidewalk vendors to sell goods. Chapter 2 shows how shifting the focus from vehicle throughput to place-making can improve a community's social capital, health, and equity.

Chapter 3 focuses on how urban recalibration can promote better environments. By *better environments* we mean fewer emissions from cars and buildings but also reduced fossil fuel consumption, stabilized climates, protected land and natural habitats, and, in general, healthier, more resourceful places in which to live, work, learn, and play. Car-dependent cities and countries consume substantially more land, fossil fuels, and natural habitat than more compact and multimodal places. They also produce significantly more local and global pollution. As climate change harms and threatens the planet and its inhabitants, urban environments designed around oversized single-occupant vehicles powered by fossil fuels look increasingly out of touch.

Chapter 4 argues that going beyond mobility can also improve economic performance, not just through reduced collisions, fatalities, pollution, and infrastructure expenditures but also by bringing people closer together and creating the types of places that are most attractive to the most productive and mobile workers. The production benefits of locating people and firms in close proximity are well established and at the heart of what makes cities the drivers of global economic growth. Walkable, transit-accessible neighborhoods with well-designed urban environments are desirable and fetch a price premium. Increasingly, finding the right balance of mobility, livability, and place-making is an essential component of attracting the kinds of high-skilled, knowledge-based industries and workers that will drive innovation and economic production in the coming decades.

2

Better Communities

Connections between and within cities are vital to the inner workings of a community. People need convenient access to schools, offices, and shopping areas to go about their lives. Unfortunately, much of twentieth-century transportation infrastructure has had damaging effects on communities. Dangerous and difficult-to-cross intersections and multilane roads have hindered people's ability to move freely and children's opportunity to play. Urban sidewalks are often unpleasant, unwalkable, or even nonexistent. Transportation infrastructure, epitomized by highways cutting through American neighborhoods in the 1960s, while connecting people on a regional level, had an unfortunate local side-effect: It reduced personal interactions within communities and obstructed their access to places.

Early modernist planners such as Le Corbusier demoted the street to a "traffic machine," as he declared in 1929 in *The City of To-morrow and Its Planning*, "a sort of factory for producing speed traffic."[1] Thirty years later, as Jane Jacobs saw the effects of New York's new highways and car-oriented superblocks on communities, she realized the importance of the street lay beyond traffic alone. She asserted that the street network is a "nervous system," communicating "the flavor, the feel, the sights," and "a major point of transaction and communication."[2] Good streets provide opportunities beyond transportation, including social interaction, memorable experiences, and business.

Modernist planners saw the city as a machine where different functions such as residential, commercial, traffic, and social gathering were discrete parts. For instance, Le Corbusier's *City of To-morrow* also prescribed a vast and grand plaza where people would socialize. But Jane Jacobs described streets and their sidewalks as "the main public spaces of the city,"[3] not the grand plazas or the parks. This simple stretch of paving can have many functions, providing opportunities for people to chat, children to play, shoppers to browse storefronts, and street vendors to sell goods. In the Global South, sidewalks are the lifeblood of cities, giving a place to food and market stalls.

We need to move away from the modernist understanding of cities as discrete parts with single-use purposes. We need to understand the compound effects of transportation infrastructure. Beyond mobility principles can be used to create better communities by improving economies and promoting environmental health. Those planning and designing our transportation infrastructure need to pay attention to the creation of places.

In this chapter we advance evidence that connecting people to places, instead of just increasing mobility, will create better communities. Better communities are safe, walkable, healthy places that promote sustainable and equitable access to a wealth of destinations by multiple modes and strengthen interpersonal connections and community interactions. Better communities are those that consider people, the environment, and the economy in the design of the transportation networks. Connections—between and within cities—are vital to sustained economic growth, prosperity, and healthy living. Connecting people to places requires environments that promote traffic safety, clean air, and recreation.

Promoting livable streets in which mobility is balanced with place-making enables people to strengthen interpersonal connections and increase social capital in concert with their neighbors, community shop owners, and family members. Having access to the street, without fear of traffic, allows physical safety and freedom. Reclaiming the street will allow people to walk more and participate in more physical activity, thereby improving their health.

Furthermore, combining sustainable transit programs with place-making strategies can promote social equity. For those without a car or easy access to public transportation, it can be very difficult to find a job where they can flourish, which has historically been a problem for women and minorities in particular. Without access to friends across the city or other stores and community meetings, people's social capital can suffer. Moreover, car-oriented environments can limit access to healthy foods, hospitals, social services, and other critical destinations for people who do not own cars.

As we will see throughout this chapter, an excessive focus on mobility challenges communities. Shifting the focus from vehicle throughput to place-making can address these challenges.

Increasing Social Capital and Sociability

Social capital has been defined as the networks and relationships between people and the idea that these relationships can bind people together for mutual benefits. Political scientist Robert Putnam defines social capital as the value of all the "social networks and the associated norms of reciprocity"[4] that a person accumulates throughout their life. "Whereas economic capital is in people's bank accounts and human capital is inside their heads," writes Alejandro Portes, "social capital inheres in the structure of their relationships."[5]

Sources of social capital can range from formal groups such as neighborhood associations to community gardens, which promote collaboration and communication between residents, to informal connections such as running groups. Both types of groups are important sources of social capital because they bring people together for mutual benefits. Greater social capital increases work performance and efficiency,[6] as well as overall happiness and life satisfaction.[7]

In his seminal 1995 article, Putnam noted that Americans' longer travel distances have increasingly disconnected them from their local family, friends, and neighbors.[8] Putman's research showed that each additional 10 minutes Americans spent commuting to work cut involvement in community affairs by 10 percent: fewer public meetings attended, less volunteering, increased voter absenteeism, and the like. Moreover, the average time devoted to informal socializing activities, whether visiting friends or hanging out in bars, fell from 85 minutes in 1965 to 57 minutes in 1995.[9] Whereas Americans used to bowl in leagues, they are increasingly "bowling alone." This, he shows, is emblematic of the weakening of social connections that happened as people in the United States live and work farther apart, a result of postwar suburbanization.

Car-oriented places do not promote the accumulation of social capital. The car journey of the typical suburbanite from the bubble of the detached single-family home to office cubicle is marked by isolation, with limited possibilities to interact socially. Urban sprawl comes with considerable "neglected social considerations," argued sociologist David Popenoe in 1979, such as "deprivation of access" and "environmental deprivation."[10] Sprawling areas not only limit access to community facilities and employment for those who cannot drive, leading to family members being "trapped" inside the home, they also lead to less stimulating urban environments where neighborhood amenities are scattered. In a Levittown survey, 50 percent of suburban teenagers said they were bored.

Another feature of modern transportation systems that directly affects quality of urban living is the severance and disruption of communities. Roads that pierce the heart of longstanding communities can cut off traditional pathways and thus limit social interactions. The mental well-being of residents can suffer when car dependence is mixed with car congestion. One study found job satisfaction and commitment fell with increased road commuting distance (but not with public transit use), and perceived traffic stress was associated with depression.[11] The 2011 IBM Commuter Pain Survey found that 42 percent of surveyed commuters felt their stress levels increased due to driving in congestion, and 35 percent said they were angrier as a result.[12]

But suburban neighborhoods could be designed to optimize for social interaction (see also chapter 7). Planners and designers can create living environments that promote visual contact and stimulate initial social contact between neighbors. Moreover, they can design, create, and plan enjoyable spaces in which people can spend time together.[13]

Even in rural areas, sustainability measures and highly developed transportation systems can be life changing. Rural transport research suggests that social capital is heavily influenced by people's mobility and whether or not they have a car, with those in possession of a car conferred higher degrees of social capital.[14] This leads to a stratification of social and economic groups, heavily favoring those of high income. Although the constant availability of transportation may be necessary in cities, by-demand transportation might be appropriate for rural areas and can give people a better way to get to work, mitigating the negative externalities that come with a lack of mobility in rural areas. Having such options can make it feasible for a person to live in a rural area instead of forcing them to move to the city, which may be unaffordable or personally undesirable. The choice to have safe, walkable environments and alternatives to driving should not be restricted to city dwellers.

The car has affected social interaction in cities as well. In his groundbreaking 1981 book *Livable Streets*, Donald Appleyard conducted a study in which he compared three streets of similar morphology and demographic makeup but with different vehicular traffic, ranging from 2,000 to 16,000 vehicles daily. In the street with a lower volume of car traffic, residents had on average three times more local connections than in the high-traffic street.[15] As Appleyard demonstrates, streets with less busy traffic enable a pedestrian experience that facilitates interpersonal interactions.

Unfortunately, American streets have been defined by street standards that privilege the car. "Many of the standards we imposed on city building," argue Donald Appleyard and Allan Jacobs, "usually in the name of health and safety-road widths, auto lane widths, and parking standards . . . actually prevent or ruin urbanity."[16] Over the century, street-width and parking standards have continually increased, taking up the majority of space for fewer people in their cars.[17] In some cities, parking lots alone account for more than a third of the metropolitan footprint.[18] As a consequence, possible social spaces have become fewer.

Urban designer Jan Gehl argues we should reclaim spaces from the car to promote *Life Between Buildings*, as is the title of his book. He argues that public space should be optimized for social interactions and daily activities.[19] His research backs this up: Copenhagen's removal of some 1,600 car park spaces in the center city over three decades—replaced by civic squares, open-air cafés, and neighborhood parks—was matched by a fourfold increase in social activities and civic engagement, such as meeting other people from different walks of life, enjoying cultural events, dining al fresco, and the simple (stress-reducing) act of taking in city life and, Cheshire cat–like, watching other people.

Necessary activities, such as going to school and work, will always happen regardless of how public space functions. However, optional activities (sunbathing, stopping to talk) will happen only if the public space is good enough to accommodate them. In other words, mobility will happen regardless of sidewalks, but social interactions and associated increases in social capital may not.

Physical characteristics that promote sociable cities on a neighborhood level include livable streets; a minimum density of residential development; a multitude of activities and resources for living including spaces to live, work, and play within a reasonable proximity to each other; and many buildings with distinct functions instead of just a few large buildings with complex functions.[20] This stands in contrast to the mono-use, car-oriented, and low-density characteristics of much of suburban sprawl.

On the level of individual public spaces, there are several ways that physical environments can facilitate sociability and the accumulation of social capital as a result.

Sociologist William Whyte in *The Social Life of Small Urban Spaces* argues that sociable places are environments with many places to sit, preferably near a busy and accessible location, and ideally not separated from pedestrian flows.[21] Whyte's work has demonstrated that people want to sit around other people, not in segregated areas, where they can easily access other parts of the city. In these social places, it is possible to people watch and gain social capital by meeting with friends or meeting new people.

Whyte also noted other elements that cause people to linger in a public space, including water features, art, and outdoor dining. He liked the waterfall in Paley Park, Manhattan, because it not only moderated temperatures but also drowned out sounds of people's conversations and passing traffic.[22] He noted how public art could be an "external stimulus" that would provoke what he called "triangulation," connecting people by prompting "strangers to talk to other strangers as if they knew each other."[23] Also, he realized the sociability potential of outdoor dining and food vendors, observing people eating, schmoozing, and standing around stalls. "If you want to seed a place with activity, put out food,"[24] he wrote.

Locating metro and bus stops near places where people are known to congregate will enhance interpersonal interactions and increase the social capital of that area. This will link more people to public transportation and could help establish a public culture that normalizes its use. This is just another example of how significant compound effects could occur when mobility is paired with place-making. However, TODs are not automatically associated with increases in social capital, and in some cases they even have a negative association. A study in New Jersey showed how TOD areas with a higher employment density—one of the goals of TOD—tended to have a lower social capital, because employment density is negatively associated with a sense of community.[25] Nevertheless, the authors acknowledged they missed subtler design details of TOD, such as walkability enhancements that might occur with good planning. (See also chapter 4 for economic benefits of TOD.)

Shared Spaces, Complete Streets, and Safety

In the 1980s, traffic engineer Hans Monderman conducted an experiment in Oudehaske, the Netherlands. He removed all road signs, signals, and road markings and made all pedestrians, bikers, and cars share roads and squares equally, creating a "shared space" (figure 2-1). As a result, all travelers paid greater attention to each other equally to keep everyone safe. Drivers were found to have reduced their speed by 40 percent because of this increase in perceived risk.[26] Monderman's trial was so successful that other towns including some in Denmark, Sweden, and Germany have taken similar measures to reduce the number of traffic accidents.

Shared spaces epitomize how balancing mobility and place-making can benefit communities. The experiment reestablished interpersonal awareness between all road users and reclaimed streets for pedestrians, allowing them to move and interact with another in new ways. By deemphasizing vehicle throughput, curbless streets become destinations. With some modifications, Monderman's concept of shared space can improve safety and sociability in larger cities as well.

One such example may be Barcelona, which is gradually creating "superblocks" out of multiple blocks in the city's Eixample district. Each of the superblocks consists of nine existing blocks of the city grid, excluding drivers other than residents and business owners from the local roads (figure 2-2). All other traffic, including cars, buses, and scooters, is pushed to the perimeter of the new superblock. As a result, Barcelona has more green space, fewer road accidents, less air pollution and noise, and better overall public health.[27] (Air pollution in Barcelona causes more than 3,500 premature deaths per year.)

Traffic calming and pedestrian safety measures can take other forms as well. Larger block sizes are known to promote faster automobile speeds, and shorter blocks with more stops will force drivers to move slower, thus reducing the severity of any collisions. Shorter blocks also promote walking, as Jane Jacobs mandated: "Streets and opportunities to turn corners must be frequent."[28]

Other traffic calming measures include speed bumps, speed cushions, raised intersections and crossings, traffic circles, chicanes, and turns in the road, all of which force cars to slow down even when they are not turning a corner. Implementing tolls on certain roads can also significantly reduce the number of cars in those areas. Smaller roads with fewer lanes, such as reducing a four-lane road to a three-lane road, could force cars to be more aware of each other and slow down.[29] A worldwide study including Japan, Australia, and Europe showed how traffic calming is a promising intervention for reducing traffic

Figure 2-1. An intersection in Drachten, a town in the north of the Netherlands based on Hans Monderman's idea of shared spaces. There are no curbs, lanes, or traffic signs, although pedestrians do have some designated crossing areas. (Source: Fietsberaad.)

Figure 2-2. A transformed intersection in Poble Nou, Barcelona, with playing areas for children where there used to be cars. (Source: Confederación de Talleres de Proyectos de Arquitectura.)

injuries and deaths.[30] All of the strategies included in this study included physical elements that could contribute to place-making, such as

- Vertical and horizontal shifts in traffic (e.g., road humps, mini-roundabouts, road narrowing)
- Optical measures (road surface treatment including color or texture), reduced horizontal visibility (shortened sightlines)
- Audible measures (rumble areas, jiggle bars)
- Redistribution of traffic (e.g., permanent or temporary blocking of road)
- Changes to road environment (increased vegetation along road, street furniture)
- Reduced speed limit zones where speeds are physically limited by traffic calming measures

There is also promise in converting one-way to two-way streets. A study in Louisville, Kentucky, showed that a conversion not only decreased traffic accidents (as well as traffic flow) but also led to the increase of livability, with reduced crime and increased property values.[31]

Some cities, including Mexico City, Bogotá, San Francisco, Philadelphia, and New York City, have even begun to implement open street programs, where roads are blocked off for several hours to allow people to walk freely, roller skate, or play games in the streets.[32]

Instead of focusing on allowing cars to travel as efficiently as possible, neighborhoods should have streets that are designed to make neighborhoods more livable to other users as well. The most comprehensive approach to benefit communities is the "complete streets" concept, a street designed for all users, not just for drivers, but also for bicyclists, transit users, and pedestrians of all ages and abilities.

Pedestrians, including people with wheelchairs, should have sidewalks and plazas that are safe and accessible, to promote walking. Pedestrian priority areas should be well lit, especially at street crossings, and pedestrians should be given longer lines of sight so that they can look out for themselves as they walk. Changing car-oriented streets to "complete streets" requires an institutional shift, including changing operating procedures so that all users are routinely considered when infrastructure improvements go through the planning, designing, building, and operating process.[33] (See chapter 8 for more about complete streets and traffic calming.)

Improving overall safety and reducing crime would benefit from such a process. A study in Austin, Texas, showed that higher density and mixed land use patterns near bus stops—all of which this book advocates—are linked to higher crime rates.[34] This complicates the seminal theory of what Jane Jacobs posited as "eyes on the street," in which compact city aspects such as walkability, mixed use, and density would lead to more people on the streets and hence more natural surveillance.[35] Densification probably clusters rather than reduces crime. This could be addressed through environmental design. A growing body of research supports the assertion that environmental design can help prevent crime and reduce the fear of crime.[36] Crime prevention through environmental design includes optimizing opportunities for natural surveillance, for instance by having more windows, lighting, and closed-circuit television and by establishing and maintaining an image that signals a positive message to users and a sense of ownership. Such strategies would deter offenders from committing crimes, by increasing their perception of being at risk of surveillance by "law-abiding" others.

Public Health and Walkability

Planning almost exclusively around the automobile at the cost of pedestrians and other modes of travel has adversely affected public health. Walking rates have decreased dramatically in the United States: Walking's share of urban trips fell from 9.3 percent in 1977 to 5.5 percent in 1995, according to the Federal Highway Administration. These lower physical activity levels alarm health professionals, because they are linked to increases in the risk of heart disease and other health problems. Spread-out cities such as Dallas and Phoenix have traffic fatality rates that are three to five times higher than Boston's or New York's.[37] Planning decisions and transportation investments should consider the health effects on communities.

Reduced physical activity, along with rising food energy intake, leads to weight gains and obesity-related illnesses such as diabetes, strokes, and heart disease.[38] Steps—putting one foot in front of the other—have been engineered out of the daily lives of many urbanites, the product of a shift toward car-oriented infrastructure and the separation of land uses that for many make walking impractical. Trips, such as going to school or picking up a loaf of bread, that a century ago our great grandparents made on foot are today made by motorized means, with serious public health consequences. In the United Kingdom, two-thirds of adults do not meet the World Health Organization standard of 30 minutes of moderate to vigorous physical activity each day, and the majority of Brits are now overweight or obese.[39]

Cities that invite walking and cycling can help reverse the trend toward sedentary urban living. A study of 30,000 adults over a 14-year period found that cycling to work reduced the risk of mortality at a given age by 39 percent relative to those who did not cycle.[40] Part of the solution is stepped-up investments in bicycle infrastructure and bike-friendly streetscapes; if you build it, they will come. A study of bike-friendly Bogotá, Colombia, found that higher road connectivity and street density increased the likelihood that residents met minimum World Health Organization standards of daily physical activity.[41]

Mixed-use and walkable areas are known to promote healthier communities. A study in Atlanta, Georgia, showed that each quartile increase of land use mix was associated with a 12.2 percent reduction in the likelihood of obesity.[42] Conversely, each additional hour spent in a car was related to a 6 percent increase in the likelihood of obesity.[43]

Urban design scholar Michael Southworth put forward the six following criteria that make up walkable pedestrian networks: connectivity, such as interconnected and continuous sidewalks; linkage with other modes, such as bus, streetcar, and train; fine-grained and varied land use patterns, as opposed to mono-use; safety; quality of path; and path context.[44] The last two of his criteria deal with perceptual urban design qualities, which are more difficult to pin down. Nevertheless, Reid Ewing and Susan Handy studied various urban design qualities that promote walkability.[45] They deemed the following as essential:

- Imageability, defined by Kevin Lynch as a quality of an urban environment that evokes a strong image in the mind of an observer.[46] Landmarks, distinctive architecture, and public art can help leave lasting impressions, lowering the threshold to taking the walk.
- Enclosure, in Gorden Cullen's words an "outdoor room,"[47] occurs when a viewer's lines of sight are blocked by buildings, creating a more intimate area. This can be achieved by creating continuous streetwalls on both sides of the street, with buildings collectively forming walls of the outdoor "room."
- Human scale, a contentious term among urban designers, loosely defined as the "size, texture, and articulation of physical elements that match the size and proportions of humans and . . . correspond to the speed at which humans walk."[48] This doesn't preclude skyscrapers; Rockefeller Center was perceived as human scale, a function of its stepped building mass, building details, pavement texture, trees, and street furniture.
- Transparency is the degree to which people perceive what lies beyond the edge of a street, such as an inviting window display as opposed to a blank wall, and can be controlled through elements including windows, porticos, and trees.
- Complexity, the number of visual differences to which a viewer is exposed over time, makes walks more interesting. Visual richness can be increased by architectural variation of buildings, rather than a single large and monotonous building, or even the constant moving of tree branches and leaves.

Besides these qualities of the urban space, safe and pedestrian-friendly streets with sidewalks, bike lanes, medians, and pedestrian crossing opportunities can significantly increase walking, as well as biking rates. Increasing the density and connectivity and improving the configuration of the street network also promotes walkable cities (figure 2-3). A California study showed that compact cities and connected streets, with fewer traffic lanes, correlate with lower rates of obesity, diabetes, and high blood pressure.[49] This

Portland, Oregon,
United States
Block size: 90m x 90m

Barcelona, Spain
Block size: 150m x 150m

Beijing, China
Block size: 500m x 500m

Figure 2-3. Block size is an important factor for walkability. A 700-meter walk through Beijing's vast superblocks could take much longer than a similar walk through a smaller grid, negatively affecting walking. (Source: Google Earth and Stefan Al.)

study illustrates how the human scale of a neighborhood is important to the health of its residents.

Trails and parks are also vital to promoting walkability and a community's health. A Georgia study suggested that proximity to places to walk, such as streets, plazas, or parks, is associated with a significant increase in levels of physical activity.[50] Trails also promote walking. A study in Knoxville, Tennessee, found that the retrofit of an urban trail in a neighborhood with a lack of connectivity led to greater levels of physical activity.[51]

Nine separate studies showed that the use of public transportation increased walking times by 8 to 33 minutes, because it typically involves some walking to stations or bus stops.[52] An increase in the use of public transport by inactive adults would lead to significant increases in the active adult population. In short, designing communities around transit hubs, public parks, trails, and mixed-use neighborhoods can provide residents opportunities to develop healthier habits.

The health benefits of reducing the automobile's footprint extend beyond active movement. Greening neighborhoods and freeing up space for playgrounds, parks, community gardens, and urban agriculture also contribute to healthier living. François Reeves, an interventional cardiologist at the Faculty of Medicine, Université Montréal, estimates improved access to healthy eating and substituting walking for car travel—by eliminating "nano-aggressors" from food (e.g., trans fats, fructose, and glucose) and air (e.g., hydrocarbons and particulates)—can reduce cardiac disease as much as 75 percent.[53] The greening of communities also reduces urban heat island effects and the amount of oil-stained runoff in streams and tributaries. Moreover, locally grown crops improve food security and shrink the environmental footprint of farm-to-kitchen produce movements.

The public health impacts of local pollution caused by automobiles are immense. We discuss these public health effects of local pollution at length in the next chapter on better environments, as well the following chapter on better economies, because the economic costs are so high.

Another important component of public health is traffic safety. Each year the transportation system kills 1.25 million people. The World Health Organization puts the total cost of global traffic injuries and fatalities at 3 percent of global GDP.[54] The social and economic costs of traffic fatalities are even higher in the Global South. Figure 2-4 plots gross national income (adjusted for purchasing power parity) against the traffic fatality rate for 172 countries reported by the World Health Organization. Each 1 percent decrease in income per capita corresponds to nearly a half percent increase in fatalities per capita. Because driving rates also decrease with income, traffic fatalities perversely affect lower-income households in lower-income cities the most. Pedestrians account for a third of traffic fatalities. (We discuss traffic safety more at length in chapter 8.) In the Global South, a small elite of drivers impose high social costs on the majority who walk or rely on transit. Road traffic fatalities also disproportionately affect the working population,

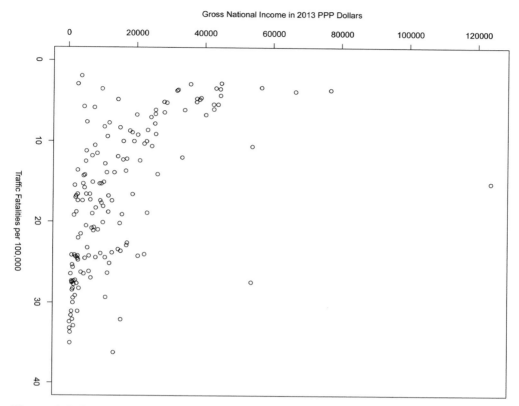

Figure 2-4. Income and traffic fatalities across 172 countries in 2013. (Source: World Health Organization.)

which tends to travel the most and at the most dangerous times of day. Given the lack of health and life insurance in the Global South, traffic fatalities and injuries impose additional costs and harm.

Social Equity, Diversity, and Opportunity

Place-making does not inherently make a community more equitable. For instance, the New Urbanist ideal of achieving compact cities through physical design fails to include social equity, accessibility, and political economy.[55] A study of TODs in Taipei shows that the increased density can be good for transit ridership but can also lead to the degradation of social equity and environmental degradation.[56] For planners and designers to create more equitable neighborhoods, they must explicitly designate such results as central to their projects.

However, the affordability, efficiency, and coverage of transit has a strong effect on employment opportunities for women and people living in poverty, who are disproportionately minorities, and on the daily lives of older adults, welfare recipients, and anyone struggling to make ends meet. Planners must consider the effects of transport infrastructure decisions on social equity, diversity, and opportunity within communities. Car-oriented cities disproportionally negatively affect women, minorities, and lower-income groups.

Women tend to work closer to home, most often because of their lower wages and larger housework responsibilities, including caring for children. A working woman is far more likely to have an employed spouse or to be a single parent with dependent children than a working man. This often means that the responsibility for taking care of children or picking them up from child care services at the end of the work day falls on her shoulders. As a result, women's responsibilities at home increase the cost of commuting.[57] A faster and more accessible transportation option would enable employees to balance their schedules more easily, work longer hours as necessary, take care of household errands, and more. Efficient transit could even enable children of appropriate ages to use public transit by themselves, alleviating the responsibilities of working mothers.[58] Improved transportation systems would enable more people to access a variety of grocery store options and thus improve overall public health, because more people would have access to healthier food and escape "food deserts."[59]

Minorities, immigrants, and low-income people have historically been cut off from dense production centers by transportation infrastructure. The federal highway system, the redlining of communities, and urban redevelopment programs all helped to exclude and restrict access to job opportunities and settlement patterns for those populations.[60] At present, many minorities are dependent on low-paying jobs that require long-distance travel, such as Latin immigrants working as house maids in southern California who rely on the public bus system, or on jobs located in and immediately around their neighborhoods that might not provide the same chance at upward mobility as a job in the city center might provide.[61]

Similarly, those dependent on temporary or extended public assistance programs would benefit from increased access to public transportation. Without adequate transportation or access to childcare services, it can be difficult for welfare participants to even go out and look for a job, which is a requisite to even receive welfare.[62] Both low-income car drivers and public transport users spend proportionally more of their income on travel than those in higher-income groups.[63] Planners and city officials need to address this inequity that places a steeper burden on those already struggling to provide for themselves and their families.

Older adults may need different transportation modifications in order to travel more freely. Most people over the age of 80 do not use the London Underground because they have difficulty accessing the stations, especially if they have medical conditions that make it harder to walk, such as arthritis or if they use a wheelchair or cane.[64] For this generation, is it not simply the number of stations available but also how to get to those stations. Are there elevators in the station? Is there adequate seating? Is the street easy to cross? Special transport services can assist them as well, including personal electronic vehicles (scooters and wheelchairs) and pickup services that they can call for transportation.

For planners and policymakers to address equity and social inclusion, it is important to recognize that certain policies to restrict car ownership and use could negatively and disproportionally affect low-income groups. Although such policies are often aimed at reducing carbon emissions, without simultaneously incentivizing the use of public transit systems and making them affordable, these policies could make car ownership unaffordable for low-income households and thus perpetuate inequality between the wealthy and poor. A study from the United Kingdom concluded, "Almost anyone living in all but the very center of our major cities needs to own a car in order to fully participate in all the activities that are considered necessary for achieving a reasonable standard of living in the twenty-first century."[65]

A successful example of people- and transit-oriented policy leading to more equitable cities is the Bus Rapid Transit (BRT) system in Bogotá, Colombia, and former Mayor Enrique Peñalosa's push to manifest social equity through the city's policies, systems, and services. The BRT campaign, although pushed through rather undemocratically, succeeded in creating a more equitable city. As a result of his policies, school attendance rose by 30 percent, the downtown core was revitalized, commuting times fell by one-fifth, and the air quality improved around the BRT routes.[66] (See chapter 9 for more on the Bogotá story.)

Transit strategies must ensure that no economic or social group is unable to take part in the city. Planners can provide more accessible transportation to food, community gardens, and mixed-use land to create a better community.[67] Compact development alleviates many of these problems, because it can provide easier access to necessities and stores and reduce social segregation, as long as the potential higher cost of housing is offset by affordable housing strategies. Moreover, a 1999 nationwide survey revealed that 83 percent of Americans want to "age in place."[68] For older adults who lose the ability to drive a car, compact and walkable environments will be vital.

Close

As we have seen in this chapter, an excessive focus on mobility challenges communities. Shifting the focus from vehicle throughput to place-making can break with these challenges and improve social capital, safe and walkable streets, and equity.

If the community is included in the process of implementation, more benefits can be achieved. Locals often understand a problem better than outside planners who themselves have never experienced the problem facing a given area. They can help modify potential solutions, ensuring their success while avoiding a solution that inhibits the functioning of the community. For instance, road planning must be sensitive to the adjacent pedestrian and retail space, to avoid impeding other sorts of travel or activity.

Collaborative or participatory planning allows people to understand the diversity of problems and solutions that exist, people's needs, and the different cultures around the world and those that make up diverse communities.[69] Diversity is important in a community, regardless of which racial or ethnic groups may reside there, and it is vital to acknowledge that everyone has different needs. These sorts of discussions are key for development and social justice. Even if a plan does not work or if there are disputes, community planning still takes steps toward creating a collaborative solution by providing a platform in which people can express their concerns.

Ethnographically informed planning methods appear promising as a tool to address community needs as well. They can be important for cities in the developing world, where a high proportion of pedestrians are engaged in informal economic activities, such as in Jakarta.[70] Annette Kim's spatial ethnography of the sidewalks of Ho Chi Minh City reveals the spatial patterns and social relations of the city's vibrant sidewalk life.[71] It highlights the cultural, aesthetic, and humanistic aspects of sidewalk life, including migrant vendors, typically missing in official planning studies.

Allowing the community to decide how to spend part of a public budget—participatory budgeting—has been shown to be a promising tool used in the United States and Latin America to reduce poverty, improve local infrastructure, and practice good governance at a local level. Studies have shown the effects of participatory budgeting to vary depending on how it is implemented in different contexts. In Porto Alegre, Brazil, where the concept was first established, participatory budgeting is successful because local municipalities are responsible for its implementation and focus on immediate interventions rather than long-term planning objectives, although the short-term focus is cited as a weakness in critical evaluations.[72] Similarly, case studies assessing the effectiveness of participatory budgeting on the national scale have revealed it to be less effective than local implementation of the policy.[73]

Public participation, whether in person or online, can help developers stay in tune with community needs and continually improve and maintain various projects. In a test of the effectiveness of a public participation geographic information system to identify national park visitor experiences, results showed that they were able to gather descriptive information about people's thoughts, perceived environmental impacts, and suggestions. This type of information allows park managers to improve parts of the park that were not as well developed and further develop the parts of parks that people enjoyed, such as animal viewing spots.[74]

Perhaps most importantly, by helping planners make the best decision for the city as a whole, members will feel more attached and invested in their community. Residents who are more invested in their community will help take better care of it, improving the community's overall happiness while increasing the amount of social capital they can derive from it. Participatory planning methods can play a vital role in improving communities.[75]

In short, shifting the focus away from mobility to place-making and transit can promote community safety, health, equity, and social capital. Such effects will only be compounded by the use of participatory planning, because the local people who help plan a change in the community will be more invested in its success.

3

Better Environments

The transportation sector's environmental footprint is immense and growing. To gain political traction and public acceptance, making places that are attractive, accessible, and highly livable must also meaningfully contribute to better environments. By *better environments* we mean fewer emissions from cars and buildings but also reduced fossil fuel consumption, stabilized climates, protected land and natural habitats, and in general, healthier, more resourceful places in which to live, work, learn, and play.

To a large extent, the urban recalibration approaches discussed in this book call for a diminished role of the private automobile in contemporary urban living. Thus, almost by definition the recalibration of cities to focus more on people and places should deliver positive environmental benefits. Are they substantial enough to matter? We think so. Some of the steadily accumulating body of evidence on the environmental benefits of sustainable cities and mobility are presented in this chapter and throughout this book. Because of the importance of climate change on the global stage, particular attention is given in this chapter to the potential impacts of better-connected and more livable places on decarbonizing cities and their environs.

Defining Sustainable Cities and Transport

In urban planning circles, the term *sustainability* is rather common and often used quite loosely, so it is important to first define what is meant by this term. Borrowing from the seminal Brundtland Report of 1987, a sustainable city is one that satisfies the needs of its residents and workforce without compromising the ability of future generations to meet their own needs within a similar cityscape. Intergenerational equity is central to the principle of sustainability. Being sustainable means an unflagging commitment to ensuring that the environmental conditions and quality of life for our children's children are at least as good as those of our generation. Air should be just as breathable, streets should be just as safe to walk and bike along, and trees and greenery should be just as abundant.

In the urban transport sector, sustainability can similarly be viewed in intergenerational terms, satisfying the current mobility needs of cities without compromising the ability of future generations to meet their own needs for movement and spatial interaction.[1] In recent times, the idea of sustainability in the urban transport sector has moved beyond a focus on ecology and the natural environment to also include economic, social, and institutional dimensions. Although this chapter's focus is on environmental sustainability, actions taken to become more economically sustainable and efficient can also confer environmental benefits, such as instituting taxation policies that also conserve energy. For instance, Japan phased in reduced ownership taxes on fuel-efficient vehicles by 25 to 50 percent in the early 2000s and imposed higher charges on large-engine vehicles and ones more than 10 years old. Overall revenues from road users have risen, while incentives, such as deeply discounted public transport fares, have been introduced to reward resourcefulness.[2]

Reducing Oil Dependence

Many of the environmental problems in the urban transport sector, such as air pollution and greenhouse gas (GHG) emissions, are rooted in its seemingly unquenchable thirst for petroleum, the automotive fuel source of choice to propel private vehicles. Any significant strides made in improving natural environments through urban recalibration must at some level contribute to reduced reliance on petroleum in the urban transport sector. Alternative fuels, such as biomass, and electric vehicles can reduce oil dependence. But so can measures that cut down on private car travel. It is in this latter domain that urban recalibration most directly contributes to better environments; for example, cities with fine-grain mixtures of land uses that shorten travel distances invite more trips by walking and cycling, thereby diminishing fuel consumption.

Reversing the transport sector's dependence on oil is a tall order. The share of the world's oil consumption accounted for by transportation rose from 45.2 percent in 1973 to 57 percent in 2016, and barring dramatic changes in current mobility practices, the sector is expected to continue to drive the growth in oil demand for years to come.[3] Cities are even more dependent on oil to move people and goods around. Worldwide, motorized urban transport relies almost entirely (95 percent) on oil-based products for its energy supply, primarily in the form of petrol and diesel.

The designs and shapes of cities, studies show, can strongly influence travel behavior, including the modes travelers opt for.[4] Some transport modes are far more energy efficient than others. The relative energy efficiencies of different forms of urban transport in eighty-four cities are shown in table 3-1.[5] Public transport is far more energy-conserving than private cars mainly because of its higher average occupancy levels. However, energy efficiencies vary by country even for public transport; for example, transit is far more energy efficient in China than the United States. Regardless of setting, promoting shifts from car travel to public transport is central to reducing the transport sector's oil dependence. Of course, shifting to nonmotorized modes such as walking and cycling can reduce oil dependence even more. Supply-side initiatives, such as bus rapid transit and bikeway improvements, can bring about such shifts, but so can demand-side and land use measures, such as parking controls and transit-oriented development. All of these measures, when well designed and managed, improve access and urban milieus.

Oil dependence not only threatens environments and political stability but also has serious social equity implications. Historically, oil prices have been highly volatile, and the world's neediest people are most vulnerable to price swings. As demand for transportation fuels rises, so do prices. In the first decade of the twenty-first century, gasoline

Table 3-1. Transport energy use by mode, worldwide and by selected countries and regions.

| Country or region | Private vehicles | Transport energy use (megajoules per passenger kilometer) | | | | | | | Assumed occupancy rates for public transport in cities (%) |
| | | Public passenger transport | | | | | | | |
		Total	Bus	Tram	Light rail	Metro	Suburban rail	Ferry	
World	2.45	—	1.05	0.52	0.56	0.46	0.61	—	—
United States	4.6	2.63	2.85	0.99	0.67	1.65	1.39	5.41	10
Canada	5	1.47	1.5	0.31	0.25	0.49	1.31	3.62	15
Australia and New Zealand	3.9	1.49	1.66	0.36	—	—	0.53	2.49	10
Western Europe	3.3	0.86	1.17	0.72	0.69	0.48	0.96	5.66	17
High-income Asia	3.3	0.58	0.84	0.36	0.34	0.19	0.24	3.64	25
Eastern Europe	2.35	0.4	0.56	0.74	1.71	0.21	0.18	4.87	—
Middle East	2.56	0.67	0.74	0.13	0.2	—	0.56	2.32	—
Latin America	2.27	0.76	0.75	—	—	0.19	0.15	—	—
Africa	1.86	0.51	0.57	—	—	—	0.49	—	—
Low-income Asia	1.78	0.64	0.66	—	0.05	0.46	0.25	2.34	—
China	1.69	0.28	0.26	—	—	0.05	—	4.9	—

Source: Peter Newman and Jeff Kenworthy, "Peak Car Use: Understanding the Demise of Automobile Dependence," *World Transport Policy and Practice* 17:2 (2011): 35–36; UN Habitat, *Planning and Design for Sustainable Urban Mobility: Global Report on Human Settlements 2013* (Nairobi: UN Habitat, 2013).

Note: This table is based on data from a sample of 84 cities in different regions. Dashes indicate data not available.

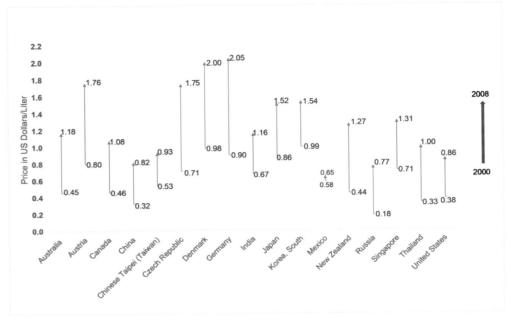

Figure 3-1. Regular unleaded gasoline prices across 17 countries, 2000–2008. (Source: U.S. Energy Information Administration, *Energy Outlook 2010* [Washington, DC: U.S. Energy Information Administration, 2010]; UN Habitat, *Planning and Design for Sustainable Urban Mobility: Global Report on Human Settlements 2013* [Nairobi: UN Habitat, 2013]).

prices steadily rose worldwide (figure 3-1). The urban poor in developing countries were especially hit hard by rising gasoline prices. In 2011, Kenya experienced a shortage in gasoline supply, followed by a 30 percent rise in gasoline prices within a few months.[6] Car owners slowly cut back on driving. Mounting gasoline prices had an immediate effect on public transport. Privately owned bus lines, called matatus, cut back on their least profitable lines and raised fares, resulting in poorer quality (and notably more crowded) services at substantially higher prices. Poor people living on the urban fringes suffered the most, with some depleting their daily earnings so that little was left for essentials such as food, and the poorest were unable to travel long distances in search of subsistence income.

Regardless of what is done to advance alternative fuel vehicles or create less automobile-dependent cities, supply-and-demand forces will ultimately require reduced reliance on petroleum. World reserves of conventional oil exceed what has been used to date, but with rapid motorization and thus increasing demands for oil, many observers believe it is unlikely that this energy source will last beyond the mid-century mark.[7] Pathways that provide a steady, minimally disruptive transition to reduced oil dependence are sorely needed. Many of the city-recalibrating ideas presented in this book, we believe, can contribute to this transition.

The Climate Challenge: Decarbonizing Cities and Transport

Oil dependence has harmed natural environments worldwide. It has increased global emissions of CO_2, the principal component of planet-warming GHGs. Climate change has catapulted toward the top of today's policy challenges for good reason. It is increasingly apparent that unless major steps are taken to decarbonize cities and regions, the global environmental and ecological consequences will be catastrophic, if not irreversible: increased flooding of low-lying areas (where most of the world's city dwellers live), more extreme weather patterns that wreak havoc on cities and claims lives, crop damage that triggers famine, and the extinction of plant and animal species.

Cities and the transportation systems that serve them have an important role to play in reducing GHG emissions and stabilizing climates. The transport sector is responsible for nearly a quarter of total energy-related CO_2 emissions worldwide, a figure that has remained fairly constant over the past four decades but could rise with increased motorization and travel in developing countries.[8] Cities themselves are responsible for a significant share of GHG emissions because they are large energy consumers: In 2011, cities were responsible for an estimated 70 percent of the world's energy-related GHG emissions.[9] Rapidly urbanizing countries contribute large amounts of GHG emission because of the energy intensity of infrastructure construction. Rapid urbanization in China, for example, has resulted in nearly half of the world's concrete and steel going to erect buildings, bridges, and other structures.[10] China's large-scale infrastructure investments are expected to account for 37 percent of global emission commitments to 2060, reflecting the high carbon emissions embodied in infrastructure buildup in the early twenty-first century.

The transportation sector itself is inextricably linked to climate change mitigation and adaptation. It is responsible for 13 percent of GHG emissions worldwide and, as noted, for nearly a quarter of energy-related emissions.[11] Three-quarters of these emissions stem from road transport.[12] By 2050 global CO_2 emissions from motor vehicle use could be three times as large as they were in 2010, accounting for 40 percent of GHG emissions.[13]

From 1973 to 2010, CO_2 emissions from the transport sector nearly doubled, from 3.4 to 6.7 billion tons.[14] Fueling meteoric rises in GHG emissions has been the growing demand for urban mobility. In the hundred-plus years of motor vehicles relying on gasoline as a fuel, the world has used approximately one trillion barrels of petroleum to move people, materials, and goods.[15] The transport sector's share of global oil demand grew from 33 percent in 1971 to 47 percent in 2002 and by one account could reach 54 percent by 2030 if past trends hold.[16] With increasing motorization and investments in roads and highways, cities find themselves in a vicious cycle: Reliance on the private car unleashes more sprawl and road building that further increases reliance on the private car. The rigid, impervious nature of transport infrastructure exacerbates climate-induced catastrophes. Paved parking and roadways contribute to natural drainage failures. A more climate-resilient transport infrastructure is urgently needed.[17]

The transportation sector is not only a contributor but also a victim of climate change. It is highly vulnerable to the effects of global warming, particularly the increased frequency and severity of flooding and excessive heat, which cause significant damage to transport infrastructure.[18] Nearly one-half of the world's cities are located on a seacoast or along a major river. These cities have historically been subject to occasional flooding, but these risks have increased in step with more frequent storm surges and high winds, both caused by global warming and rising sea levels. Transport systems are often the first to bear the brunt of major flooding. Inundated highways and collapsed bridge supports can result. Yet it is the same transport system that we rely on for mass evacuation. When transport systems fail, they can have crippling economic effects. The submerging of roads along America's Gulf Coast during the next 50 to 100 years could cost, by one estimate, hundreds of billions of dollars.[19]

There is no one-size-fits-all approach to transport-related GHG mitigation. This is partly because transport's footprint varies widely across cities, accounting for 11 percent of GHG emissions in Shanghai and Beijing, 20 percent in New York City and London, 35 percent in Rio de Janeiro and Mexico City, 45 percent in Houston and Atlanta, and 60 percent in São Paulo.[20] Levels of energy consumption for transport and thus GHG emissions vary significantly even between cities with similar GDPs, depending on urban form, financing and taxation policies, and the quality and affordability of alternative modes. As cities become more compact and dense, CO_2 emissions from transport generally decline.[21] For instance, Austria's urban areas are more than four times denser than Australia's and generate only 60 percent of the amount of CO_2 per capita that Australia's urban areas generate.[22] Mode share is also an important factor: Energy consumption levels universally fall as the share of trips on public transport and nonmotorized modes increases. In 2008, per capita energy consumption in the transport sector was 2.8 times higher in the United States than in Japan and more than 4 times higher than in Germany.[23] One of the reasons is that in Japan, 40 percent of all urban motorized trips are by public transport, compared with just 4 percent in the United States.[24] Indeed, GHG emissions per passenger of public transport (bus, rail, and trams) is about one-twelfth that of the car.[25]

Transport-related emissions vary at the national level as well. The transport emissions per capita in North America are more than four times the global average, whereas in most of Asia and Africa they are but a third of the global average.[26] The overall CO_2 emissions per capita in the United States are sometimes 2.5 times higher than in China, but in the case of transport emissions they are 12 times higher. Clearly climate mitigation must take a different form city by city, country by country. Although emissions per capita in the Global South pale in comparison with those in the United States, Australia, and most parts of Europe, cities in the Global South are among the fastest-growing and largest contributors to climate change. Any plan to reduce global emissions must consider the fast-growing cities of Asia, Africa, and Latin America.

Regardless of setting, some common mitigation steps, notably the decarbonization of the transport sector's fuel supply, will be needed to stabilize climates and cleanse cities.[27] However, technology alone will be insufficient. Reduced motorized travel has a role to play as well. The post-oil city of tomorrow will need to be one that allows people to easily get around by foot, two-wheelers, buses, and trains. This will require stronger linkages of transport and urbanization and increased investments in green infrastructure. Investments that improve the connectivity of pedestrian, bicycle, and transit networks and the attractiveness of living and working in compact, mixed-use settings—that is, cities with green mobility and well-designed places—are part of the solution.

It may well be that it is too late for appreciable inroads to be made in reducing carbon emissions and that bigger payoffs are to come from focusing on climate adaptation than mitigation. Climate adaptation will require marked changes in how cities are designed and where development is located. New development in flood-prone locations must be curtailed or even banned. Infrastructure must be designed to withstand high temperatures (e.g., to reduce the buckling of rail tracks). Drainage systems need to move floodwaters away from infrastructure. In general, transport infrastructure and the cities they serve need more built-in resilience. They must be more resourceful, more robust, and more flexible, whether through form-based zoning codes that bring buildings closer together, elevated tramways that can withstand flooding and storm surges, or bus rapid transit improvements that allow a quick reconfiguration of routes as emergencies dictate.

Design reforms that can withstand the wrath of extreme weather patterns and increase resilience are particularly crucial in developing countries, the world's most rapidly urbanizing and motorizing settings. It is the Jakartas, Mumbais, and Dar es Salaams of the world where major strides must be made in building climate-proof urban systems. Poor residents of cities in the Global South are among the most vulnerable to changing weather patterns and rising sea levels, because they often live in ecologically vulnerable lands and are least able to afford to move or adapt to climate change. Decarbonizing cities and urban transport would benefit the neediest inhabitants of the world's neediest countries.

Local Pollution

GHGs are a global form of pollution. Also worrisome are local pollutants. Worldwide, only 160 million people live in cities with clean, healthy air—that is, in compliance with World Health Organization (WHO) guidelines.[28] WHO estimates that 80 percent of urban dwellers live in cities with excessive amounts of particulates and other pollutants, contributing to 5.4 percent of annual deaths worldwide. Oxides of sulfur and nitrogen (SO_x and

NO_x) and ozone (O_3), outdoor air pollutants, are particularly problematic in cities because of their high concentrations and levels of exposure. Long-term, repeated exposure to high levels of ozone and particulates can diminish lung function and trigger asthma and other respiratory illnesses. Worldwide, some 3 million people died prematurely in 2012 because of air pollution, about four times as many as a decade earlier.[29]

The urban transport sector is a major contributor to local air pollution. It is the biggest emitting sector in the developed world and increasingly responsible for air quality problems in developing countries. Of the global cities with more than 100,000 residents that exceed WHO clean air standards, 98 percent are in low- and middle-income countries.[30] Although the most polluted cities are clustered in Africa and the Middle East, air pollution has exacted its biggest toll in China and India, where poor air quality has been associated with billions of years of lost life.[31] In China, home to some of the world's most polluted cities, about half of the pollutants that form photochemical smog come from the tailpipes of cars, trucks, and motorized two-wheelers.[32] The urban transport sector's footprint is even greater in Central and Eastern Europe. There, 80 percent of total air pollutants in most capital cities, including Ashgabat, Dushanbe, Moscow, Tbilisi, Tashkent, and Yerevan, come from cars and trucks.[33]

In many developing cities, air pollution stems to a significant degree from the prevalence of old, poorly maintained vehicles that run on dirty fuels, such as high-sulfur diesels and leaded gasoline. In India, many auto rickshaw drivers illegally adulterate their gasoline with up to 30 percent kerosene and 10 percent lubricating oil to economize on fuel costs, but hydrocarbon and particulate emissions increase exponentially as a result.[34] In some developing cities, lax regulatory standards are also to blame, allowing them to become the dumping grounds for gross emitters, such as decrepit imported vehicles from Western Europe and Eastern Asia. Also to blame are fiscal policies. In Uganda, for example, the import duty on second-hand vehicles of 56 percent is so high that many residents cannot do away with old cars (on average, 12 years of age) to acquire newer, less-polluting ones.[35]

Sources of transport-sector emissions are altogether different in most developed cities. There, trucks and freight carriers are the chief culprits behind rising mobile-source emissions. Even though large commercial vehicles make up less than 10 percent of road traffic in most European cities, they can cause half of all nitrogen dioxide emissions (a contributor to the formation of photochemical smog), about a third of particulate matter, and more than 20 percent of GHG emissions.[36] Goods movement clearly must be part of the urban recalibration equation in many parts of the world, whether in the form of electric consolidated freight vehicles or urban agriculture that, besides greening neighborhoods and increasing food security, reduces the need to ship in fruits and vegetables.

Another form of local pollution is unwanted noise. Here again, motor vehicles, and especially heavy trucks, are a significant source of the problem. In Moscow, around three-quarters of the population lives in areas with transport noise levels that exceed WHO standards.[37] Noisy streets pose even greater hearing risks in crowded cities of the developing world. Studies show that prolonged exposure to loud traffic can cause irreversible hearing loss, disrupt sleep, increase stress levels, and in general diminish the quality of urban living.[38]

Many of the ideas for recalibrating the design of cities reviewed in this book increase urban densities. Yet compact living increases exposure to both noise and air pollution, which is often cited by critics as a rationale for lowering urban densities. However, compact mixed-use environments also reduce motorized traffic. Car-free pedestrian zones, found in some of the most compact cities of the world, are attractive in part because they are less noisy. Public policies, regulations, and clean technologies—whether in the form of promoting bike sharing, restricting cars in crowded districts, or decarbonizing fuel supplies—clearly have an important role to play in creating healthy and livable urban futures.

There is also an important environmental justice dimension to cleansing local air basins and mitigating traffic noise. Often those affected the most—the poor, the young, and older adults living near freeways and other infrastructure—contribute the least to pollution because they travel less and rely more on transit or nonmotorized modes. This holds in wealthy and poor societies alike. In the world's poorest cities, informal settlements often pop up on unstable or contaminated land, downwind of factories, or near large infrastructure, such as freeways or freight corridors, that make the sites unattractive to private real estate developers. Flooding, mudslides, deafening noise levels, and exposure to extreme weather events are all too common. As with global pollution, reducing local emissions and exposures among all urban dwellers is critically important to advancing environmentally just urban futures.

Environmental Mitigation and Urban Recalibration

Significant environmental benefits can accrue from a shift in focus away from mobility and more to places. Place-making that makes high-density living more attractive while promoting eco-friendly transport such as cycling—made more possible through compact growth—reduces energy consumption and tailpipe emissions through shortening of trips and modal shifts. For example, an Australian study found that annual energy consumption of suburban households was 50 percent higher than that of households in the urban center, explained primarily by greater car use and longer journeys.[39] Compact development, which becomes more acceptable to middle-class households when supplemented by greenery and aesthetics, can curb other environmental costs associated with car-dependent sprawl: premature consumption of open space and prime agricultural land, fragmentation of natural habitats, reduced biodiversity, and disruption of local ecosystems from dissecting roads. Widened roads may take away land for pedestrians, play areas, and green spaces. Trees that once were the lungs of communities and habitat to birds and wildlife are continually being lost to roads.

An important feature of compact, mixed-use development is that trips are shortened. Cities that promote shorter trips by slower modes are among the world's most sustainable places. They reduce the vehicle miles traveled (VMT) per inhabitant, the strongest correlate of environmental adversity in the transport sector: As VMT per person goes up, so do energy consumption, land takings, pavement coverage, and tailpipe emissions. Mixed land uses also encourage cycling by allowing trip chaining and efficient tours (e.g., tying together a trip to work, shopping, and a fitness center as part of the same bike trip). Urban containment can also contribute to climate change mitigation by preserving the carbon sequestration capacity of surrounding natural and agricultural areas.[40] Urban greening and landscaping, made possible by compact development, can reduce the urban heat island effect. Along with building design features such as reflective materials (e.g., white roofs) that absorb less solar radiation, place-making enhancements that replace pavement with green spaces and create tree canopies help cool dense environments.[41]

As discussed in chapter 7, pedestrian-friendly and transit-oriented growth produces environmental synergies. For example, clean technologies are enabled by low-impact patterns of growth. Electric vehicles with limited driving ranges become more viable in compact, mixed-use settings of short-distance travel. By one estimate, compact development combined with technological improvements (e.g., more fuel-efficient vehicles) can reduce GHG emissions by 15 to 20 percent.[42] Of course, CO_2 emissions will decline only if electricity comes from renewable sources such as wind and solar or low-carbon stocks such as biofuels. Fortunately, this is increasingly the case. As discussed in chapter 7, the green TODs of Scandinavia yield scale economies that in turn reduce energy consumption of buildings and make the on-site production of clean energy such as biofuels economically feasible.

Physical "hardware" measures can also combine with policy "software" measures to make a difference. Smart growth and efficient pricing reinforce each other, for example, with positive environmental outcomes. A 2006 experiment in Portland, Oregon, replaced gasoline taxes with VMT charges, levied on 183 households that volunteered for the experiment. Some motorists paid a flat VMT charge, whereas others paid higher rates during peak times. The largest VMT and associated tailpipe emission reductions were recorded among households in compact, mixed-use neighborhoods that paid congestion charges, compared with little change in travel among those living in lower-density areas and paying flat rates.[43] A general equilibrium model of urban regions in Organisation for Economic Co-operation and Development countries reached similar conclusions, finding that "urban density policies and congestion charges reduce the overall cost of meeting GHG emission reduction targets more than economy-wide policies, such as a carbon tax, introduced by themselves."[44]

Close

Rising GHG emissions and global temperatures as well as levels of photochemical smog and particulates in urban air basins underscore the urgency of weaning the transport sector from its dependency on oil and more generally auto-mobility. Increased connectivity of green modes and place-making enhancements that promote compact, mixed-use living, we believe, are critically important to decarbonizing cities of the future. They contribute to better environments.

Governments are increasingly committed to shrinking the environmental footprint of the urban transport sector. The European Union has set a 2050 target of zero carbon emissions from transport in cities.[45] Environmentally progressive cities with world-class public transport and cycling infrastructure, such as Copenhagen and Stockholm, are leading the charge in decarbonizing their urban transport sectors. New communities, on greenfields as well as brownfields, are also fully committed to green, low-carbon mobility. Eco-friendly communities such as Vauban, Germany, and Hammarby Sjöstad, Sweden, discussed in chapter 7, have embraced core principles of sustainable urbanism and mobility: a diminished presence of the private car, substantial cycling and pedestrian infrastructure, green buildings and architecture, tramways that offer central-city circulation, dramatically reduced parking, and a built form that creates shorter trips and promotes slower modes. Thus important progress is being made, but more is needed, especially in developing cities, where motorization rates and VMT per capita continue to rise.

4

Better Economies

Connections—between and within cities—are vital to sustained economic growth, prosperity, and healthy living. Country roads connect farmers to markets and agricultural extension services, allowing the sale of crop surpluses and increasing food security. Metro lines connect skilled labor to good-paying downtown jobs. Bikeways also have utilitarian value plus the added bonus of promoting active travel and providing access to nature and the great outdoors. For avid cyclists, they make work–live–play balance possible. Decades of research convincingly shows that transport infrastructure is among the most powerful tools available for growing local and regional economies and enhancing quality of life.

In the language of microeconomics, transport is an essential factor input to economic production. It links raw materials to factories, finished products to distribution centers and retail outlets, and skilled labor to service industry jobs. Lowering transport costs increases firm productivity and profits. For cities of several hundred thousand inhabitants and more, tall office buildings owe their existence, in part, to metros and commuter rail lines that funnel sufficient numbers of high-skilled workers needed to achieve agglomeration economies, the economic benefits of clustered development. Concentrated growth, as in the form of downtown office towers, facilitates face-to-face contacts, interfirm exchanges, and knowledge spillovers, critical elements of knowledge-based economies. What's more, regional highway and transit networks expand laborsheds and tradesheds, the geographic territory from which firms draw in labor and commercially transact. In so doing, they facilitate firm–worker matching. As the geographic reach of labor markets increases, so does the likelihood that a company can recruit and hire the right person for the job and a worker can find the best job for her or his skill set and career aspirations. In much of the developed world, of course, enlarged laborsheds equate with sprawl and the high environmental and social costs that go with it. Whether enlarged laborsheds mean a more automobile-dependent urban form depends in good part on how new growth is managed and organized and the kinds of transport investments made. It also depends on focusing more on places than movement, and the connections between them.

The environmental agenda that is central to urban recalibration must not ignore the economic underpinnings of virtually all public choices. In market economies, consumers freely choose between competing goods and services so as to maximize personal well-being, constrained by regulations and controls introduced by politicians and policymakers. Elected officials similarly seek to optimize their well-being, politically speaking, by appeasing their constituents. Often this means enacting policies that create jobs and increase incomes, even if air quality suffers as a result. Environmental initiatives, however well-intended, must operate in the context of contemporary political and economic realities.

The timing of impacts, be they more breathable air or walkable neighborhoods, is crucial. Consider any number of measures aimed at shrinking environmental footprints, such as curbing sprawl via growth boundaries, stabilizing climates by decarbonizing fuel supplies, or cleansing the air through natural gas propulsion. Such measures appeal to the natural instincts of humankind to pass on a world to their offspring that is as livable, breathable, enjoyable, and productive as that of the present generation. However, a fundamental dilemma of all campaigns to create sustainable urban futures is that they unfold slowly and often take considerable time for the hoped-for environmental benefits and payoffs to materialize. They are at odds with political systems and 2- to 4-year election cycles that those who make tough policy choices—elected officials—live in. Within short political time horizons, other pressing needs, such as job creation and stimulating private investments, are apt to command more attention than environmental considerations. Voters and constituents demand so. Thus, linking the urban recalibration agenda to measurable and fairly immediate economic gains is critically important to advancing the green movement.

A logical way to know what's important to politicians is to ask them. Over the past decade, surveys of mayors worldwide consistently show transport infrastructure to be among the most important and pressing local issues they face, at the top of the list of public investments needed to make cities globally competitive.[1] A 2007 survey revealed that solving transportation issues was the number-one local priority in the eyes of 522 decision makers across twenty-five global cities.[2] In response to the question, "What should mayors do to make their cities more competitive for business?," posed in the 2010 Liveanomics survey by the Economist Intelligence Unit, 61 percent of mayors said "Improve public transport/roads," nearly twice the share that cited the second most common response, "Improve education."[3] Transport is the number-one concern even in the wealthiest countries with the most fully developed infrastructure. From a 2014 survey of more than 70 U.S. mayors, for example, transportation infrastructure topped the list of public investments that could spur economic growth.[4] The 2016 Menino survey of more than 100 U.S. mayors identified infrastructure, including roads and transit, as the top priority for federal aid.[5]

Transport is often viewed as critical to the economic well-being of developing cities. A recent KPMG/World Bank survey of senior managers of 100 midsize Tanzanian companies found that among public investments needed to successfully conduct their businesses, transportation was the most important, more so than electric power and communications.[6] Transport infrastructure is never sufficient, in and of itself, to turn around economic fortunes, and this is particularly so in the Global South, where governing capacities are weak and institutional reforms are needed if progress is to be made.

Making a convincing link between sustainable cities and economic performance is critical to moving the urban recalibration agenda forward. Demonstrating that walkable communities, transit-oriented development, and livable places can grow local economies, by itself, is probably not sufficient to gain sustained political support. However, the connection to economic benefits is indisputably a necessary precondition to bringing politicians on board. Translating such strategies into job formation, stepped-up private investments, attraction of new firms, increased labor productivity, and stronger real estate market performance will resonate more with politicians than metrics such as reductions in vehicle miles traveled (VMT), metric tons of carbon emissions, or acreage of farmland conversion. Yes, green jobs and low-impact manufacturing can stimulate economies in sustainable ways. However, so can making cities and places less traffic clogged, more visually and instinctively attractive, enjoyable to walk in, and accessible for everyday activities.

Urban theorists have floated the idea that economic progress is tied to striking a workable balance between transport infrastructure and place-making.[7] Quality of life, we are told, is an important feature of an economically competitive city. The previously cited 2016 Merino survey of U.S. mayors underscored this. Among U.S. cities with more than 300,000 inhabitants, quality of life was rated as the top policy priority, cited by 30 percent of mayors who were interviewed. Furthermore, amenity-oriented, place-based investments, some assert, can help regenerate once-declining urban districts.[8] In an early Urban Land Institute publication on place-making, Geoffrey Booth maintained that residents and employers are increasingly seeking out vibrant, pedestrian-friendly live–work–shop places, what was called the "place-making dividend."[9] Place-making is today widely understood as crucial to economic vibrancy, especially in core cities. A city's endowment of cultural assets and distinctive architecture can be an economic boon not only because it attracts visitors but also because it attracts and helps retain educated and skilled workers.[10] Such amenities not only help create distinctive, memorable places but also define the kinds of low-impact, harmonious transport services needed to bring people to them, often in the form of walkways, bikeways, and tramways.

The escalating count of "dead malls" throughout America's suburbs reflects the cold market reality of failing to appeal to the growing demand for attractive, less car-cluttered places to shop and to be. Even shopping malls that underwent dramatic facelifts in the past two decades have gone under because of their placelessness. The once highly popular Owings Mills Mall in North Bethesda, Maryland, which was renovated in 1998 but closed in 2016, succumbed to competition from more pedestrian-friendly, human-scale open shopping centers. A Web site, deadmalls.com, has been created to chronicle the grave-yard of malls that dot America's suburbs. Chapter 6 reviews several successful efforts to repurpose and reinvent car-centric shopping malls by transforming them into mixed-use projects with 24/7 personas.

Perhaps more than anyone, Richard Florida has elevated the role of urban amenities and place-making as an economic development tool. Florida has attributed the resurgence of large cities such as New York and Boston to their so-called cultural, aesthetic, and consumerism advantages, ones that help them attract knowledge-based workers and the "creative class."[11] Cities that offer amenities such as cafés, clubs, bars, galleries, and public spaces that appeal to the iPhone generation correlate with the presence of knowledge workers and economic growth, even if they are "old and cold" (New York or Boston, London or Berlin, Melbourne or Tokyo).[12] People-oriented "third places" that enrich land use mixes are increasingly vital in the heated competition for good-paying jobs in the twenty-first-century global marketplace.

This chapter marshals evidence on the economic benefits of creating more livable, less car-oriented places. Evidence is still trickling in, and not everyone is convinced about the link between livability and economic performance. Besides statistical studies, insights from qualitative research are also mentioned in this chapter. Politicians live in a world of best-case examples and anecdotes. Research shows that politicians retain case-based information more readily than empirical numbers.[13] To politicians, evidence on better economies is best conveyed through better stories.

Lifestyle Preferences and Economics

Market trends are a harbinger of what's in store for cities and suburbs of the future. Shifting demographics, household structures, lifestyle preferences, and consumer values suggest a different built environment and urban fabric 30 years ahead compared with 30 years ago. More and more Americans, Australians, and Europeans are choosing to live in settings where they are less dependent on their cars because reducing air pollution and energy use matters to them.[14] A 2011 survey of more than two thousand adult Americans found seven times more people said the neighborhood where a house is located is a bigger consideration in deciding where to live than the size of the house.[15] Walking to restaurants, businesses, schools, and other amenities was the most appealing neighbor-hood feature for many respondents. To many 20- and 30-somethings, walkable communities are equated with a downsized environmental footprint and energy efficiency, with the added benefit of burning calories during everyday activities. If green buildings and solar panels dot the landscape and rooftops, all the better. Notes one economist with the Urban Land Institute, "Energy efficiency is becoming the new granite countertops; it's a necessary feature to sell the property."[16]

Shifting preferences are about more than evolving tastes; they are partly a reaction to bona fide problems associated with car-oriented, suburban living.[17] Numerous studies have linked sprawl to rising obesity rates, which are reaching epidemic levels in parts of the United States and Europe and increasingly places such as China and India.[18] Behavioral research shows that out of a number of daily activities, commuting has the most negative effect on peoples' moods.[19] Happiness economists similarly tell us that commuters who live an hour away from work need to earn 40 percent more money than they currently do to be as satisfied with their lives as noncommuters.[20]

The fact that the Millennial generation—those from their late teens to mid-30s—are increasingly forsaking car ownership and driver's licenses, at least in the United States, Canada, Western Europe, and Australia, speaks volumes about where consumer demand is heading. From 2000 to 2010, the share of 14- to 34-year-olds in the United States without a driver's license rose from 21 percent to 26 percent.[21] Over roughly the same period, the annual number of vehicle miles traveled by America's young people fell 23 percent. Although the recession played a role in these declines, more recent data reveal that this trend holds even in more buoyant economic times. Only 69 percent of America's 19-year-olds had licenses in 2014, compared with 87.3 percent in 1983, a 21 percent drop.[22] Shifting lifestyle choices partly account for this trend, but so do new information technologies. In cities such as San Francisco, New York, and London, app-based ride-hail services such as Uber and Lyft have flourished in part because tech-savvy young professionals find it easier and more convenient to call for a car on demand than own one, automatically charging the expense to their debit cards.[23] Such services make living in mixed-use urban villages with many everyday activities within a 3- or 4-minute walk all the more possible.

The trend toward a less automobile-dominated lifestyle can have direct long-term economic repercussions, at least in terms of the personal pocketbook. Money freed up from not owning, using, or maintaining a car, arguably one of the most rapidly depreciating assets around, can be directed to other things, including owning a home, one of the most rapidly appreciating assets, especially in gentrified districts.

The growing demand for homes in walkable communities is reflected by land price premiums. Traditional walkable neighborhoods near transit weathered the real estate market downturn of the past decade better than anywhere else. In 2000, for instance, the highest price per square foot in the Washington, DC, metro area was in the leafy suburbs of Great Falls, Virginia. Ten years later, townhouses in the hip and urbane Dupont Circle neighborhood of Washington were worth 70 percent more per square foot than property in Great Falls. Similar stories could be told in many U.S. rail-served cities with reasonably robust regional economies, at least robust enough to rebound from the Great Recession of 2007–2011.

Recent surveys and markets further underscore the desirability for walkable places, even in better economic times. A 2013 community preference survey by the National Association of Realtors (NAR) showed that 60 percent of Americans favored neighborhoods with mixes of houses and stores, whereas only 35 percent favored ones that rely on driving to get around.[24] Millennials are particularly drawn to walkable places: According to the American Planning Association, 56 percent want to live in more walkable neighborhoods with mixed uses.[25] Furthermore, the 2015 NAR survey found that 83 percent of Millennials like walking, compared with 71 percent who like driving (the lowest percentage of any generation).[26] In terms of asking rents, one study found that among America's thirty largest metro areas, walkable urban places commanded premiums of 66 percent for multifamily and 71 percent for retail properties compared with car-dependent suburban locations over the 2010–2015 period.[27] A related study found similar premiums based on sales transactions: In metropolitan Washington, DC, homes in walkable urban neighborhoods sold for 70 percent more per square foot than those in car-dependent areas.[28]

Mixing walkability and transit access is a particularly profitable combination. Trend-line data from the TOD Index, prepared by John Renne, reveals this, even in the world's most car-dependent society, the United States.[29] The index tracks home values in zip codes associated with 1,444 train stations in thirty-nine regions across the United States. Figure 4-1 shows that for the period from mid-1996 to the end of 2016, median TOD home values per square foot rose more than fourfold, substantially outperforming national trends (reflected by Zillow median home values). Since the start of America's economic recovery in early 2012, TOD home values have grown 57 percent, compared with the national growth of 32 percent. Similar patterns were found for rental markets.[30] Even though rental and home prices per square foot for TODs are higher, a combination of smaller units and lower outlays for daily travel makes TOD living more affordable. The TOD Index report estimates that TOD residents average more than $10,000 in extra disposable income per year than the typical American.

The preference for compact, mixed-use, walkable settings extends to commercial and office real estate projects. For the past 15 years, surveys of nonresidential developers by the Urban Land Institute and PricewaterhouseCoopers have consistently shown the top investment prospects to be areas close to transit stations, in pedestrian-oriented suburban business districts, and in central business districts. Least appealing have been car-dependent settings such as suburban strip commercial centers, suburban business parks,

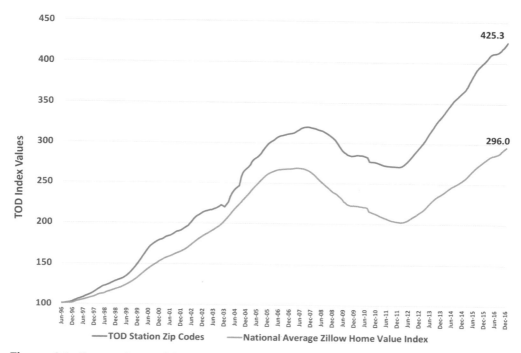

Figure 4-1. Comparison of home values in U.S. cities: TOD zip codes versus Zillow national home values, 1996–2016. (Source: Renne-Greschner TOD Index, https://todindex .com/.)

and exurbia. Real estate prices reflect these preferences: Since 2010, offices in mixed-use, walkable locales in America's thirty largest metro areas have commanded rent premiums some 90 percent above properties in car-oriented suburban locales.[31] Smart investment money has gravitated to lively, 18-hour, 7-days-a-week urban and suburban districts rather than mono-use developments that operate only during the day, Monday through Friday.

Companies increasingly realize that offices close to residences, shops, recreational outlets, and educational centers—once called multiuse centers and now often referred to as live-work-learn-play (LWLP) places—appeal to highly sought young professionals. The 2010 U.S. census showed that nearly two-thirds (64 percent) of college-educated 25- to 34-year-olds said they looked for a job after they chose the city where they wanted to live. Where most want to live is in walkable districts with Starbuck's-like away-from-home-and-work places to hang out, surf the Internet, chat with other locals, and work on their laptops, known as "third places." And where educated Millennials go, so do employers and retailers. Over the past 5 years, America's fastest job growth has been in urban areas, reversing the past few decades of job suburbanization.[32]

The Big Picture

For marshalling the evidence on better economies, we start at the macro level. City-level comparisons are often belittled by academics for their simplicity and vulnerability to spurious inferences. However, politicians and news editors love them. If nothing else, they can confirm the findings of more rigorous disaggregate studies, making them more accessible to nonacademics and the broader public. The following is some evidence on cities and economic performance at the macro, "from 30,000 feet above" level.

One of the first studies to suggest that auto-centric sprawl can be a drag on the economy was by Jeffrey Kenworthy and Felix Laube.[33] Theirs is among the most widely cited macro-scale studies on transport and economic performance. Using data from forty-six international cities over the 1960 to 1990 period, the authors found that gross regional product per capita was generally higher in less auto-dependent cities. Their conclusion: "Car use does not necessarily increase with increasing wealth, but tends to fall in the most wealthy cities."[34] In an updated study titled "Decoupling Urban Car Use and Metropolitan GDP Growth," Kenworthy documented a decline in passenger kilometers traveled per unit of gross domestic product (GDP) for thirty-seven of forty-two high-income cities over the 1995 to 2005 period.[35] Another widely cited and more recent macro study, *Growing Wealthier*, reached similar conclusions. Prepared by the Center for Clean Air Policy, the study found that U.S. states with low VMT per capita tended to have higher GDP per capita.[36] Peter Newman and Jeffrey Kenworthy's recent book, *The End of Automobile Dependence*, echoed this finding: The six most walkable U.S. cities averaged a 38 percent higher per capita GDP than other medium to large cities.[37]

These studies, it bears noting, relied on simple correlations and for the most part introduced few statistical controls. This hampers the ability to draw causal inferences. Other researchers have reached opposite conclusions, finding that physical travel and wealth creation tend to reinforce each other. Travel, they argue, is both a catalyst and consequence of economic interaction. Using data for the United States as a whole over the 1936–2007 period, a study conducted for a libertarian think tank, the Cascade Policy Institute, found travel and wealth to be positively associated with each other.[38] Based on Granger causality testing, moreover, changes in VMT were found to more strongly explain changes in GDP than vice versa. That is, more rather than less physical travel, the researchers argued, was associated with economic growth.

Further muddying the waters are exceptions that can be found when tracking trends for individual metropolitan areas. For two U.S. regions with productive public transit systems and comparatively strong regional economies—Washington, DC, and Portland, Oregon—incomes grew faster than travel during the 2001–2006 period (figure 4-2). For many medium-sized U.S. cities without urban rail systems, there's little relationship between

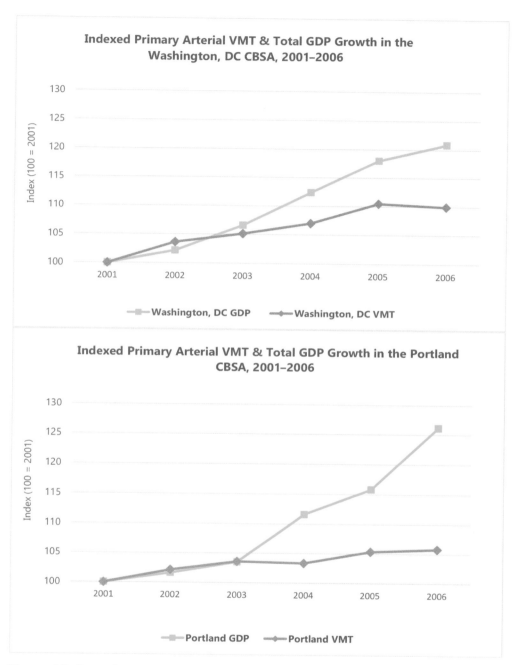

Figure 4-2. Growth trends in GDP and VMT, *(a)* Washington, DC, and *(b)* Portland, Oregon, 2001–2006. (Data provided courtesy of the Center for Clean Air Policy [CCAP], Washington, DC. Adapted from charts produced by C. Kooshian of CCAP for the World Symposium on Transport and Land Use Research, Whistler, BC, July 2011.)

travel and income. It might very well be that in auto-oriented cities, travel and commerce feed off each other, but in denser, more transit-oriented places, such as Washington and Portland, they do not. Construct validity might also be at play. That is, travel, or VMT per capita, could be a poor explanatory metric, and what really matters is interaction, be it in the form of economic transactions or social network building.

Measuring relationships between transport, urban form, and economic outcomes at finer geographic scales is complicated by the fact that economic transactions often span large territories, so pinpointing the location of wealth creation is difficult. More disaggregate studies have shown that compact and highly accessible districts within cities tend to have higher levels of labor productivity.[39] A study of twenty-seven subregions in the San Francisco Bay Area found labor productivity rose with increases in highway travel speeds, employment densities, and job accessibility levels. Disaggregate findings drawn from one or a few metropolitan areas, however, raise questions about external validity, or the generalizability of results to other places.

Another relevant question that can be addressed from macro data concerns modes of travel and economic well-being. It is commonly held that wealthy places allow more private car consumption, which in most instances equates with less transit usage. After all, transit is most heavily used by the poor, and thus the same should hold for cities; that is, lower-income ones might be expected to average higher transit usage. A city-level database from the International Association of Public Transport (UITP) calls this into question. Table 4-1, prepared from the UITP database, suggests that low VMT and high

Table 4-1. Transit ridership, VMT, and GDP among 9 global cities.

	Transit trips per person per year	VMT per person per year	GDP per person (US$, 2005)
Hong Kong	627	4,880	$27,600
Zurich	533	8,690	$41,600
Munich	534	9,670	$45,800
Singapore	484	9,240	$28,900
Stockholm	346	7,210	$32,700
Curitiba	334	7,900	$ 6,800
Copenhagen	268	8,700	$34,100
Chicago	73	12,000	$40,000
Melbourne	105	11,400	$22,800

Source: International Association of Public Transport, Mobility in Cities Database, 2006.

transit ridership are not synonymous with low economic performance. European cities with world-class transit systems, such as Zurich and Munich, average high GDP per capita as well as high transit ridership and modest VMT per capita. More car-dependent cities such as Chicago and Melbourne average lower GDP per capita on a parity purchasing power basis. Zurich is one of the wealthiest cities in the world, and its high per capita levels of transit ridership are matched by some of the highest commercial real estate values in the world (Bahnhoffstrasse), high worldwide rankings in quality of life (almost always in the top five),[40] one of the lowest vehicle ownership rates in the developed world (40 percent of households have no cars), and some of the best air quality of any European city. In Zurich, car-limited living, world-class transit, green urbanism, and prosperity go hand in hand.[41]

Access and Land Markets

Much of the scholarly literature on urban transport and economic performance has focused on property markets. If transportation delivers benefits in the form of improved access and connectivity, this is reflected in real estate prices. There is a finite, limited supply of land parcels with great access to jobs, shopping, parkland, and other urban attractions. In the competition for accessible locations, people and institutions bid up the prices of the most accessible properties. Land markets effectively capitalize the accessibility benefits of transportation improvements that connect places.

Freeways and Motorways

Most research on improved access and real estate market performance has concentrated on roadway networks, mostly because in the developed world at least, far more travel occurs in cars and trucks than trains and buses. Freeways and other high-performance road investments are indispensable features of the industrialized world. Limited-access, grade-separated freeway systems drive down the costs of moving the two main components of economic production: capital and labor.[42] Studies show that under the right conditions, urban land markets capitalize the benefit of proximity to freeway interchanges, especially for nonresidential uses.[43] What, one might ask, are the right conditions? For the most part, rapid population and employment growth, matched by worsening traffic congestion, must be present if nearby properties are to capitalize the accessibility benefits conferred by highways and freeways.[44] Even then, other preconditions, such as supportive zoning and complementary infrastructure, must also be present if significant property value increases are to occur.[45] Additionally, research shows that land use impacts of roadways tend to be more redistributive than generative, shifting growth that would have occurred somewhere to one part of a region. In buoyant economic times, infrastructure generally "crowds in" investment, attracting private capital. Under stagnant conditions, however, it can "crowd out" private investment, effectively channeling private wealth into public goods and services. Moreover, studies show, transport infrastructure is incapable, by itself, of turning around lagging economies and distressed urban areas.[46]

A California study concluded that land value appreciation attributable to highway investments can depend on network structure and the composition of economic growth.[47] The marginal accessibility benefits of an improvement to an already extensive roadway network might be small. Site features also matter. For commercial activities that rely on visibility, exposure, and ease of site access, such as motels and convenience retail, land appreciation is often limited to parcels close to an interchange.[48]

Public Transit

Research has long established that proximity to high-performance transit corridors gets capitalized into higher land prices and comparatively strong real estate market performance. Mixed land uses, as reflected by overlay zones, are associated with even stronger capitalization effects.[49] Condos in amenity-dominated mixed-use neighborhoods experience much higher capitalization effects than single-family houses, even in sprawling cities such as Phoenix and San Diego.[50] Privately funded rail investments, such as Portland, Oregon's streetcar system, demonstrate that property owners are often willing, even eager, to invest in transit lines that benefit both them and the population as a whole.

Evidence on the benefits of being close to rail transit in the world's most rapidly motorizing and modernizing places, megacities of the developing world, is also beginning to accumulate. A recent study of eighty-five office properties in Bangkok showed a monthly rent premium of being 1 kilometer closer to a transit station of 19 Baht, or US$0.58, per square meter.[51] The elasticity of office rents and distance of metrorail stops was –0.06; in other words, a doubling of distance from metrorail was associated with a 6 percent drop in rents. However, proximity alone does not always translate into markedly higher real estate prices. Studies show that proximity combined with high-quality urban design and place-making can bolster land values even more. Hong Kong's Rail + Property (R+P) program, for instance, was found to generate 25 percent higher profits when air-rights development projects were combined with streetscape, landscaping, and other place-making enhancements.[52] See chapter 7 for further discussions on Hong Kong's experiences.

Transport Infrastructure in the Global South

In the Global South, insufficient roadways, transit infrastructure, and sidewalks often hinder economic development. According to a World Bank report, Asian cities dedicate only about a third as much space to roadways as American cities, constraining goods movement and economic growth.[53] Underinvestment is even worse in Africa, where the World Bank estimates that meeting infrastructure needs would cost $93 billion a year—approximately

15 percent of regional GDP.[54] Although transportation accounts for just 20 percent of this need, the report focuses entirely on regional transportation and emphasizes freight movement. The need is perhaps even greater in metropolitan areas.

Although there is general agreement that transportation infrastructure is insufficient in cities in the Global South, there is less agreement on how to close this gap. New infrastructure is expensive and competes with a host of other pressing needs such as education, health, and public safety. Furthermore, an emphasis on highway construction, despite strong and growing evidence that new highways do not reduce congestion,[55] has too often exacerbated problems by encouraging sprawl, dividing neighborhoods, breaking up the local road network, destroying the quality of pedestrian spaces, and inducing car ownership. Beijing has built six urban ring roads to accommodate its meteoric growth in car population, yet they have failed to reduce congestion or improve regional access.

In developing cities, new transit investments are rarely integrated with land development and existing transportation networks. Bogotá's highly acclaimed bus rapid transit (BRT) system, TransMilenio, failed to live up to its city-shaping potential in large part because system designers focused on maximizing mobility at minimum cost.[56] This meant siting TransMilenio lines in the median of busy motorways and distressed urban districts to economize on land acquisition costs, thereby suppressing development potential. In the Global South, the almost singular focus on moving the maximum numbers of people cheaply has trumped other considerations when adding transportation infrastructure.

Road Restraints, Pedestrianization, and Economic Performance

Freeways and thoroughfares are widely known to increase economic productivity and commercial property values. In the quest to strike a balance between mobility and livability, might things work in reverse? Might less roadway capacity and perhaps the outright tearing down of freeways and motorways actually yield economic benefits?

Over the past three decades, many European cities have brought livability and pedestrian safety to the forefront of transportation planning, opting for programs that tame and reduce dependence on the private car.[57] Traffic calming is one such approach, pioneered by Dutch planners who have added speed humps, realigned roads, necked down intersections, and planted trees and flowerpots in the middle of streets to slow down traffic. With traffic calming, automobile passage is secondary. Early studies of traffic calming found slowing traffic was often associated with higher property values, healthier commerce, and safer places.[58] After traffic calming its streets in the early 1990s, the city of Heidelberg, Germany, witnessed a 31 percent reduction in accidents and 44 percent fewer casualties.[59]

Empirical evidence reveals a host of benefits from street redesigns and auto-restraint measures. A study of pedestrianization in German cities recorded increases in pedestrian flows, transit ridership, land values, and retail sales transactions as well as property conversions to more intensive land uses, matched by fewer traffic accidents and fatalities.[60] Research on more than 100 cases of road capacity reductions (e.g., car-free zones, pedestrian street conversions, and street and bridge closures) in Europe, North America, Japan, and Australia found an average overall reduction in motorized traffic of 25 percent and, for the most part, positive economic outcomes.[61]

As discussed in chapter 8, more radical measures such as freeway removals and motorway-to-greenway conversions have also conferred economic benefits, as revealed by land prices and firm locations. In the early 2000s, Seoul, South Korea, embarked on a program of urban regeneration that included reclaiming urban space consumed by roads and highways, especially space used to funnel new-town inhabitants in and out of the central city.[62] The removal of a 6-kilometer elevated freeway in the heart of Seoul, Cheong Gye Cheon, replaced by a pedestrian-friendly greenway, sparked a radical transformation of central-city Seoul, including the conversion of dilapidated structures to modern midrise buildings.[63] At the same time that roadway capacity was reduced, new and expanded BRT and metrorail services were introduced. Land price premiums of 15 percent or more were recorded for residences within 300 meters of BRT stops and along the greenway.[64] Office and commercial rents were noticeably higher with a greenway than with an elevated freeway.[65] Moreover, there was an uptick in employment densities and professional offices along the corridor after the freeway-to-greenway conversion.[66] In a crowded, land-constrained city such as Seoul, better access and neighborhood environments prompted property owners and developers to intensify land uses along BRT and greenway corridors, mainly in the form of converting single-family residences to multifamily units and mixed-use projects. Similar economic benefits and land use densification have been recorded after the replacement of freeways with boulevards and greenways in San Francisco and Boston.[67]

Urban Amenities and Nature

So far, our attention has focused on the economics of transport facilities and transit-oriented locations. Place-making, of course, involves other elements of built and natural environments besides transport hardware and infrastructure. Urban amenities are a cardinal feature of place-making. Research from the United Kingdom has shown that the economic benefits of enhancing urban quality are of a similar order of magnitude as those conferred by public transport or pedestrianization improvements.[68] Moreover, studies from the United States consistently show that quality-of-place variables are associated with positive employment and human capital outcomes in large and midsized cities alike.[69]

Land value assessments have been carried out in the past on a number of different site amenities as well as dis-amenities, including open space, waste facilities, building designs, streetscapes, and waterfronts. As an externality, a site amenity or dis-amenity typically exerts its price influences on a specific aspect of a property, such as a view or proximity.[70] In middle- and upper-income settings, property owners are often willing to pay for aesthetics and architectural design to increase property premiums.[71] However, the impacts of nature are less clear. In the case of open space, studies show the land price impacts vary tremendously. Open space can increase land prices by its intrinsic qualities (e.g., greenery, spaciousness) but also by reducing the amount of developable land available. However, the noise and foot traffic generated by nearby popular parks and open areas can be viewed as a nuisance by residential property owners.[72] Proximity to nuisances such as toxic waste sites or airport flight paths universally lowers property values, with residential parcels losing the most.[73] Other forms of neighborhood amenities rarely overcome such nuisances. For example, one study showed that average land prices were no different in nicely landscaped districts than in less lavish ones with similar levels of traffic congestion.[74]

Research also shows that the land price effects of open space vary by size and type. One study found that small neighborhood parks increased residential property values the most.[75] Another study found that natural area parks were more highly valued than urban parks.[76] A Portland, Oregon, study found that proximity to private parks and golf courses increased residential sales prices.[77] In general, research shows, the benefits of open space accrue mostly to residential properties in areas that are denser, have higher household incomes, and are closer to central business areas.[78]

The impacts of open space and public amenities on nonresidential properties are less clear. Factors such as access to labor and customers are overriding considerations when firms or businesses choose a location. Urban parks might have amenity value, but they might also cut down on foot traffic, which many shops depend on. Urban economists such as Ed Glaeser contend that parks, greenery, open space, and waterfront improvements can help cities attract skilled workers and knowledge-based industries in addition to stabilizing declining neighborhoods.[79] One study in greater Los Angeles found that public amenities such as parks influenced the location patterns of firms.[80]

Community Designs and Economic Performance

We close this chapter with a brief review of the little evidence that exists on the influences of contemporary design genres, such as New Urbanism and neotraditional development, on economic outcomes. The evidence remains sketchy, and commentary is mostly anecdotal, thus our discussions are brief.

Matched-pair studies, wherein communities with similar household incomes and locations within a region are compared, show that smart growth communities, those with smaller lots, mixed land uses, sidewalk networks, and neighborhood centers, economically outperform car-oriented, residential-only places. Price premiums can range from 40 to 100 percent.[81] Moreover, studies show such neighborhoods better hold their premium values over time.[82] A recent Portland, Oregon, study found single-family homes that are closer to the city and have traditional neighborhood design features held their values more during the 2008–2009 economic downturn than comparison properties.[83] Community comparisons of walking- and car-oriented places also show that value premiums multiply when coupled with energy-conserving architecture and green urbanism. A case in point is Hammarby Sjöstad, an eco-community built on a former brownfield site on the edge of central Stockholm, which studies show enjoys a housing price premium over more car-oriented traditional suburbs with otherwise similar demographics and household incomes.[84]

Shifting development practices also speak to shifting market preferences. In the United States, open-air shopping centers fashioned after main streets have been built at a far more rapid pace over the past decade than enclosed malls enveloped by surface parking.[85] Ground-floor retail and "third place" offerings have become de rigueur for mixed-use and transit-oriented developments. For nearly a decade, the Urban Land Institute's *Emerging Trends in Real Estate* publication has shown that human-scale, people-oriented places with an accent on livability and social engagement outperform the best-performing enclosed malls by most market indicators.[86] This seems to hold in the Global North and South.

Although this chapter has focused on economic versus financial impacts, to many civic leaders, the fiscal implications of urban form can be just as if not more important. It is well established that sprawl is costly to service, whether in the form of extending sewer lines, logging more miles on school buses, or opening new fire stations in once remote settings. A study by the Florida Department of Community Affairs found that the infrastructure needed to serve a house in a spread-out, conventional suburban subdivision cost nearly twice as much (more than $15,000 in 2010 currency) as it costs to serve a house closer to existing job centers.[87] For the United States as a whole, *The Cost of Sprawl 2000* study estimated that during the first quarter of the twenty-first century, a controlled-growth versus uncontrolled-growth scenario would save nearly US$40 billion annually in public service expenditures.[88] A study of metropolitan Toronto estimated that developments with 66 people per hectare cost 40 percent more to serve than those with 152 people per hectare.[89] Calgary's mayor, Naheed Nenshi, successfully ran on a campaign of eliminating such "sprawl subsidies." Recalibrating urban growth to reduce car dependence is all the more critical in light of rapid motorization and modernization in the Global South. The new Climate Economy project of the Global Commission on the Economy and Climate estimates that more compact urban growth could reduce urban infrastructure capital outlays by more than US$3 trillion over the next 15 years.[90]

Close

As part of a city's economic development strategy, finding the right balance of mobility, livability, and place-making can be expected to gain importance in the increasingly heated global competition for high-skilled, knowledge-based industries and workers. Even cities with traditional manufacturing and basic-industry economies have much to gain through a balanced approach to connectivity and place-making. Places such as Detroit, Michigan, a poster child of aging Rust Belt cities, are aggressively investing in greenways, cultural amenities, mixed-use places that promote natural surveillance, and streetscape enhancements and are even contemplating freeway teardowns. Cities that advance sustainable transport modes, embrace walkability, and focus on community-building and place-making will be best positioned to attract high-value growth in years to come. To explore the challenges of recalibrating the planning and design of cities to create better future environments, communities, and economies, and thematic examples of where such challenges have been successfully taken on, we now turn to part two of this book.

PART II

Contexts and Cases

The next four chapters review different contexts for moving beyond mobility through urban recalibration. Case experiences—some successful, some less so—are discussed for each of the four contexts.

Chapter 5 examines the physical, social, and economic transformations of core districts in European and North American cities in the wake of postindustrialization. Experiences with redeveloping and regenerating docklands, warehouse districts, industrial sites, and abandoned rail corridors are reviewed, drawing case insights from Europe and the United States.

Whereas brownfield redevelopment has occurred mostly on central former industrial sites, a different type of metamorphosis is occurring in the suburbs: the transformation of sprawling, single-use employment centers and campus-style office parks into mixed-use, "complete" communities. Chapter 6 probes experiences with office park retrofits and edge city transformations in the San Francisco Bay Area and northern Virginia, among other settings. Other suburban transformations reviewed in the chapter include the infill and greening of surface parking at shopping malls as well land-hungry uses such as racetracks and multiplex movie theaters.

Infilling parking lots around urban rail transit stations with a mix of housing, retail, and pedestrian-oriented activities is yet another form of urban recalibration, as reviewed in chapter 7. Transit-oriented development (TOD) has gained popularity worldwide as a way to shrink the urban transportation sector's immense environmental footprint in addition to promoting broader social aims, such as community building and place-making. Chapter 7 draws on international cases in reviewing TOD typologies, transit-oriented designs and place-making, and revenue generation through value capture. Niche forms of TOD tied to green urbanism, adaptive reuse of industrial sites, and the creation of kid-friendly communities are also reviewed.

Chapter 8 closes out part two with an exploration of a different kind of recalibration happening in cities worldwide: the contraction and reassignment of valuable real estate that had been given over to roads to more people-oriented uses. Experiences with traffic calming, car-free districts, road dieting, green connectors, and freeway-to-greenway conversions are reviewed and assessed in the chapter.

Though not exhaustive in its coverage, together the different contexts and cases reviewed in part two provide ample illustrations and hopefully useful examples that other places can adapt and apply in recalibrating cityscapes and, in so doing, becoming better, more livable communities.

5

Urban Transformations

The transformation of the core city is a global phenomenon found in virtually every major postindustrial city in the United States and Europe, parallel with back-to-city migration. Chapter 9 focuses on urban and suburban transformations of the Global South; its fundamentally different conditions merit a separate chapter. The projects discussed in this chapter concern the reuse of former industrial properties of Western cities, including docklands, warehouse districts, and freight rails. Although there are many more cases of urban transformation, here we focus on the upgrade of former industrial transportation sites to accentuate the overall argument of the book: an urban recalibration from conduits to move goods to people-oriented places with a strong accent on aesthetics, amenities, and place-making.

Since the 1970s, the term *urban regeneration* has been used to denote the reuse of brownfield sites in postindustrial cities, generally defined as the physical, economic, and social renewal of an area that has been subjected to decline.[1] Urban regeneration concerns the redevelopment of brownfield sites, which, compared with greenfield development, is much more challenging and potentially a lot more risky and costly, because it generally requires remediation of contaminated sites, demolition of structures, and the upgrading of obsolete or aging infrastructure. Therefore, making the economics work is critically important. However, not all brownfield redevelopment can be considered urban regeneration. Only when the reuse of core city industrial land is championed by governments through *proactive* economic redevelopment policies do we speak of urban regeneration.

As promising as urban regeneration may be, it is also controversial, seen as gentrification and the widening of inequality. Critics argue that the focus should lie on people excluded from the benefits of property-led urban regeneration.[2] When this issue is addressed, urban transformations can be ways for postindustrial cities to retool the industrial engines that built their cities and create better communities, reduce environmental footprints, and benefit economies.

Globalization, containerization, and the rise of the postindustrial economy have changed the makeup of Western cities. Docklands and warehouse districts in Western cities became underused when the use of standardized containers moved shipping to deep-water ports and companies increasingly outsourced manufacturing to countries with lower labor costs. Meanwhile, the rise of the trucking industry led to the abandonment of thousands of rail lines. These former industrial sites can be given a new purpose in the postindustrial city, although some forms of manufacturing in these former industrial districts still exist. A new post–2009 recession trend is the emergence of the artisanal or "maker" economy on former industrial sites, such as small and young companies that produce craft products ranging from furniture to microbrews.[3]

As urban industrial sites became vacant, populations moved back to cities, a reversal of the postwar exodus to the suburbs. In the United States, mostly younger people migrated into center cities, a phenomenon researcher Moos called "youthification."[4] In 1990 most American cities had even age distributions, with young adults making up 22–25 percent of the population of urban centers. By 2012, they made up 25–40 percent or more of the population within 2 miles of city centers.[5] Above all, well-educated young adults reside in metropolitan areas. Two-thirds of America's 25- to 34-year-olds with a bachelor's degree live in the nation's metropolitan areas with populations of a million or more.[6]

A similar phenomenon occurred in Europe. Manchester, England, lost 17.5 percent of its population between 1971 and 1981 as its industrial dominance decayed. Then, between 2001 and 2011, census data revealed that the city's population increased by 20 percent, now at a median age of 29. What helped trigger the city's rebound was the British government relocating many functions out of high-priced London, including the BBC headquarters, which helped create a MediaCityUK on the site of the former Manchester docks. Meanwhile, throughout the city, old red-brick warehouses became lofts and nightclubs.

Design and a sense of place help make urban regeneration successful.[7] Built to withstand the pressures of industrial processes, many factories and warehouses were built to last, and their high-vaulted ceilings and thick ceilings lend an industrial aesthetic that has become all too fashionable. A study by the National Trust for Historic Preservation shows that established neighborhoods with a mix of older, smaller buildings perform better than districts with larger, newer structures when tested against a range of social, economic, and environmental outcome measures.[8] Older buildings provide historic authenticity, an original identity, and what Kevin Lynch referred to as "imagability."[9] With a few adjustments, typically the opening of ground floor walls to create a more attractive street edge and let in light, they can be adapted into museums, incubator offices, and residential lofts. The reuse of an existing industrial site also has environmental benefits: It avoids new construction and sprawl and saves embodied energy—all the energy used to build and maintain the structure (from fuel to labor). Moreover, adaptive reuse has social benefits, because it can preserve a piece of history that is meaningful to communities. In short, urban regeneration can catalyze positive change by repurposing industrial infrastructure and through place-making.

Dockland Conversions

This section focuses on three cases of dockland conversions: London, Rotterdam, and Buffalo. The London Docklands was the first large-scale dockland redevelopment focused not just on infrastructure but also on place-making. Rotterdam used its dockland conversion to reinvent its entire image, through contemporary architecture, transit, and place-making, most notably through the iconic Erasmus Bridge. Across the Atlantic, Buffalo, New York, redeveloped its Canalside docklands through creative place-making and historic preservation.

London Docklands

London's Eastern Docklands is the first example of a large masterplanned transformation of a derelict industrial area to drive urban growth, focused not just on infrastructure but also on transforming the quality of the place, building pedestrian networks, a public realm, and iconic buildings. The conversion was spurred by huge government tax breaks and infrastructure investments, such as the Docklands light-rail line.[10] Once the world's largest dock system, an area of 8½ square miles, the Port of London employed 100,000 people in the 1930s. But the port suffered greatly in the 1960s, as many of the industries the port depended on, such as manufacturing, left the Greater London area, and much of the remaining shipping moved downstream to the deep-water container ports as the shipping industry modernized. By 1981, 60 percent of the land and enclosed water in the area was derelict, vacant, or underused.[11] The road network surrounding the port was frequently congested, and private investment in the declining area was scarce because of its depressed image and poor accessibility.

The creation of the London Docklands Development Corporation (LDDC) by directive of the Local Government, Planning & Land Act of 1980, a national act, marked a turning point. The British government had historically sought to shape urban growth through new-town projects on greenfields. But many new-town experiments failed to achieve their long-term objectives.[12] By the early 1980s, the national government sought to shift the focus to regenerating former inner-city industrial cities, what planner Harvey Perloff called as a form of "New Towns Intown."[13]

The objective of the LDDC was to create an urban development corporation to secure the regeneration of the area "by bringing land and buildings into effective use, encouraging the development of existing and new industry and commerce, creating an attractive environment and ensuring that housing and social facilities are available to encourage people to live and work in the area."[14] The LDDC was not meant to fund commercial activity directly or engage in community development or public housing (although in practice the LDDC later became active in providing social facilities). Instead, the LDDC was tasked with preparing sites for development and guiding the regeneration project according to loose, flexible, and internally created plans for the area.

The crowning achievement of the LDDC period, which lasted from 1981 to the corporation's disbandment in 1998, was the regeneration of the Canary Wharf area (figure 5-1). The focal point was One Canada Square, a fifty-story skyscraper designed by César Pelli. The tallest office building in the United Kingdom when it was completed in 1990, it quickly became the flagship property of the Canary Wharf district. According to urban designer Carmona, "For the first time, design was seen not as a barrier to innovation and a cost on investment, but instead as a means to establish a new and marketable sense of place."[15] Despite a property bust in the early 1990s, the Docklands continued to grow as a financial center and soon became the second-largest financial services district, after the City of London. Today, the area is one of the main focal points of the future growth of London, with an additional 200,000 jobs and 20,000 new housing units planned for the area by 2026, according to the London Plan of 2004.

As part of the regeneration effort, some of the iconic warehouse structures along the Thames have been repurposed for various uses, including residential flats. The Georgian-era West India Docks were preserved for the Museum of the London Docklands, keeping alive the area's maritime history. Other warehouses serve London's vital tourism industry, such as the Hilton Docklands Hotel. Preservation and reuse of the industrial architecture have helped the district stay true to its historical maritime context, seen by critics as a welcome contrast to the modern American-style corporate architecture prevalent in Canary Wharf's skyscrapers.

The expansion of transportation infrastructure to the Docklands was integral to the area's development, ultimately comprising almost 50 percent of the LDDC's £1.86 billion public investment in the district.[16] A lack of connectivity to the rest of London slowed early attempts at development, until the Docklands Light Railway opened in 1987, with two lines directly linking the Docklands to the City of London and Stratford. The £77-million price tag for the initial two lines of driverless railway was a fraction of the £500 earmarked for road building,[17] with costs kept low through adaptive reuse of a number of lengths of preexisting redundant railway viaduct. After continual expansions from 1991 through today, the system is by far the most used light-rail system in the United Kingdom, carrying 110 million passengers on seven lines (an average of 300,000 passengers

Figure 5-1. Canary Wharf *(top)* before and *(bottom)* after transformation. Where previously were derelict docklands, now stands a new financial district. (Source: *[top]* IanVisits, Flickr, *[bottom]* Martin Deutsch, Flickr.)

per day) in 2014.[18] The Jubilee Line Extension, opened in 1999, provided an even faster and more convenient rail connection from Canary Wharf to much of Central London. The Crossrail project, projected to open in 2018, will link Canary Wharf and Canning Town to Heathrow Airport and the wider southeast England region.

The regeneration of the London Docklands is not without its critics, however. In the absence of an overarching formal plan, private-driven regeneration produced a limited amount of public space and a jumbled architectural style, occasionally referencing the neighborhood's industrial past but often rejecting it in favor of an American-style sub-urbs-and-skyscrapers aesthetic, capped with a Canary Wharf masterplan by Chicago firm SOM. Much of the housing built, particularly in the early days of the project, was focused on bringing in wealthy residents from outside the area, built in gated communities. Most of the jobs created in the booming Canary Wharf district were in the financial sector and not open to the area's working-class population due to a lack of education. Despite 20 years of sustained investment, fifteen of seventeen Tower Hamlets wards remained among the top 5 percent of the United Kingdom's most deprived wards as of 2002.[19] In fact, of the £4 billion of public investment in the project in the 1980s and 1990s, only £110 million went to social housing projects.

Moreover, the docklands area south of Canary Wharfs lagged behind, characterized by a series of disconnected privatized compounds. But the 2000 Millennium Quarter Master Plan was the first public sector attempt to proactively chart the direction of this area.[20] Moving beyond a two-dimensional zoning approach to a three-dimensional urban design framework, it established a continuous and connected urban fabric with new residential and office spaces, as well as diverse public open and civic spaces, including public squares and gardens. A permeable network of pedestrian routes were laid out across the area, including routes promoting internal movements within the site. Blocks were planned containing buildings with active frontages at the ground level, to promote a vibrant public realm.

The London Docklands conversion from derelict, underused industrial space into a bustling new financial center and transit-linked hub and a network of public space demonstrates the possibilities present to postindustrial cities. Even though the Docklands conversion may have failed to incorporate a unified architectural image, its economic success kick-started a wave of urban regeneration projects across Western cities. As the urban design plans for the area were refined over the years, the London Docklands conversion demonstrates an urban recalibration away from just designing infrastructure to allow workers and residents to move in and out of the Docklands to a focus on designing a community, with a special attention to the quality of place.

Kop van Zuid, Rotterdam

Rotterdam's Kop van Zuid is a prime example of the power of urban regeneration focused on place-making to drive a reinvention of a city's image, in the face of deindustrialization and offshoring port activities. As in many other ports around the developed world, the containerization of shipping and deindustrialization in the late twentieth century left large areas of Rotterdam's industrial waterfront obsolete as newer, larger port areas opened nearer to the sea. The Kop van Zuid, a peninsula located on the south bank of the Nieuwe Maas River opposite Rotterdam's city center, was one of the areas hardest hit by this change in fortunes for older port areas. Before its regeneration, the Kop van Zuid formed a stark physical barrier of industrial use separating the city's northern and southern halves.

The city identified the Kop van Zuid as integral to realizing the city's full potential in a new masterplan, published in 1986, for its proximity to the water and potential to reconnect the city's separate halves. This new regeneration scheme was intended to provide 5,300 housing units, and 400,000 square meters of office space, as well as hotels and a new convention center, although enough flexibility was left to accommodate changing market conditions as demand for housing in the area grew.[21] By 2010, the area was estimated to be home to 15,000 people and 18,000 jobs.[22]

High-quality architecture and urban design has been a defining feature of the transformation. Iconic buildings by some of the world's leading architects, including the KPN Tower by Renzo Piano, the World Port Center by Norman Foster, and De Rotterdam by Rem Koolhaas (OMA), dominate the skyline and help cement Rotterdam's reputation as "Manhattan on the Maas." Some remnants of the pier's erstwhile shipping days have been repurposed, including the Holland America Line's old headquarters (now the Hotel New York; figure 5-2), and the Entrepot building (now a food market with restaurants). The area's history is kept alive through creative public art, and the waterfront is now accessible to pedestrians, reconnecting the people of Rotterdam to the city's maritime history.

Figure 5-2. The repurposed former headquarters of the Holland America Line, now Hotel New York (right), gives historic identity to the Kop Van Zuid, Rotterdam. (Source: Kees Torn, Flickr.)

Much like in London's Docklands, transportation infrastructure improvements were central to the regeneration scheme. Transportation initiatives, including an underground subway stop and a new tram line, provided greatly improved access to the transformed area. Most important to the redevelopment has been the stately Erasmus Bridge (completed in 1996 and nicknamed "The Swan"), which soars over the river and provides a direct connection by car, tram, bicycle, and foot between the north and south sides of the river (figure 5-3). Notably, the Rotterdam City Council chose the most expensive of the three designs presented for the bridge, but the boldness of the resulting landmark helped solidify Rotterdam's reputation as forward-thinking architectural city, gave a progressive context to subsequent development on the Wilhelminapier, and provided private investors a reason to feel confident in the city's commitment to development.

The Kop van Zuid project also attempted to redistribute economic gain. The area was redeveloped according to the Dutch "Complete Cities" principle, part of the nation's 1994 Major Cities Policy (*Grotestedenbeleid*), which emphasizes three pillars of sustainability: social, economic, and environmental development policy. The policy favors a mixture of uses and income levels in development, as evidenced by the Kop van Zuid's creation of the Anopolis social housing units, as well as a government program that helped

Figure 5-3. The Erasmus bridge (left) provides a new landmark for the Kop Van Zuid and Rotterdam, among icons by Renzo Piano (center right) and Rem Koolhaas (right). (Source: Roman Boed, Flickr.)

channel new jobs to the local population. The regeneration of Kop van Zuid and its heavy emphasis on place-making, transit, and equity is playing a leading role in making Rotterdam's economy attractive to creative, knowledge-driven industries such as design, and employees of those industries.[23]

Canalside, Buffalo

Across the Atlantic, the city of Buffalo, New York, is showing how even without iconic skyscrapers, urban transformations can have substantial positive effects on a declining city. The Canalside redevelopment project along Buffalo's waterfront is using creative place-making and historic preservation to reconnect residents to the city's industrial past and provide a locus of civic pride and an icy skate in winter.

For most of the nineteenth century, Buffalo was the world's leading transshipment port for grain, thanks to its advantageous position at the western end of the Erie Canal, which opened in 1825 and provided the first direct connection from the Great Lakes to the Atlantic Ocean. However, the plummeting cost of overland rail transportation and later truck transportation left the Erie Canal obsolete and sent the Canal District neighborhood into a precipitous decline. Urban renewal projects along the downtown waterfront in the mid-twentieth century, including an elevated freeway and a hockey arena, bulldozed the neighborhood's remnants and left the area unrecognizable from its industrial heyday, once the "portal to the west," a port district bustling with commercial activity, which helped transform Buffalo into a vibrant metropolis.

For years, Buffalo searched for a large private investment to revitalize the area. After the hockey arena's closure in 2006, the Erie Canal Harbor Development Corporation (ECHDC, a state agency formed to promote economic growth around Buffalo's harbor) failed in its search for a big-box retailer to fill the enormous vacant space. With no investors to be found, Buffalo had to rethink its approach to regeneration and decided to invest $300 million in public infrastructure and attractions to entice independent private investment.[24]

The centerpieces of Canalside are its recreations of the historic transportation networks that once served the area—the Erie Canal and Commercial Slip (which connected the canal to the mouth of the Buffalo River)—on the site of the former hockey arena and the vacant land surrounding it. Remarkably, the portion of the Commercial Slip where the hockey arena once stood now sits on top of a freezing system preserved from the old building. During the winter, the canal is frozen and serves as a 35,000-square-foot public skating rink. The traditional street grid, once lost to urban renewal, has been revived and paved with cobblestones, slowing automobile traffic. A large open lawn between the resuscitated streets is used for concerts in the summertime. Kayaks and canoes are available for rent on the waterfront boardwalk, and thanks to an effort by the ECHDC to dredge toxic soils from the Buffalo River, the harbor area is once again safe for fishing (figure 5-4). Further afield, the state of New York has converted a derelict piece of industrial land on the Lake Erie waterfront to a state park, while lining the outer harbor with bicycle and pedestrian trails. For the first time in decades, visitors to Buffalo's waterfront can look northwest across the lake to Canada from public land, providing an important visual reminder of the city's international connections.

Historic preservation is key to the project. Historically accurate replicas of bow truss bridges that spanned the original canals now span the reconstructed ones. The original foundations of a few Canal District buildings were unearthed by archaeologists during the construction of the Commercial Slip and are now preserved for visitors to explore as part of an outdoor exhibit on the history of the Canal District. America's largest inland naval park, the Buffalo Naval and Military Park, sits across a truss bridge from the restored foundations. Historical tours of Silo City, the grain elevator graveyard that still looms over the Buffalo River, depart from the boardwalk and give visitors an up-close-and-personal view of the industrial engineering works that powered the city's nineteenth-century boom. Musical and spoken-word performances inside the silos take advantage of the unique acoustics.

The fully reconstructed Commercial Slip opened in late 2014 and has already attracted private investment in the form of a large hotel and a hockey-themed convention center that hosts hockey tournaments in two NHL-sized indoor rinks, the most expensive privately funded single building in Buffalo's history. Though early in the process, Buffalo's new genius locus demonstrates the power of historically sensitive regeneration to revive the fortunes of a city in decline.

Redevelopment of Warehouse Districts

Many of the best-known urban transformations have occurred in former warehouse districts, such as the SoHo and Meatpacking districts in New York. As we will see in chapter 7, the Pearl District in Portland, Oregon, is an example of an urban transformation of a warehouse district into a mixed-use community through small, episodic infill, guided by a large vision around transit corridors. This section includes the redevelopment of warehouse districts in Charlotte, North Carolina, and Barcelona. Charlotte is an example of urban regeneration through a publicly funded rail corridor and a masterplan guiding private-sector development and place-making. Barcelona established a municipal development corporation to redevelop its industrial Poble Nou district, simultaneously stimulating the tech industry.

Southside Charlotte, North Carolina

An organic, project-by-project method is transforming Charlotte, North Carolina's Southside from a once-stagnant textile manufacturing and warehouse industrial zone into a vibrant, mixed-use live–work–play–learn corridor. Neighborhoods to the south of

Figure 5-4. Canalside, Buffalo, *(top)* before regeneration and *(bottom)* after. Tables with movable chairs allow for various activities at the newly accessible waterfront. (Source: *[top]* George Burns, Wikimedia Commons; *[bottom]* Dommatarese, Wikimedia Commons.)

downtown Charlotte have historically been preferred residential addresses, but over time, commercial industrial encroachment caused this area to languish. This changed when Charlotte's 10-mile Lynx light-rail system opened in 2007. Light-rail services triggered a steady wave of new condo-apartment construction projects and small-scale retail centers along the light-rail path, including renovated mills and factory buildings. The units were marketed to downtown professionals seeking a convenient, rail-served location outside the urban core in which to live. This private-sector development, supported through the community investment in light rail, was guided by the 2005 SouthEnd Transit Station Area Plan, which provided a vision for the entire district, including guidance about density and scale, most notably for the areas around the light-rail stations.

Studies show that Charlotte's South End housing and retail plazas have enjoyed sizable rent premiums since light-rail services were introduced.[25] The 208-unit Fountains @ South End project plays up its proximity to transit, marketing itself as a "connected place." The project has a first-floor transit lobby adorned with several large-screen monitors connected to outside cameras that continuously scan up and down the train tracks. Residents can sip on a latte and peruse the morning paper in the comforts of the lobby, whisking off to the nearby platform when alerted by the overhead monitor that a train is approaching.

22@Barcelona

22@Barcelona is an urban regeneration example of converting factories and warehouses into lofts, nightclubs, and galleries, as well as stimulating the tech industry. Poble Nou, in Barcelona, used to be nicknamed the "Catalan Manchester" in the nineteenth century, the heart of Catalan industry. But as industry moved outside the city in the twentieth century, the neighborhood fell into decay. In 2000, the city of Barcelona saw the then-derelict area as an opportunity to establish an innovation district and promote economic growth. The city council approved a new ordinance aimed to transform the industrial area by forming a municipal development corporation, 22@Barcelona. The 500-acre area covered 115 city blocks, one of Europe's largest urban regeneration projects.

The development corporation created value by rezoning the area from industrial to services. It then captured this value through development fees, allowing it to spend a total of 1 billion euros on public improvements, including public realm upgrades, open space, four thousand social housing units, bicycle lanes, a pneumatic solid-waste disposal system, and knowledge-based infrastructure such as incubators, R&D centers, fiberoptic grids, and Wi-Fi connections.[26] The agency also collaborated with universities to relocate research and academic activities to the district. The entire redevelopment stimulated the creation of 42,000 jobs by 2008.

Figure 5-5. A biker and light-rail on Barcelona's famed Avenida Diagonal pass Poble Nou's new ZeroZero tower (right), which hosts the headquarters of Telefónica. (Source: Thierry llansades, Flickr.)

Place-making played a central role in the project, including a district-wide heritage protection plan for 114 buildings. It also included new iconic architecture, with large towers reserved for the city's Avenida Diagonal, the famed street bordering Poble Nou, which also housed a new streetcar system (figure 5-5).

Rail-to-Greenway Conversions

Imposing linear systems, such as railways, can sever communities, generate noise, and, whether through visual blight or disruption, reduce the quality of urban living. Reclaiming these lands can trigger an urban renaissance. This section focuses on the reassignment of disused, dysfunctional, or disruptive transport infrastructure to greenways.

The rise of the trucking industry in the twentieth century led to the abandonment of hundreds of thousands of miles of railroad right-of-way as transportation shifted from the rails to the road. In America, the working rail system shrank from a peak of 270,000 miles to 141,000 in 1990.[27] Rails-to-trails are transformations of these defunct rail corridors into trails for active mobility and recreation. Successful rail-to-trail conversions can have significant social, economic, and health benefits for surrounding communities in both urban and rural contexts by attracting development, increasing physical activity, and reducing automobile dependence. Rails-to-trails conversions can put derelict land into productive use while preserving rail transportation routes that may prove to be vital again in the future. In the United States, the National Trails Systems Act of 1983 established a "railbanking" system that allows private railroads to transfer management of a railroad right-of-way to a public or private trail manager for use as a recreational trail without having to legally abandon the easement. The right-of-way is thereby preserved for use as a rail line if the need to return it to active use for industrial or passenger rail service were ever to arise.[28]

Rails-to-trails projects can promote an active lifestyle and improve community health by providing an alternative to the automobile for short trips. Studies in both urban and rural areas have shown that rails-to-trails projects are associated with increased rates of physical activity in nearby communities due to increased nonmotorized connectivity.[29] Rail trails can also serve as important commuter links by connecting users in residential areas to public transportation networks, such as the Minuteman Bikeway in suburban Boston, or directly from suburban areas to downtown, such as the Capital Crescent Trail in Washington, DC.

Although rails-to-trails are the most common form, greenways often follow rights-of-way reserved for other types of infrastructure, including canal towpaths, sewer pipes, and utilities. Maintenance of the Washington & Old Dominion Trail, a 45-mile rail-to-trail conversion in northern Virginia, is funded largely through an agreement to share its right-of-way with a fiberoptic service provider.[30] The London Greenway follows the path of the active Northern Outfall Sewer for 4½ miles through east London, with signs made from old sewer pipes reminding visitors of the park's dual infrastructural use at access points along the route.

This section includes some of the most famous rail-to-trail conversions, including the High Line in New York, the BeltLine in Atlanta, the Great Allegheny Passage from Pittsburgh to Washington, DC, and Gleisdreieck Park in Berlin.

The High Line, New York City

The High Line, a 1½-mile-long linear park that runs on a raised viaduct through New York City's Chelsea and Meatpacking District neighborhoods, demonstrates the potential of rail-to-trail conversions to spur economic growth (figure 5-6). Inspired by the Promenade Plantée in Paris, a group called Friends of the High Line formed to save the derelict structure vacated by the West Side Line from demolition and preserve it as an aerial greenway. The High Line was built in three phases between 2006 and 2014 using $152 million in public funding and more than $300 million in private donations.[31] It draws more than six million visitors per year and has established itself as one of New York's premiere tourist

Figure 5-6. The High Line, an elevated freight rail repurposed into a park, spurred the redevelopment of Chelsea, with iconic architecture including from Frank Gehry (left). (Source: David Berkowitz, Wikimedia Commons.)

attractions.[32] Traversing through a tunnel of buildings three stories above street level provides a novel way of experiencing the city and unique angles from which to view the city's streetlife. The design by architects Diller and Scofidio and landscape architect James Corner left some of the rails intact, to remind visitors of the park's industrial roots.

The High Line's economic impact on its surrounding neighborhoods has been profound. To gain support for the park from property owners, the city created a special zoning district that allowed property owners to sell their air rights above the High Line to be reallocated to selected areas within the neighborhood, allowing densification of the area surrounding the park and justifying the city's investment.[33] The New York City Planning Department in 2011 estimated that twenty-nine new projects built since 2006 around the High Line accounted for 2,558 residential units, one thousand hotel rooms, and 423,000 square feet of office space and drew more than $2 billion in private investment and twelve thousand new jobs.[34] One study calculated that the High Line increased property tax receipts within one-third of a mile of the park by $100 million in 2010, nearly repaying the city's investment in just 1 year.[35] Critics of the project have pointed out that the benefits of the park have not been experienced evenly across the economic spectrum, because lower-income residents have been displaced by gentrification of the surrounding neighborhood, and the application process for vendors along the park's route favors the well capitalized over the more modest vendors found at street level.[36]

Repurposing large elevated rail structures is often less expensive than demolishing them, and thus the High Line is inspiring copycat projects in other cities—often referred to as the High Line Effect—including the Reading Viaduct in Philadelphia, the Bloomingdale Trail in Chicago, and the Hofbogen in Rotterdam.[37] Although each of these projects has the potential to positively transform its surroundings, the success of the High Line relies on Manhattan's uniquely dense context and is unlikely to be repeated quite so profoundly elsewhere. Similarly, the air rights transfer scheme would not be nearly as lucrative in an area lacking the land values of Manhattan.

The Atlanta BeltLine

The Atlanta BeltLine is an ambitious project to build a 22-mile loop of rail transportation, 33 miles of multiuse trails, and 1,300 acres of parks on (mostly) abandoned railways surrounding the core of Atlanta, Georgia, over 25 years (figure 5-7).[38] When complete, this so-called "Emerald Necklace" (borrowing a term from Frederick Law Olmsted) will connect forty-two neighborhoods through high-quality public transportation and 20-foot-wide pedestrian and bicycle superhighways. First proposed in a 1999 graduate thesis by Georgia Tech student Ryan Gravel, the project broke ground in 2006 after an extensive public engagement and planning process, and the first trail section of the project opened in 2008. The initial portions of the project were funded using a special tax allocation district agreement between the City of Atlanta, Atlanta Public Schools, and Fulton County, wherein the jurisdictions agreed to dedicate future property tax revenue increases along the BeltLine corridor over the next 25 years to construction on the BeltLine. In 2016, Atlanta voters approved a sales tax referendum worth an estimated $2.5 billion over the next 40 years to fund public transportation, including $66 million to complete the BeltLine.

Although to date only a few stretches of the multiuse trail portion of the project are complete, the project is already having a large economic impact on surrounding neighborhoods. Since 2005, more than fifty projects and $1 billion in private investment have taken place in the BeltLine corridor.[39] As with the High Line, however, critics of the BeltLine point to displacement of low-income residents associated with rising land values as a sign that the economic gains realized by the BeltLine are not universally enjoyed across the economic spectrum.[40]

The Great Allegheny Passage

The Great Allegheny Passage demonstrates the potential of rails-to-trails projects to drive economic growth even in rural areas. It stretches 150 miles from Pittsburgh, Pennsylvania, to Cumberland, Maryland, where it connects to the Chesapeake & Ohio Canal

Figure 5-7. *(top)* **The Eastside section of the Atlanta BeltLine stimulated the construction of** *(bottom)* **historic South Ward Park.** (Source: Atlanta Beltline, Flickr.)

Towpath, forming an unbroken 335-mile stretch of nonmotorized trail all the way from Pittsburgh to Washington, DC.[41] The trail began in sections starting in 1978, and in 2001 a series of connected trails was rechristened the Great Allegheny Passage as the first 100-mile continuous stretch was completed between Meyersdale and McKeesport. Along its route, the trail passes by industrial artifacts and historical sites that connect users to the region's industrial and Civil War past.

The Great Allegheny Passage attracts many visitors to an area hit hard by job losses in the mining industry. According to estimates by the Trail Town Program, the Great Allegheny Passage carried more than 800,000 trips along the corridor between Cumberland and Pittsburgh in 2015. One survey found that two-thirds of businesses noted at least some increase in revenue because of proximity to the trail, with direct spending in the local economy by trail users exceeding $40 million.[42] As the Great Allegheny Passage shows, rails-to-trails have the potential to spur economic development in rural areas as well.

Gleisdreieck Park, Berlin

Berlin has long been a metropolis with green fingers. The newest and in many ways most impressive is the Gleisdreieck Park greenway in the trendy Kreuzberg district (figure 5-8). *Gleisdreieck,* which means "triangle of rails," was formed by the intersection of separate railway lines that had entered Berlin from the south since the mid-nineteenth century. Railway lines, sheds, and warehouses of three old railway stations lay dormant for much of the post–World War II period, with the 31 hectares of prime, centrally located land becoming run down and neglected. For decades, this strategically located freight depot wasteland served as a place to dump waste and rubbish.

After many years of public involvement, a plan to preserve native vegetation and open space interlaced by a network of mostly north–south bikeway connectors was approved, and the project opened in 2013. Almost immediately this centrally located corridor in one of Berlin's hippest districts triggered a mammoth building boom, with the greenway today flanked by midrise, mixed-income housing towers and ground-floor commercial uses that give the corridor a defined edge. Eco-friendly, mixed-use development now occupies some 16 hectares of redeveloped land alongside the park. Green buildings populated by diverse generations, cultures, and social backgrounds, in harmony with nature, have made the Gleisdreieck district a popular leisure and socializing destination.

Gleisdreieck does not ignore its past. Rather, it embraces its railway heritage by keeping remnants of rail tracks, bridges, and railsheds intact throughout the corridor. A high-speed inter-city express railway continues to run through the development, functionally and symbolically linking the past and future.

Gleisdreieck Park's success lies in striking a workable balance between connectivity and place-making. U-Bahn and S-Bahn train services are a 5- to 10-minute walk away for most residents. World-class bicycle infrastructure provides direct and mostly conflict-free

Figure 5-8. Railway-to-greenway conversion, Gleisdreieck Park, Berlin, Germany. (Source: A. Savin, Wikimedia Commons.)

connections to Berlin's urban centers. Gleisdreieck Park provides central Berlin with a new green lung, a much-valued amenity that in turn has attracted residents and businesses drawn to green mobility choices, be they walking, cycling, or transit riding.

Close

The projects discussed in this chapter concerned the reuse of former industrial properties of Western cities, including docklands, warehouse districts, and freight rails. These cases show how urban regeneration, when proactively guided by governments and with a focus on both transit and place-making, can achieve better communities, better environments, and better economies. As migration to postindustrial cities is expected to continue the next decades, governments can retool the sites that made up their industrial engines. Although the cases in this chapter focused on cities in the West, urban regeneration is also a new buzzword in China, where the economy has shifted from industrial to postindustrial in the period of only one generation, and art factories and "creative cluster" industrial areas proliferate, such as the 798 factory complex in Beijing.[43] There, too, the power of adaptive reuse is evident, judging from all the couples taking wedding photos in front of old factories and abandoned rail tracks.

6

Suburban Transformations

Suburbanization is a truly global phenomenon, fueled over the past half-century by modernization, motorization, and growing affluence of cities and their inhabitants. Also at play are the location-liberating effects of information technologies, the desire to escape central-city crime and congestion, and a general preference for more spacious, large-lot living as household incomes rise. The first wave of suburbanization—residents moving to dormitory communities, triggered by streetcar investments in the late nineteenth century—was soon followed by a second phase: retailers migrating outward to be closer to consumers. Suburbanization's third wave saw companies and businesses following suit, leaving downtowns and setting up shop in office parks and corporate centers to be closer to labor markets and to save on rents, that is, the suburbanization of employment.[1] With regional activities, and thus trip origins and destinations, spread all over the map, to no surprise the private automobile steadily gained ascendancy over these three waves of suburbanization. Suburban gridlock and environmental problems associated with it soon followed.[2]

This chapter focuses on the quest for place-making and vibrancy for activities tied to suburbanization's second and third waves: commercial retail shops and workplaces. Although the private car enabled retailers to spread out across metro areas, in truth it led to concentrations and consolidations of commercial activities, in the form of shopping plazas, big-box outlets, and indoor malls. In the pre-automobile era, retail activities could be found on nearly every city block, with mom-and-pop stores, cozy restaurants, and the local butcher shop intermingled among central-city residences. With the car, there became fewer establishments in fewer locations but with much bigger footprints and much, much more parking. Car-led retailing also ushered in a new era of "placeless-ness," punctuated by gargantuan asphalt parking lots, a fairly generic shopping center design template, and the banality of commercial strip development.

Suburban workplaces have likewise struggled to become attractive destinations or noteworthy places, for the most part also a product of their automobile orientation. As superhighways opened up vast expanses of land for new development, workplaces began to stretch outward rather than upward. Campus-style office parks, adorned with manicured open spaces and enveloped by expansive surface parking lots, quickly became the design *de rigueur* for suburban workplaces across much of the United States, Canada, Australia, and, with time, continental Europe.[3] The physical separation of office complexes and insular building designs discouraged walking and the kind of everyday, face-to-face interactions found on downtown streets. By the mid- to late 1980s, another type of suburban workplace was taking form: "edge cities," which in contrast to masterplanned office parks were mostly disconnected assemblages of midrise office towers and retail establishments, giving them downtown-like qualities without much in the way of pedestrian infrastructure or amenities.[4] Their compact, mixed-use yet auto-oriented designs predictably resulted in edge cities experiencing some of the worst traffic conditions anywhere. Over time, some observers began to characterize America's suburban landscapes as mostly edgeless, marked by loose constellations of sprawling corporate enclaves, business parks, standalone office buildings, big-box retailers, and power centers.[5] Edgeless-ness and placeless-ness became synonymous.

The rapid-fire pace of job decentralization has been particularly pronounced in the world's most automobile-dependent society, the United States. In the 1980s, about a quarter of metropolitan jobs were in America's suburbs.[6] By 2002, all U.S. metropolitan areas, with the exception of New York and Chicago, had the majority of office space outside traditional downtowns.[7] By 2006, more than 60 percent of U.S. metropolitan office space was in the suburbs.[8] And by 2014, 67.5 percent of employment in the fifty largest U.S. metro areas was in suburbs.[9]

An about-face in where U.S. companies locate could be in the works, at least for some kinds of jobs. As an indicator that place increasingly matters, the preference for suburban, car-oriented workplaces appears to be waning and maybe even reversing.[10] During the 2002–2007 period of economic expansion, the 3-mile ring around U.S. city centers saw employment growth of barely one-tenth of a percent per year. By contrast, outlying areas grew ten times as fast. But from 2007 to 2011, the period coinciding with the onset and early recovery of the Great Recession, the picture abruptly changed. Among forty-one one U.S. metro areas, center city jobs increased 0.5 percent per year while employment in the periphery fell 0.1 percent per annum. Whereas only seven city centers outperformed their peripheries in job growth over the 2002–2007 period, twenty-one of forty-one did so in 2007–2011. More recent data suggest a balancing of job growth between America's suburbs and cities. Between 2010 and 2014, the number of jobs in America's fifty largest metro areas increased by 9 percent in suburbs and 6 percent in urban areas.[11] The opening of densely packed call centers and data-handling services has accounted for some of the recent gains in suburban jobs. However, better-paying knowledge-based jobs continue to flock mainly to urban cores.

Changes in America's economic geography reflect powerful market forces such as globalization and increasing international competition, prompting firms to consolidate, reposition themselves, and cut costs. But so have other factors. These include the high energy demands and enlarged carbon footprint of traditional suburban development, increases in commuting times matched by less time spent with families and friends, a growing recognition that physical isolation reduces innovation by lessening opportunities for workers to interact and exchange ideas, and employee discontent with such seemingly trivial but actually important things as having to eat at the same company cafeteria each day.[12] The collective weight of such factors has prompted more and more firms to set up shop or relocate to more traditional, pedestrian-friendly neighborhoods and commercial districts. A recent report from NAIOP, a commercial real estate development association, showed that U.S. office tenants prefer walkable urban locations, either in cities or mixed-use suburban centers, by a four-to-one margin over typical suburban office parks.[13] Shifting preferences are also reflected in real estate prices. In America's thirty biggest metro areas, office space in walkable urban districts is almost twice as valuable as in car-oriented suburban ones.[14]

Notwithstanding such trends and preferences, the reality is that a huge stock of automobile-oriented shopping centers, strip malls, and business parks continue to dot the suburbs of America and elsewhere. Are they simply to be boarded up and abandoned? Or might they be reimagined, reinvented, redesigned? One of the saving graces of huge surface parking lots is they can be easily torn up and rebuilt upon. They offer a clean slate of preassembled real estate that without too much in the way of demolition or relocation expenses can be redirected to other uses, presumably with more of a sense of place, less auto-centricity, and better connectivity.

Fortunately, suburban landscapes are malleable and for the most part can be easily adapted, modified, and reused. Adaptive reuse is gaining traction in the suburbs of America and beyond. A number of jobs-only land uses have been diversified in recent years, in the form of infill and densification, the addition of housing and retail uses, and the breaking up of superblocks through the construction of internal pathways and trail systems. Real estate prices reflect this market shift: In 2008, for example, mixed-use office clusters had already enjoyed a healthy price premium relative to single-use, campus-style office development, and since then this premium has increased.[15] The "citification of suburbia," foretold by Masotti and Haden some four decades ago, is today in full swing.[16]

It is not so much center cities and central business districts (CBDs) that employers are seeking but rather their attributes: vibrancy, diversity, walkability, and good transit access. For the most part, live–work–play, mixed-use environments with good transit connectivity are limited to traditional urban cores. Suburban transformations are about changing that.

In many ways, suburbs are the low-hanging fruit in the quest to create sustainable, highly livable, and more accessible places. Their vast supplies of skipped-over yet infill-able lands combined with their outsized carbon footprints make them as suitable as anywhere for large-scale, impactful changes. In the United States, low-density suburbs consume two to three times more energy per capita than central cities.[17] Moreover, finan-cially strapped local governments shoulder the burden of funding infrastructure expan-sions to serve sprawl.[18] Chronic illnesses such as diabetes and heart disease stem in part from sedentary living, made all the worse when people substitute driving for walking and cycling.[19] Changing how people live, work, shop, and play in the suburbs through physical transformations of built environments stands to conserve energy, save money, and improve public health. Fortunately, markets and lifestyle preferences are moving in this direction. What is needed are proactive public policies to usher them along more smoothly and swiftly.

Possibilities for transforming car-oriented suburban workplaces have captured the attention of architects and urban designers in recent years. The Miami-based design firm of Duany Plater-Zyberk and Company (DPZ) has applied the New Urbanist transect prin-ciple to visualize how a campus-style office park (S7 on the transect) can be converted to an urban core zone (T5 in the transect zone). Contemporary office parks, what DPZ calls a "random, train wreck pattern" of buildings, should be infilled and altered so that work-places and supportive land uses are oriented to the street and inviting to pedestrians.[20] In *Sprawl Repair Manual*, Galina Tachiera similarly represents how a sprawling office park might be transformed into a mixed-use center, as shown in figure 6-1.[21] Once repaired, the modified workplace is akin to the pre-automobile city, albeit with a postindustrial twist: no smokestacks, slaughterhouses, and other nuisances that dotted the late-nine-teenth-century city. Others, such as architect Paul Lukez, propose an "adaptive design process" that gradually phases in such eco-friendly, eye-pleasing design elements as street trees, permeable paving, internal cycle paths, and building gateways.[22] In *Retrofitting Sub-urbia*, architects Ellen Dunham-Jones and June Williamson call for similar transforma-tions to temper the "banalities of late-20th century suburban development," remind-ing us that such metamorphoses pose more than physical design challenges. Successful suburban retrofits, they contend, require careful attention to the sociological, cultural, and financial–economic roots of the past half-century of suburban growth as well. For

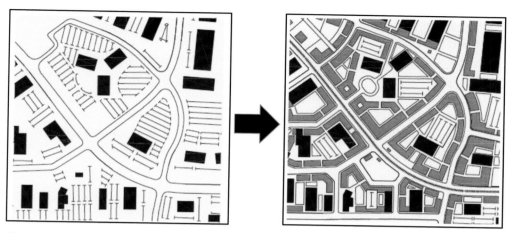

Figure 6-1. Transforming a business campus to an urban center. (Source: Galina Tachieva, *Sprawl Repair Manual*, Washington DC: Island Press, 2010, p. 165.)

example, longstanding practices of social exclusion, such as through large-lot zoning or shunning the need for working-class housing, are today being challenged on legal and moral grounds. As a result, suburban retrofits must be socially inclusive, providing on-site affordable housing, for example. Exploiting modern financial tools can also be critical to success. The formation of business improvement districts, use of tax increment financing, or creation of zoning overlay districts can affect the bottom line of any large-scale suburban redesign.

Office Park Retrofits

Office parks are as car oriented as anywhere. Not surprisingly they have been among the first large-scale suburban projects to be adapted, transformed, and repurposed.

The first office park transformations occurred in the early 2000s in suburban enclaves such as Hyattsville, Maryland, and Westwood, Massachusetts.[23] The surface parking lots that enveloped Hyattsville's ten-story office towers were systematically infilled and transformed, giving way to a new pedestrian-friendly main street and a mix of uses that created a 7-days-a-week, 18-hours-a-day place. What was a series of standalone, indistinguishable midrise office buildings had been transformed into an active and vibrant University Town Center.

In the greater Boston area, property owners have sought to reinvent the suburban office park, in the words of one developer, "taking a page from urban revitalization that transformed old mill and factory buildings into mixed-use developments of housing, retail, and office spaces."[24] Today, dozens of suburban office park "redos" involving billions of dollars are under way across eastern Massachusetts. The combination of aging, outdated buildings, some a half century old, and increased competition from mixed-use urban centers is driving the change.

Also driving the change in many places are market realities. As younger workers return to the city, and employers follow, isolated campuses of low-slung buildings, parking lots, and company cafeterias face significant challenges, from new competitors to aging facilities to high vacancy rates.[25] Remarks one Massachusetts property developer, "People are looking for something different; it's the entire 'live, work, play' environment that people want. They don't want to go to just an office park with a cafeteria and parking lots."[26] What knowledge-industry talent wants, employers and thus office developers must provide if they are to remain competitive.

The transportation and environmental benefits of going from a jobs-only compound to a mixed-use center can be substantial. Mixed-use activity centers, research shows, average much higher rates of trips that are internal (i.e., within the mixed-use site) and by foot than the typical office campus.[27] Vehicle miles per worker and per resident thus tend to be lower. The energy savings and air quality benefits of shorter and more walking trips have been matched by lower parking demands, largely due to a higher share of workers who carpool or take transit to work. Office-only development prompts many workers to auto-commute because they would otherwise be virtually stranded without a car, unable to meet a colleague off-site or take care of personal errands after work. Putting restaurants, retail shops, health clubs, and grocers on site liberates workers from the need to have a personal car. This, research shows, boosts the share of suburban office workers who commute by carpool, vanpool, and public transit.[28] Mixed land uses also allow shared parking; for example, parking for office workers can be used by theatergoers in the evening and on weekends, shrinking parking supplies by up to 20 percent.[29]

The one asset that sprawling office parks and other monofunctional suburban uses have is real estate, particularly surface parking space. They are thus ripe for infill. Almost all are overparked, relics of an era when, almost regardless of context, all office parks had to have five or six parking spaces per 1,000 square feet of development. Lenders and insurers demanded so. What has resulted is "a self-selected, circular process that is widely believed to have resulted in excessive minimum parking requirements."[30] Except for call centers and crowded workspaces of 200 square feet per employee, experiences in the suburbs of Denver, Washington, DC, and Atlanta reveal that less parking is needed when office space is within a walkable distance of a rail station or where Millennials, drawn to transit, cycling, Uber, and other less traditional modes, make up a significant share of the workforce.[31] Freed-up parking thus facilitates suburban transformations.

Two of the largest suburban employment campuses in the San Francisco Bay Area, Bishop Ranch and Hacienda Business Park, are being transformed into mixed-use centers, owing to market trends and smart-growth pressures. Both projects were described in the 1989 book *America's Suburban Centers* as quintessential car-oriented, campus-style workplaces. Their very survival in the twenty-first-century postindustrial marketplace will

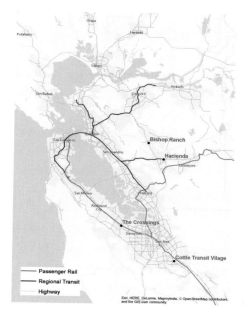

Figure 6-2. Case locations in the San Francisco Bay Area.

depend on becoming more complete, better-connected places. A third Bay Area office park retrofit reviewed in this section, in the sprawling Silicon Valley of Santa Clara County, is close to three urban rail stops and thus by proximity as well as design is taking on the persona of mixed-use suburban transit-oriented development (TOD). Figure 6-2 maps the locations of the Bay Area projects reviewed in this chapter.

Bishop Ranch, San Ramon, California

One of the San Francisco Bay Area's largest suburban employment concentrations is Bishop Ranch, located off of Interstate 680 in the city of San Ramon in Contra Costa County. Bishop Ranch Office Park opened in 1978 at the leading edge of the San Francisco Bay Area's suburban office market boom. The original Bishop Ranch project was unabashedly auto-centric, with nearly all of its building floor space devoted to housing white-collar office workers. Buildings stood in isolation, inward-focused and enveloped by paved parking. Over the past three decades, the project has slowly but steadily diversified its land use and intensified activities through strategic infill, much of it on former parking lots. What in the late 1970s was a largely vacant field with a handful of stand-alone low-slung office buildings three decades later had been filled in with a mix of office and commercial activities interlaced by pedestrian-ways, pretty much executing the figure 6-1 schema on repairing suburban office parks.

Guiding Bishop Ranch's transformation has been the City of San Ramon's City Center Project plan. Relying on broad-based community input, the plan calls for many of the activities found throughout most suburban townships to be concentrated within walking distance of each other. Adhering to this simple but important concept, Bishop Ranch is becoming a mixed-use urban center, featuring substantial amounts of new retail development, hotel space, mixed-income housing, flexible office space, civic parks, and a new City Hall and town center. Public spaces and connected pathways are identified in the plan as critical to enhancing the project's pedestrian-friendliness.

Bishop Ranch's transformation from a mono-hub of employment to a complete work–live–shop–learn–play community marks a paradigm shift in suburban office design. It has meant discarding the design template of shielding companies from each other and providing 5 parking spaces per 1,000 square feet of office space. Commercial lenders, insurance underwriters, fire marshals, and others beholden to the twentieth-century model of suburban workplace design had to be brought on board before the retrofit could be greenlighted.

Ironically, Bishop Ranch was originally envisaged as a community where suburbanites could live and work. However, the original planned unit development proposal with ranch-style housing prompted a citizens' revolt. This led to the creation of San Ramon as a municipality to control such development and invoke the NIMBY (Not in My Back Yard) rule. It took a quarter century to change the mindset of local residents and financial institutions. Adding some 500 housing units, retail shops, entertainment uses, and lodging services to what had been a large-scale, 9-to-5 employment hub was a monumental achievement given the reticence of local residents to accept almost any form of new growth. But a proactive, inclusive planning process, combined with growing discontent with auto-oriented development, paved the way for a sea change in local attitudes about Bishop Ranch's future.

In 2015, the first phase of Bishop Ranch's transformation began, adding a fourteen-screen movie theater, restaurants and shops, an upmarket hotel, hundreds of residential units, and four office buildings totaling 800,000 square feet to the project. As prominent is the makeover of Bishop Ranch's signature building, the 1.8-million-square-foot former headquarters of AT&T, transforming it into a modern high-tech campus amid retail plazas and nearby housing, and in so doing creating an attractive work–live–shop–play corporate setting. Designers hope that the kind of people-oriented, high-amenity, eco-friendly work environments found at the headquarters of Google, Apple, and Facebook in the Silicon Valley, some 30 miles to the south, can be brought to this once car-oriented office park in the East Bay.

Besides trying to create a stronger sense of place in suburbia, the owners of Bishop Ranch have sought to lure tenants with eco-minded workers to the project by launching electric car and bike-share programs and operating bus shuttles to and from the nearest Bay Area Rapid Transit (BART) rail station, some 6 miles away. Bridging the "first-mile/last-mile" connectivity gap to transit is an Achilles heel for many sprawling corporate campuses like Bishop Ranch. In this respect, Bishop Ranch is poised to become a bona fide pace-setter. In March 2017, two twelve-passenger autonomous shuttles, called EasyMile, began operating as a pilot project with the hope of eventually connecting Bishop Ranch to BART, without a driver. Should they catch on, such autonomous technologies, discussed further in chapter 10, could be as transformational in suburban campus settings as anywhere.

Hacienda, Pleasanton, California

Hacienda lies 10 miles south of Bishop Ranch, in the town of Pleasanton in eastern Alameda County. Like Bishop Ranch, most of Hacienda took shape during the San Francisco Bay Area's 1980s office building boom. San Francisco's office rents had become prohibitively high at this time, yet the market was still clamoring for office space. Hacienda became one of the major catchments for relocated central-city jobs.

The desire to blend in figured prominently in initial decisions governing Hacienda's building designs and placements, landscaping, and site organization. The delicate relationship between the built and natural environment was particularly evident in Hacienda Business Park's design guidelines, which specified that interior zones of the complex should recall the "orchard or grove-like character typical of California farm communities."[32] This meant, of course, the project would be spread out and auto-oriented. The choice of Hacienda's 860-acre site was considered ideal because of its proximity to the interchanges of two major freeways and the plan to open a nearby BART rail transit station.

The first major land use shift for Hacienda came as the office boom waned in the late 1990s. Recognizing the growing market for a live-near-work lifestyle and disdain for long-haul commuting, within a 10-year period more than 1,550 residential units were added to the once jobs-only office park. Although jobs still far outnumber residents, Hacienda has become home to those drawn to the logic of "efficient location," that is, those willing to trade higher condominium and duplex prices in return for lower transportation costs. For many, the economics make sense. In robust real estate markets such as the San Francisco Bay Area, housing appreciates in value. By comparison, few commodities lose value faster than a car.

From its inception in 1983 to two decades later (figure 6-3), Hacienda's land coverage (from buildings) jumped from 5 percent to nearly 70 percent. The addition of housing, corporate offices, lodging, and retail services has not only enriched land use offerings but has also brought buildings—and thus potential trip origins and destinations—closer together. This in turn has shortened trips and reduced shares of trips by car.

Hacienda's metamorphosis from a car-oriented business park is reflected by the increased density and connectivity of its interior road network. Most notable has been the addition of a fine-grained road pattern serving new residential enclaves on the eastern side

Figure 6-3. Hacienda site development. From *(top)* a sparsely developed office park in 1984 to *(bottom)* an infilled, mixed-use center 2 decades later. (Photos by Hacienda Business Park Association.)

of the project. This has helped break up the project's superblock design and along with a few additional links has created more of a gridlike road layout. Hacienda's improved connectivity is revealed by the project's higher connectivity index (links/nodes), from a value of 1.96 in 1990 to 2.10 in 2007. The development's road density (lineal distance of roads divided by land area) increased by a similar magnitude. Increased connectivity is part of Hacienda's legacy as a destination that invites alternatives to private car travel. The business park was one of America's first large-scale employment centers to aggressively pursue transportation demand management (TDM).[33] TDM offerings to Hacienda's employees today include free shuttle access to the nearby BART station, guaranteed ride home programs, and ride-matching services. Bike sharing and car sharing are also available.

Cottle Transit Village, San Jose, California

San Jose is the Bay Area's most populous city. Yet despite having operated light-rail transit for more than 20 years and a bevy of pro-TOD policies, most growth has taken place away from transit stops. This has been especially so in the Silicon Valley, the world's tech capital that today remains mostly dotted by sprawling office campuses enveloped by asphalt parking. Although some of the valley's office complexes are adjacent to light-rail stops, they are not always transit-oriented or transit-inviting in their layouts and designs (figure 6-4).

This is now changing, in part because civic leaders and the Silicon Valley's tech titans are demanding so. Besides the valley's terrible traffic and severe shortages of affordable housing, expected climate-induced sea level rises threaten the very livelihood of some of the world's technology powerhouses unless there is an abrupt course correction (figure 6-5).

Among the most notable urban recalibrations in the San Jose area has been the infill and transformation of office parks near rail stops to compact, mixed-use transit villages. The largest is Cottle Transit Village, which enjoys an unusually high level of transit access, lying within walking distance of two light-rail stations and a Caltrain commuter rail stop (figure 6-6). The former IBM campus that once occupied this 172-acre triangular parcel, now owned by HGST, a data storage technology company, has been "rightsized" and diversified. HGST opted to demolish the site's 1.3 million square feet of horizontally scaled office buildings, replacing them with midrise office and commercial towers. Freed-up land is being infilled with retail, green infrastructure, public spaces, and some 3,000 housing units, with the highest densities (sixty units per residential acre) situated closest to transit stops. Cottle Transit Village is the most prominent of some seventy "active, walkable, bicycle-friendly, transit-oriented, mixed-use urban settings" called for in the Envision San Jose 2040 General Plan.[34] Public policies are not the only reason for this course correction. Market realities have also played a role. Remarked the master planner of the Cottle Transit Village project, "Employers and employees both want denser, more urban, integrated mixed use environments and do not want to be in a business park."[35]

Figure 6-4. Boxes and asphalt: transit-adjacent development along the Tasman East light-rail corridor, Santa Clara County, California. If one squints hard enough, a light-rail train can be seen approaching the intersection in the right photo, surrounded by a sea of asphalt. (Photos by *[left]* Erick Haas; *[right]* Cisco Corporation.)

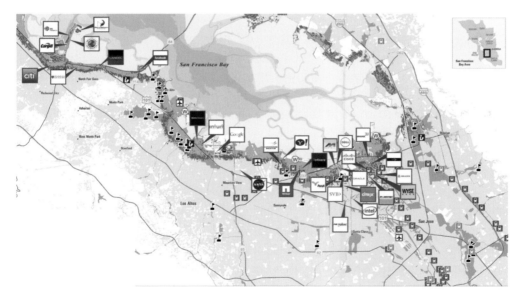

Figure 6-5. Climate change and projected shoreline shifts in the South Bay by 2067. Under business-as-usual scenarios, rising sea levels threaten to inundate the headquarters of many of the world's technology leaders. Companies in red zones will be under water if the bay shore rises 55 inches within the next half century. (Source: GreenInfo Network.)

Edge City to Suburban TOD: Tysons, Virginia

One of America's most substantial suburban transformations is slated for Tysons in northern Virginia, what long has been considered the "mother of all edge cities."[36] Tysons epitomizes all that can go wrong when a massive car-oriented employment center is hastily created on the urban edge: nightmarish traffic conditions, a deplorable walking

Figure 6-6. Cottle Transit Village. This transformed mixed-use TOD is surrounded by two light-rail stations and a Caltrains commuter rail stop. (Photo by Urban Land Institute.)

environment, and except for its shopping malls, a place that is largely abandoned on weekends. What was a quaint intersection of two county roads 50 years ago had by the late twentieth century been transformed into a jam-packed two-tiered interchange with ten lanes of traffic heading to America's twelfth-biggest employment center. By the early 2000s, entire office building complexes stood empty, victims of speculative overbuilding and companies seeking nicer working environments. Today, the 4.3-square-mile "tangle of parking lots and office parks" has a staggering 160,000 parking spaces for 120,000 employees.[37]

The announcement of plans in the early 2000s to extend the Washington Metrorail system to the Dulles International Airport and site four new stations in Tysons created an unparalleled opportunity to change directions. Noted urbanologist Christopher Leinberger calls "the redevelopment of Tysons . . . the most important urban redevelopment in the country, possibly in the world. If they do this right, it'll be the model. Just as it was the model of edge cities, it will be the model of the urbanization of the suburbs. It's that big."[38]

The prescription devised by local planners and citizen activists is to morph from a massive car-oriented employment hub to a balanced, mixed-use community of higher densities, one that gives priority to walking and transit over the private car. The approved plan, shown in figure 6-7, calls for concentrating 95 percent of Tysons's future growth within a 3-minute walk of the four planned Metrorail stops and three planned tram circular routes. Six times as much housing as currently exists is to be built on the 1,700-acre

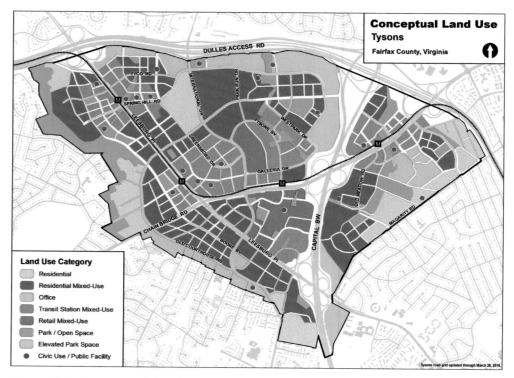

Figure 6-7. Conceptual land use plan for the transformed Tysons. (Source: Fairfax County Zoning and Planning Department.)

Tysons site, most of it within walking distance of a rail stop, bringing the total housing count to some fifty thousand units. Some 200,000 new jobs are also to locate near transit corridors. Densities will drop off precipitously, wedding-cake style, beyond one-quarter mile of stations, giving clear edges and definition to Tysons's four TODs. Since the plan's approval by the Fairfax County planning board in 2009, the $2.6-billion Metrorail extension has opened, developers have invested $400 million in new commercial and residential development, and three new Fortune 500 companies have moved into Tysons. New developments embrace their proximity to metrorail. The Ascent, a twenty-six-story posh apartment tower, has a Wi-Fi–enabled lobby where residents can watch a large flat-screen TV for potential delays at the metro stop, a 3-minute walk away.

A major component of the Tysons retrofit plan involves breaking up the current super-block structure by creating new local streets, bikeways, and internal trails, resulting in a more fine-grained, modified gridlike street pattern, as revealed in figure 6-7. Planners hope that a permeable and articulated roadway pattern will encourage nonmotorized access (i.e., walking and cycling) to stations and increase internal capture (i.e., boost the shares of trips made by residents and workers within Tysons's borders). The traditional suburban practice of park-and-ride access will also be jettisoned in favor of walk-and-ride, bike-and-ride, and bus-and-ride. In many ways, the plan aims to mimic the highly successful transit-oriented development found some 10 miles inward from Tysons along the Rosslyn–Ballston corridor of Arlington County.[39] Unlike in the Rosslyn–Ballston corridor, however, the decision was made to build Tysons's metro line above ground to save on construction costs. This decision, decried by local smart-growth advocates, could prevent the kind of seamless integration of transit and development that Arlington achieved with a subway alignment.[40]

High-rise developing is beginning to take form around Tysons's rail stops; however, as is often the case in suburban station areas, road infrastructure still dominates (figure 6-8). To help turn this around, Fairfax County's planning department has held numerous design charrettes over the years, soliciting inputs from local residents, workers, and businesses on the kind of urban environment preferred. A common sentiment is to create a more people-oriented milieu and marginalize the mobility role of the private car. Midrise, mixed-use projects such as the Commons of McLean market themselves as being surrounded by "park space, not parking spaces."

The consensus view is it will take some time for the Tysons transformation to take shape. Notes one developer, "It took 40 years to get to this point, and significant changes

Figure 6-8. High-rises cluster near a Tysons metro rail stop. Road infrastructure dominates the immediate station area. (Photo by Bill O'Leary.)

are going to take another couple of decades."[41] The challenges of inserting stations and TOD into an edge city not planned for them are immense, and thus the retrofit will no doubt change course over time. However, having a thoughtful, cogent plan in place will ensure that each plan revision will not fundamentally change the goal of creating a more transit-oriented, pedestrian-friendly future Tysons.

Tysons, of course, is an extreme case of a mega-complex transformation. Most office-oriented edge cities are not served by rail. Extensions of existing rail lines are one way to help jumpstart conversions. However, more likely to resonate and find political acceptance are road-based solutions. They could include inserting dedicated-lane bus rapid transit (BRT) services along major arteries feeding transformed centers. After all, higher densities and mixed-use activities are the very land use patterns needed to sustain successful BRT services.[42] Also possible is the creation of multiway boulevards that separate high-speed traffic from slower local traffic, offering ease of site access and a higher-quality pedestrian environment. As discussed in chapter 8, road capacity reductions and traffic-calming treatments might also play a role in creating better-connected and livable places. The co-development of land use changes with high-quality multimodal transportation options offers the best hope of placing large-scale suburban developments, whether on the scale of Tysons or smaller, on more sustainable pathways.

Revamped Malls and Shopping Centers

Another prominent, exceptionally auto-centric feature of suburban landscapes is the shopping center and indoor mall. Typically parking lots cover an area two to three times the size of the footprint of a suburban center or mall. Built to serve parking demands for weekends before Christmas, for much of the year these same parking lots sit half empty. Vast stretches of asphalt enclosed by arterial loops isolate shopping malls from the rest of suburbia, lengthening trip distances and all but eliminating foot access. It is ironic that motorists will cruise up and down parking lot aisles seeking a parking spot as close to mall entrances as possible. Three or four minutes might be spent looking for a space that ends up putting them 50 feet closer to the entrance. They will then enter the mall and walk a mile or more. Such behavior speaks to the value of place-making. Mall parking lots are about as dreadful places to walk as any. Being in a well-lit, temperature-controlled, high-amenity shopping complex where one can pass a different storefront every 5 seconds offers the kind of sensory stimulation and variety of all good, people-oriented places.

Shopping centers and malls often taint the neighborhoods that surround them. Besides forming superblocks and breaking up street patterns, they often form blank facades, have poor or nonexistent transit access, and impose noise and air pollution on abutting properties. Dying malls often produce dying, dysfunctional surroundings.

Just as with office parks and edge cities, developers are seeking to redefine and reinvent shopping centers and malls to meet the growing demand for walkable, urban-like neighborhoods—even in the suburbs. Shopping centers, once the antithesis of such a life, are attractive because they are huge properties with massive, easy-to-build-on parking lots, often with good freeway access and sometimes near rail stops.[43]

Car-oriented complexes from the 1970s are being overhauled and remade all across the United States and Canada to attract twenty-first-century tenants and their customers. Complete mall teardowns and replacements are also occurring. Mini-villages with open-air designs and popular shops, eateries, and offices today occupy acres that a decade earlier were filled with parked cars. Among the first was the demolition of an outdated, underused strip center in Mountain View, California, near the Silicon Valley (see figure 6-2), replaced by a mixed-use, pedestrian-friendly community called the Crossings, near a Caltrain commuter rail stop (figure 6-9). Some of the project's 835 upscale apartment units prominently sit above ground-floor retail. Other shopping-mall-to-walkable-community transformations are in the works in places such as Rockville, Maryland, and Alexandria, Virginia, outside of Washington, DC.

Even viable shopping malls are being repositioned and reinvented as mixed-use destinations. One such case is Northgate Mall, which since opening in 1950 has been the hub of north Seattle's retail activities. In 2001, the mall was updated and expanded, which included the addition of new surface parking. In a bid to create a less auto-centric place and more of a town center environment, an agreement was later reached between the land owner and the City of Seattle to fill 8 acres of parking with 500 housing units and 3 acres of open space, called Thornton Place (figure 6-10). This parking-lot-to-upscale-apartment project makeover was made possible by the addition of a new transit hub near the mall and west of Thornton Place. Stepped-up bus services along with the planned extension of light-rail services to the district have reduced the need for parking. Being near transit is also a bonus: According to the Urban Land Institute, transit centers are among the most promising retail expansion opportunities outside of downtowns.[44] In addition to Thornton Place, several nearby mixed-use projects have recently opened, adding to the live–shop–play qualities of the emerging town center.

The daylighting of a former culverted creek that meanders near Thornton Place has been an especially welcome addition to the area. The parklike bioswale has improved water quality, restored the area's natural habitat, and reduced heat island effects. A popular walkway hugs the open creek, providing a pleasant curvilinear pathway for an evening stroll (figure 6-10). As a testament to the value of greenery, a two-bedroom, two-bath apartment on Thornton Place's "Creekside" leases for 25 percent more per month than a comparable-size unit on the project's "Plaza Side" (i.e., facing the mall).[45]

Other successful shopping malls are also not content to rest on their laurels, following the lead of Northgate Mall to diversify land uses by infilling parking lots. One of the largest is Belmar in the suburbs of Denver, a mixed retail–office–housing development of 1.15 million square feet on the former Villa Italia mall.[46] The Denver suburb of Englewood

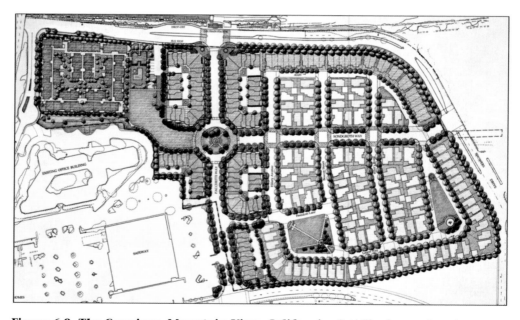

Figure 6-9. The Crossings, Mountain View, California. *(top)* The former shopping center was converted to *(bottom)* a compact, mixed-use walkable community with a modified grid street pattern. (Source: Calthorpe and Associates.)

Figure 6-10. Shopping mall infill: Thornton Place, Northgate Mall, north Seattle.
From *(top)* mall parking lot to *(bottom)* condos and a daylit park. Regreening has occurred at the
LEEDS-ND pilot project through the daylighting of a former culverted creek. (Photos by *[top]*
Landscape Architecture Foundation; *[bottom]* walkingseattle.blogspot.)

converted the languishing Cinderella City mall into a lively mixed-use, transit-served complex called CityCenter Englewood that includes shops, housing, city offices, a library, and an outdoor museum. In Edina, Minnesota, three buildings with a total of 232 luxury apartments were recently built on the southeast corner of the parking lot of Southdale Mall, America's oldest fully enclosed, climate-controlled mall. During the winter when it is often below freezing, the ability to walk to nearby restaurants and shops in a temperature-controlled mall has appeal. Apartment add-ons to shopping mall parking lots have also recently occurred in Phoenix, Raleigh, and Atlanta. Elsewhere, defunct malls are being repurposed, such as in Austin, where the 81-acre Highland Mall is home to the new Austin Community College campus and new apartments, offices, and retail are being built on more than a million square feet of surface parking. In Nashville, the Vanderbilt Medical Center has taken over much of the 100 Oaks Mall, which boosted sales at the remaining retail shops in the mall and breathed life into the neighborhood surrounding 100 Oaks. Few activities enliven an area and create a 24/7 persona more than colleges and university research centers.

Other Suburban Retrofits

A variety of other longstanding suburban land uses are also being converted, infilled, and diversified, driven by market and demographic shifts. In the wake of business park and shopping mall transformations, other suburban destinations being redesigned include golf courses, car dealerships, race tracks, garden apartment complexes, and entire commercial strip corridors.[47]

In Florida, state tax credits have allowed lightly used, heavily weeded suburban golf courses to be built on and transformed into mixed-use centers. Demographics and lifestyle shifts have largely been at play, with young adults opting to swing golf clubs far less than their parents. Florida's brownfield cleanup funds helped finance the conversion of the DeLand Country Club to a pedestrian-friendly shopping plaza, anchored by a Publix grocery store. Race tracks, another huge sports venue, are also being converted. The red-hot real estate market between San Francisco and the Silicon Valley is witnessing the conversion of the Bay Meadows horse track to a mixed-use urban village, complete with upscale housing, five new office complexes, a retail plaza, and a private high school.

Former multiplex movie theaters have also been transformed, as in Fairfax County, Virginia. There, an aging movie theater set in a sea of parking was recently bulldozed and redeveloped as the Mosaic District, featuring more than a half-million square feet of upscale boutiques, restaurants, common areas for community events, and office space. Nearly a thousand residential units and townhouses have also been added along with a 148-unit hotel.[48]

Entire commercial strips are also undergoing a facelift. The 5-kilometer Aurora car-oriented commercial strip in Shoreline, north of Seattle, is being converted to a pedestrian-friendly "complete street" through widened sidewalks, extensive landscaping and streetscaping, underground utility lines, a multimodal trail paralleling the road, center turn lanes converted to tree-lined medians, public plazas, and street art. To guide the particularly challenging task of redeveloping closed car dealerships, the nonprofit organization Sustainable Long Island has prepared design and implementation guidelines for four suburban communities east of New York City. In greater London, older garden apartments on the city's edges are being replaced by denser housing with neighborhood retail services. This has been mostly in reaction to skyrocketing rents but also shifting household preferences. It is safe to say that in reasonably healthy real estate markets, any suburban activity that is isolated from others and dependent on car access—be it a shopping plaza, golf course, or car dealership—is ripe for conversion. Increasingly, the market demands it.

Close

In the 2012 report on *Shifting Suburbs*, the Urban Land Institute identified several precursors to successful transformations of outdated suburban development.[49] Among these were the formation of public–private partnerships (to spread risks and rewards), investment in supportive infrastructure such as BRT, an emphasis on place management (i.e., adding festivals, concerts, and farmers' markets), proactive planning, stakeholder engagement, and improved connectivity through investment in pedestrian and trail networks. Such preconditions have been in place and played roles, to varying degrees, in the suburban retrofits and transformations reviewed in this chapter.

Connectivity can be particularly crucial to any successful suburban transformation. Many far-flung suburban locations are disconnected. A highly walkable mixed-use community might be built, but if it is fairly isolated and suffers from a last mile problem, it will struggle to survive financially. If enough transformations occur to create a critical mass of compact, mixed-use communities, the last mile problem will disappear. Thus, as suburban transformations scale up and become common, almost by default urbanized regions will invite short-distance travel by slower, eco-friendly modes.

The enormous footprints of suburban development have historically been a double-edged sword, on one hand increasing car dependence but on the other providing fairly easy-to-build-on land parcels to later infill and redevelop. Thus, thinly spread development, wide grassy knolls between buildings, and surface parking have been a backdoor form of land banking, providing large tracts of land to build meaningful-scale infill projects if and when the market demands it. Parking lot conversions have occurred at rail stations, shopping malls, drive-in theaters, and car dealerships, mostly in the United States but increasingly elsewhere as well. Wide suburban arterials provide room to reassign road space to more sustainable modes, such as cycle tracks for bicycles and dedicated lanes for BRT. Just as suburban communities are diversifying (i.e., complete communities), so are suburban streets (i.e., complete streets). Adaptive reuse of former industrial sites, shopping centers, or roadway corridors can face hidden costs, such as for remediation of contaminated sites. However, such one-time expenses pale in comparison to the high long-term costs of sprawling, auto-dependent growth. Public policies must provide the kinds of tax credits and financial support needed to make desirable and justifiable land conversions, if need be with funds coming from high-impact development and travel (e.g., funding through sprawl taxes and carbon fees). Such tools should also go toward ensuring that suburban transformations are socially inclusive. If transformations end up as little more than high-end boutique retailing and chi-chi development, and those in the service industries are largely priced out, they will not become complete communities.

As with any massive change, resistance can be expected from those who benefit from the status quo (e.g., developers of suburban tract housing) or who associate suburban transformations with more congested roads, more crowded schools, and longer lines at the grocery store (e.g., existing residents). Many suburbanites might welcome the construction of bike paths and trailways to nearby destinations but oppose plans to infill a shopping mall or office parking. Fears of increased traffic can be assuaged if suburban transformations are designed and mobility services delivered so as to appreciably shorten trips and promote cycling, walking, ridesharing, and transit use. Local buy-in is also more likely if an inclusive, participatory planning process is in place, allowing the kinds of compromises and sharing of ideas often needed to moderate NIMBY resistance. Local inputs also increase the likelihood that the kinds of place-making elements local residents want will be built into retrofitted suburban projects.

7

Transit-Oriented Development

Public transport is touted worldwide not only for its ability to relieve traffic congestion, reduce energy consumption, and cleanse the air but also for its ability to support sustainable patterns of urban development.[1] One would be hard-pressed to find a policy document today on climate change, smart growth, or social inclusion that did not enthusiastically support expanding the role of public transit.

The coupling of public transport investments and urban development—what can broadly be defined as transit-oriented development (TOD)—yields the most efficient and sustainable type of cityscape.[2] TODs embrace many of the same urban design features of all places that aim to promote more walking and transit riding and less driving: pedestrian-friendly designs such as safe and attractive sidewalks; small city blocks and a highly connected gridlike street network; mixed land uses that place many destinations close to each other, including small storefront ground-floor retail in commercial districts; sufficiently high densities to justify high-quality and frequent public transport services; and community hubs and civic places that promote social interaction and a sense of belonging. TODs thus are compact, mixed-use, highly walkable places that take advantage of being close to a major transit access point. Within the community, movement is principally by foot. For travel out of the community, often too far to walk and not always easily bikable, transit becomes the preferred travel means. Transit stops thus serve as the conduit for connecting highly walkable, active urban districts and their hinterlands. In many ways, then, TOD is POD, or pedestrian-oriented development. Five-minute ped-sheds are interlinked by high-quality, high-capacity public transit.

Well-designed TODs not only increase ridership by drawing more travelers out of cars and into trains and buses but can also serve as hubs for organizing community development and revitalizing distressed urban districts.[3] Worldwide, the best TODs serve as focal points for regenerating, enriching, and enlivening local communities—places not only to pass through en route to a station but also to *be*, whether for shopping, socializing, attending public celebrations, demonstrations, outdoor concerts, farmers' markets, or any other activity that builds community.[4]

TOD's growing popularity lies in part in its broad appeal. If there is any place on the city map where nearly everyone agrees that it makes sense to concentrate urban growth, it is in and around rail stations and major transit stops. Everyone—politicians, environmental advocates, real estate developers, or lay citizens—relates to the idea that putting trip origins and destinations within walking distance of stations is beneficial environmentally, socially, and economically. Many employers also understand the importance of good transit access: State Farm Insurance recently chose three metro areas (Atlanta, Phoenix, and Dallas) to be home to new, transit-served office hubs principally because they have urban rail systems with plans for further expansion.[5] Yet for most transit corridors, TODs are more the exception than the rule. If the expansive surface parking lots (what some real estate developers have called "underperforming asphalt") and marginal neighborhoods found near many rail stops are any indication, going from the theory of TOD to real-world implementation is often an uphill struggle.

TOD is hardly a new idea. In the pre-automobile era of the late nineteenth and early twentieth centuries, most urban development concentrated along streetcar and interurban rail corridors. Modern-day TODs create the kinds of neighborhoods found around transit stations 100-plus years ago. In *The Returning City: Historic Presentation and Transit in the Age of Civic Revival*, the pedestrian-friendly designs and regional connectivity of early TODs are noted: "The transit villages that came of age in the late nineteenth century exhibited all the characteristics modern TOD proponents describe as ideal for today, including a coherent transportation pattern that worked within each transit village at the pedestrian scale and multiplied efficiently throughout corridors and regions, connecting neighborhoods and suburban towns to the urban core via public transportation."[6]

This chapter examines transit stations and their surrounding neighborhoods as platforms for building communities that help move us beyond mobility. International examples of TOD as both transit access points and community hubs are presented. Before reviewing these experiences, it is important first to examine the role of public transport in the twenty-first-century city, and in particular, how stations might span the spectrum of being mobility versus place-making hubs, or some combination thereof.

The TOD Process: Planning and Typologies

TODs do not spontaneously sprout around transit stations. They are mostly the products of market forces and conscientious, strategic planning efforts to channel and nurture transit-supportive growth. The economic drivers of large-scale clustered development around train and busway stops are often pent-up market demands for growth in employment sectors that benefit from agglomeration and spatial clustering (e.g., knowledge-based industries and services). Employment gains in such fields as finance, law, real estate, and architectural design promote mid- and high-rise development to facilitate face-to-face interactions, knowledge transfers, and deal-making.[7] Transit hubs are where such businesses naturally gravitate. Basic employment jobs in turn spawn business-serving subclusters as well as tertiary demand for housing, some of which can end up near transit stations. Making sure they do means preparing station-area transit plans that identify the functional roles and urban design qualities of station catchments that appeal to prospective tenants, backed up with effective implementation tools.

Defining the future roles of transit station areas often starts with a typology of TODs. TOD typologies can be defined in terms of *land uses* (e.g., predominantly employment, predominantly residential, or balanced/mixed use), *market catchments* (e.g., regional, sub-regional/district, or community/neighborhood), *development intensities* (e.g., high-density, medium-density, low-rise), and *market activity* (e.g., strong, emerging, or static). For successful TOD to take shape, every station and its surroundings can and should be classified in terms of these four characteristics.

In the case of Portland, Oregon, America's most successful TOD region, such an approach toward building TOD typologies has been in place over the past decade. As described later, factors such as trends in land prices and building densities as well as urban design features (e.g., average block sizes and street connectivity indices) have been used to classify metro Portland's existing and planned rail stations. Station areas with a mix of strong real estate market trends and transit-supportive built environments are targeted for proactive TOD planning and public-sector leveraging. This means preparing specific station-area TOD plans and introducing supportive land use zoning and complementary infrastructure investments (e.g., sidewalk enhancements, expanded sewerage trunkline capacities). In neighborhoods with more tepid local real estate markets for which TOD is desired for social or environmental reasons, financial incentives such as property tax abatements and low-interest loans might also be introduced to entice private investors.

Node versus Place

If a transit station is to be more than a jumping-off point to catch a fast train or bus, its functional role should be defined along a spectrum of *node* versus *place*. The absence of TODs in many parts of the world often reflects the inherent tension between the place-making and logistical roles of stations.[8] On one hand, stations are logistical nodes wherein cars, buses, minibuses, taxis, delivery trucks, pedestrians, and cyclists converge for accessing transit. Intermodal connections are inherently messy. They are a patchwork of weaving, merging, and conflicting traffic streams. They are hardly people-oriented places where folks want to be; rather, most of us want to get out of stations and on to our intended destinations as quickly, safely, and efficiently as possible. Thus, in the design of such stations and their surroundings, function takes precedence over form. Engineering principles win out over the visions and aims of architects and planners. Safety and efficiency considerations override all others.

At the other end of the spectrum are stations and their immediate environs that are places to be. As a place, a TOD can serve both functionally and symbolically as the centerpiece of a community. Here, form takes precedence over function. In terms of physical designs, architecture and urban planning subsume engineering. Place-oriented TODs emphasize the design qualities of all attractive, human-scale developments, places that are comfortable, memorable, legible, connected, engaging, and amenity-oriented and instill safety through natural surveillance and Jane Jacobs–style "eyes on the street." Such place- and people-oriented TODs aim to not only boost transit ridership but also enliven community life, build social capital, be inclusive and diverse through the provision of mixed-income housing and services, provide clean and safe car-free environments for walking and mulling, and stimulate commerce and economic activities. Making place-oriented TODs affordable and inclusive is a particular challenge because urban amenities and high-end designs inevitably increase project costs. Development incentives, such as density bonuses and tax credits for including mixed-income housing and retail, are one way to promote affordable place-oriented TODs. Effectively, the revenue gains conferred by high-quality transit-proximate development end up cross-subsidizing below-market-rate housing and retail. This occurs only if there is a proactive local government committed to social inclusion and sustainable transport.

Absent efforts to build TOD typologies and define stations along the place–node spectrum, functionality almost always precedes form, due to factors such as statutory design codes and insurance liability and indemnification concerns. Whenever the intermodal connectivity and logistical needs of a station take precedence, the resulting road designs and parking layouts can seriously detract from the quality of walking, sitting, waiting, and conversing. What nearby development that does take place is likely to be transit-adjacent than transit-oriented (i.e., TAD, the "evil twin" of TOD). TADs are massings of buildings near major transit stops. TODs too have clustered buildings, but through thoughtful designs and attention to details they are also communities that instill a sense of place and identity, offer high-quality walking environments, have architectural integration, and provide attractive civic spaces.

With limited institutional capacities and resources to conduct strategic planning, many cities designing and building TODs give little thought to the functional roles of specific stations. Defined roles should weigh both market realities and the physical, historical, and cultural assets of a neighborhood. Community values and preferences also matter. Stations with a residential orientation might be good candidates for place-making roles. Those with more commercial orientations might be better suited as intermodal connection and transfer points. Failure to define the functional roles of stations and create TOD typologies can mean stations try to play both place-making and logistical roles, and as a consequence they may do neither particularly well.

Nodes of Access

Though not sufficient, being close to transit stops is a precondition of TOD. Compact cities put many residents and workers within walking distances of major stops. A recent study by the Institute for Transportation Development and Policy (ITDP) showed that higher urban densities are associated with higher shares of residents living within 1 kilometer of high-quality transit (defined as urban rail and bus rapid transit [BRT]).[9] The relationship was stronger across the thirteen Organisation for Economic Co-operation and Development (OECD) metro areas examined in the study vis-à-vis twelve non-OECD metro areas (figure 7-1). This partly reflects history: Rapid urbanization and modernization happened in the pre-automobile era in most European and North American cities, creating more transit-accessible built forms; elsewhere, rapid growth occurred mostly during the automobile era. Other factors, such as a stronger tradition of urban planning in Europe and North America and the favoring of well-to-do populations in the alignment of metros in many developing cities, also explain differences.

TODs as Places

The use of the railway station as a focal point for community building and rejuvenation finds its roots in Scandinavian town planning during the post–World War II period.[10] On the outskirts of Stockholm and Copenhagen, rail stations are physically, functionally, and symbolically the hubs of communities. In masterplanned new towns that orbit Stockholm, such as Vällingby and Skarholmen, the rail stop sits squarely in the town center.[11] Upon exiting the station, one steps into a car-free public square surrounded by shops, restaurants, schools, and community facilities. The civic square, often adorned with benches, water fountains, and greenery, is the community's central gathering spot, a place to relax and socialize and a setting for special events, whether national holidays, public celebrations, parades, or social demonstrations. Sometimes, the square does double duty as a place for farmers to sell their produce or street artists to perform, changing chameleon-like from an open-air market one day to a concert venue the next. The

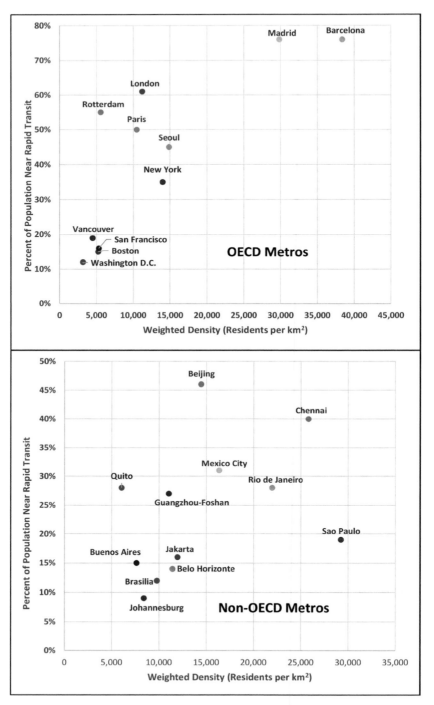

Figure 7-1. Comparison of PNT (People Near Transit) and population densities among OECD and non-OECD metro areas. (Adapted from ITDP, "People Near Transit: Improving Accessibility and Rapid Transit Coverage in Large Cities," 2016).

assortment of flower stalls, sidewalk cafes, newsstands, and outdoor vendors dotting the square, combined with the musings and conversations of residents sitting in the square, retirees playing chess, and everyday encounters among friends, adds color and breathes life into the community. Thus, a community's rail station and its surroundings are more than a jumping-off point. As attractive, lively districts, they become places people are naturally drawn to. When done well, Scandinavian TODs are places to be, not just to pass through.[12]

The place-making potential of rail stations was a focus of the 1997 book *Transit Villages in the 21st Century*. The term *village* conjures images of close-knit places where people meet, socialize, and catch up on local happenings. Transit villages were defined as just such places, focused on train stations:

> *The centerpiece of the transit village is the transit station itself and the civic and public spaces that surround it. The transit station is what connects village residents and workers to the rest of the region, providing convenient and ready access to downtowns, major activity centers like sports stadiums, and other popular destinations. The surrounding public spaces or open grounds serve the important function of being a community gathering spot, a site for special events, and a place for celebrations—a modern-day version of the Greek agora.*[13]

TOD Planning and Typologies in Portland

Cities at the forefront of advancing smart growth have laid the groundwork for TOD planning. To no surprise, Portland, Oregon, is one such city. Portland is well known for its proactivity in halting sprawl and promoting transit, highlighted by a rigid urban growth boundary and redevelopment of once-stagnant districts along light-rail and bus transit corridors. The city also wins kudos for having developed a thoughtful, market-sensitive approach to prioritizing TOD planning activities.[14] Realizing that TOD is not suitable for all areas and adhering to the idea that a limited number of successful TODs is preferable to a large number of both good and bad, the city has fashioned a compelling set of criteria for focusing TOD energies.

Two key criteria are used to create TOD place types in Portland: *market strength* and a *TOD score* (which accounts for the influences of urban form and activities on transit use). Both criteria are applied to neighborhoods surrounding stations (roughly half-mile rings from stations) and weigh existing and planned development and activities. Market strength gauges the real estate health of a neighborhood based on such factors as residential and commercial sales prices per square foot, absorption rates of net leasable space, and vacancy rates. Market characteristics largely define the future land use program of a station area and what are considered to be achievable development types in terms of density envelopes and urban design features. The TOD score accounts for the bones of a neighborhood, in terms of physical factors that now or in the future influence ridership, notably urban densities (e.g., residents and employees per net acre), average block size, availability and quality of urban living infrastructure, access to and connectivity of bikeways and sidewalks, and transit service frequency. Circularity exists in that these factors are codependent (e.g., higher densities induce more frequent transit services and vice versa). Figure 7-2 shows the TOD score ratings for fifty-seven station areas in Portland Metro as of 2010, with darker shades representing blocks and subareas that scored high in terms of transit ridership potential.

Based on three ordinal ranks of the two criteria, Portland planners have come up with nine categories of TODs. Figure 7-3 displays these using a two-way plot of station scores, with market strength occupying the horizontal axis and urban form and activity on the vertical axis. Markets are either static, emerging, or strong. The TOD score of ridership potential ranges from low (transit adjacent) to medium (transit related) to high (transit oriented). Each station is plotted along the two axes and falls into one of the nine types. (In figure 7-3, colors of the station dots represent Portland's five light-rail corridors.) The TOD types and stations that lie in the upper-right corner of the graph have the greatest potential for leveraging TOD. They are the low-hanging fruit, meant to get TOD on the ground as soon as possible. Accordingly, they have top priority for planning action. Zoning changes and local infrastructure improvements viewed as necessary to entice private

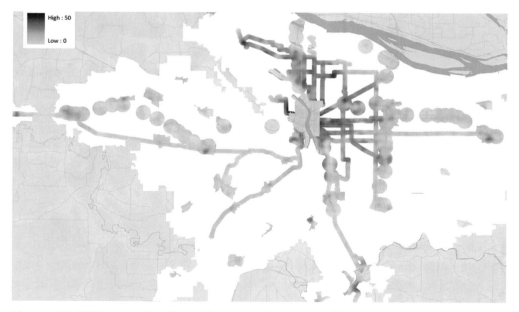

Figure 7-2. TOD scores for 57 station areas in metropolitan Portland. On a 1–50 scale, darker-shaded areas within half-mile rings of stations are subareas and blocks with the highest TOD potential in terms of ridership generation. (Source: Portland Metro.)

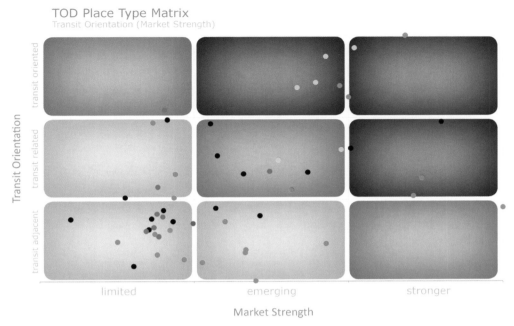

Figure 7-3. Two-way plot of urban form and activity versus market activity. The most promising TODs lie in the upper-right corner of the plot. (Source: Portland Metro.)

investments are quickly made around these stations. With success on the ground, Portland planners hope they also provide good case examples from which other neighborhoods can learn and adapt to local circumstances.

Because nine is a large number, Metro Portland planners opted for a simpler three-group typology: infill + enhance, catalyze + connect, and plan + partner. Infill + enhance areas are the most "TOD ready." Some need little public support, whereas others are transforming more slowly and could benefit from proactive measures that prime the development pump. The Hollywood light-rail station is one such example.[15] The Hollywood neighborhood has the densities, land use diversity, pedestrian infrastructure, and transportation assets of a vibrant urban district. High-density, mixed-use infill is slowly occurring around the Hollywood station, although there currently is no direct connection to the rail stop. Accordingly, the city aims to improve pedestrian and cycling connections to the station itself as an enhancement to the Hollywood infill TOD. The second cluster, catalyze + connect, characterizes areas with either a strong transit orientation but limited market support or transit-related urban form and emerging market support. These areas offer some physical or market foundation for supporting TOD but need public-sector help, such as targeted investments in living infrastructure, to catalyze private investments. Lastly, plan + partner communities are the lowest-priority areas because of their lack of key market and physical features needed for successful TOD. Nonetheless, the

Portland region has made important transit investments in these areas and continues to monitor their needs to allow the full value of these investments to be captured someday.

In Portland, moving from TOD planning to execution generally proceeds through a process of pilot testing a limited number of TODs, preparing specific station area plans, fashioning a TOD implementation strategy, and ongoing monitoring, evaluation, and adjustments. Portland's TOD planning, design, and implementation is a never-ending process as new opportunities arise and changing circumstances unfold. According to Portland Metro, among the benefits conferred by aggressive TOD planning and implementation over the first decade of the twenty-first century have been less private car travel, reflected by a 20 percent reduction in per capita VMT; $1.1 billion savings in transportation costs; $1.5 billion savings in travel time costs; and as a reflection of TOD's place-making premium, an in-migration of 25- to 34-year-olds that was five times faster than for the United States as a whole.[16]

Portland also offers insights into the challenges of planning and building TODs as connected places. Connectivity and place-making have been central to the city's quest to be highly livable, breathable, and affordable. Two cases of TOD place-making are reviewed later in this chapter—one successful (the Pearl District), the other less so (the Beaverton Round).

TOD Design and Guidelines

In addition to the kind of strategic planning done in Portland, design guidelines can be a useful instrument for translating transit-oriented design principles to on-the-ground projects. Hundreds and hundreds of transit-supportive design guidelines have been prepared over the past quarter century that promote TOD. Produced mainly by transit agencies, their aim is to set standards and offer illustrations of how project designs can promote transit riding and facilitate transit operations. North American transit agencies were the first to introduce TOD design guidelines. In 1993, twenty-six transit agencies in the United States and Canada had published guidelines.[17] By the early 2000s, this number had more than doubled.[18]

Past reviews of transit-supportive guidelines reveal that they address and set standards for key factors known to affect transit ridership and operations: land use densities, vehicle parking, sidewalk provisions, mixes of land uses, bicycle facilities, and pedestrian connectivity.[19] Rail transit agencies tend to stress minimum residential densities needed for cost-effective services. San Francisco's Bay Area Rapid Transit (BART) system, for instance, calls for a minimum of forty units per acre for individual multifamily housing projects and an overall station area average of twenty units per gross acre. Some U.S. rail authorities, such as the Chicago Transit Authority, have created station typologies, similar to those of Portland Metro, that recommend different urban design approaches and standards (e.g., minimum residential densities and parking levels) for each TOD place type.

Design standards embraced by most transit agencies are often indistinguishable from those set by New Urbanists and other advocates of less car-oriented built environments.[20] Typically, a grid of small, navigable city blocks with complete and interconnected networks of sidewalks and bikeways is called for. Mixed land uses and diversity are also promoted, not only to enliven and activate urban landscapes, as advocated by New Urbanists, but also to create "24/7" places that generate transit trips at night and on weekends. The Metropolitan Atlanta Rapid Transit Authority (MARTA) *Transit-Oriented Development Guidelines* (2010), for example, make the point that mixed-use projects help fill trains and buses in off-peak periods, thus increasing transit's daily load factors and fare-box recovery rates. MARTA encourages the use of TOD Overlay Districts to intermix land uses so as to generate all-day, all-week transit trips in transit-served corridors.

Of course, suburban transit agencies face the stiffest challenges in creating built environments that are conducive to transit riding. Some, such as Pace Transit, the operator of more than 200 bus routes in the suburbs of metropolitan Chicago, have risen to the challenge. Pace was one of the first suburban transit operators in the United States to actively promote TOD, having prepared design guidelines, available as both hard-copy reports and video tapes, as early as 1993.[21] The agency recently updated and disseminated its guidelines with a user-friendly interactive Web site.[22] A unique feature of Pace's new and improved online guidelines is the packaging of information and illustrations for different audiences, notably elected officials, municipal staff, developers, architects and engineers, transportation professionals, and residents and businesses. One section of the guidelines details all components of a typical transit trip, highlighting the needs of the rider, the development, the transit station, transit vehicles, and "the public walk." A section on "The Public Realm" suggests good design practices for everything from road layouts and streetscape designs to scaling and platting city blocks (figure 7-4). A companion section on "The Private Realm" shows transit-supportive examples of project land uses, densities, parking management, and building designs, emphasizing suburban settings.

Only recently have transit-oriented design manuals begun to address the more nuanced issue of place-making. This is partly because transit agencies (versus, say, design firms) have mostly produced guidelines, placing operational topics such as ease of bus turning maneuvers and access to bus stops above all else. This emphasis brings us back to the tension of stations as places versus nodes. Should roads leading to and within transit station areas be narrowed to create human-scale, pedestrian-friendly environs or generously widened to accommodate the turning radii of 50-foot buses? Understandably, safety considerations have mostly governed such design decisions. For many transit properties, this means accommodating the needs of buses, delivery trucks, and kiss-and-ride maneuvers, even if pedestrians and cyclists are inconvenienced. Design considerations are shifting, however. Recent transit-oriented design guidelines in Chicago, San Francisco, Denver, and Austin elevate the importance of place-making in some station settings. For

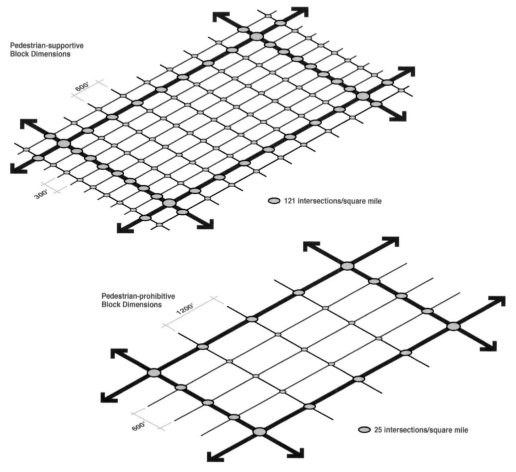

Pedestrian-supportive
Block Dimensions

600'

300'

○ 121 intersections/square mile

Pedestrian-prohibitive
Block Dimensions

1200'

600'

○ 25 intersections/square mile

Figure 7-4. Options for scaling and designing blocks and road frontages. (Source: Pace Bus, *Transit Supportive Guidelines for the Chicagoland Region*, 2013.)

stations seeking to become the centerpieces of surrounding communities and hubs for social engagement, all emphasize the importance of high-quality, human-scale designs that make transit stations, among other things, "the heart of special places" and "iconic elements" of neighborhood landscapes.

The TOD Standard

The ITDP is a highly influential nongovernment organization active on the global stage, devoted to advancing sustainable transportation and development. Over the years, ITDP has gained a reputation as an honest broker in representing the interests of cyclists, pedestrians, and transit users in the programming of multi-million-dollar loans from international development banks to developing countries.

In 2013, ITDP released *The TOD Standard*, a case-based, illustrative document aimed at promoting TODs that are highly walkable and that effectively integrate station areas with their surroundings. In effect, the document is TOD design guidelines aimed at a global audience. A panel of TOD experts advised ITDP staff throughout the project. Eight key objectives that contribute to environmentally sustainable TOD were identified in the *Standard*, each weighted according to what experts consider to be their relative importance:

- *Walking*: a public realm that is safe, complete, active, comfortable, and vibrant (15 pts.)
- *Cycling*: a cycling network that is safe and complete, with ample and secure parking and storage (5 pts.)
- *Connectivity*: walking and cycling routes that are short, direct, and varied, more so than driving routes (15 pts.)
- *Transit service*: high-quality transit that is accessible by foot (0 pts. since this is a prerequisite)
- *Mixed land uses:* diverse and complementary land uses that shorten trip lengths (15 pts.)
- *Density:* residential and job densities sufficient to support high-quality transit (15 pts.)
- *Compactness:* developments that infill built-up areas and improve access to other transit hubs (15 pts.)
- *Shifting:* land devoted to off- and on-street parking and driveways is reduced (20 pts.)

Based on these criteria, ITDP scored thirty-one TOD projects around the world. Scoring the highest, with 99 points out of 100, was the Central Saint Giles TOD, a mixed-use, infill project in Central London adjacent to the Tottenham Court Road tube station (figure 7-5). Central Saint Giles features an eleven-story office building that houses Google, NBC Universal, and other new-economy tenants as well as high-end ground-floor shops and restaurants; a fifteen-story residential tower with 109 units, about half of which are priced below market rate (in return for the developer being able to add two floors to the project); and a publicly accessible pedestrian plaza located between the site's two main buildings, surrounded by ground-floor retail and restaurant space. As an infill project in a built-up area, Central Saint Giles contributes to an uninterrupted expanse of high-quality urbanism. It also has a sense of place: an interior courtyard that, weather permitting, invites people to sit, chat, and take in the surroundings. Although the project achieves good quantitative balance between jobs, housing, and retail, qualitatively the match is less than perfect. For instance, restaurants and shops cater to the high-income profile of well-paid tech industry workers but are hardly affordable to working-class residents. This

Figure 7-5. Central Saint Giles, London. This colorful mixed-use TOD in central London fills in a built-up area, earning it the "best TOD" rating in ITDP's *TOD Standard*, 2013. (Photo provided courtesy of Institute of Transportation Development and Policy. Photo credit: Ömer Çavusoglu.)

underscores the importance of rating developments not only on quantitative metrics but on more qualitative and interpretative ones as well. The second edition of *The TOD Standard*, released in mid-2017, increases the importance of affordability and mixed-income development in the scoring of TODs.

Place Identity: Oakland's Fruitvale Station

Place identity has been important to a number of TODs in the United States, especially those in once-downtrodden neighborhoods that have been reinvigorated. Oakland's Fruitvale district is one such case. The Fruitvale neighborhood remained fairly stagnant during its first three decades of BART metrorail services, attracting little in the way of commercial investments or neighborhood upgrading. As with many BART stations, the vast expanse of surface parking surrounding the Fruitvale station suppressed rail transit's ability to spawn compact, mixed-use TOD, as envisaged when the system was first planned.[23] Thanks to a broad-based partnership of public, private, and philanthropic interests and funding support, a compact, mixed-use village huddled around the Fruitvale station has begun to take form over the past decade.[24] In keeping with the design principles of successful transit-oriented places, one of the signature features of the Fruitvale Transit Village has been an active public realm that is friendly to pedestrians and cyclists.[25]

Kickstarting Fruitvale's transformation was the redevelopment of 5.9 acres of surface parking lots into more than 140,000 square feet of retail, commercial office, and community service space. A two-block pedestrian spine rimmed with ground-floor retail and above-level offices and lofts was designed to connect the BART station to the neighborhood's historical commercial street, International Boulevard (figure 7-6). Of course, people do not experience a community at an oblique angle or from plan view, like birds soaring above. Rather, they experience it on the street. Accordingly, local planners relied on a series of design charrettes to generate on-the-street images of how, over time, the International Boulevard main street might be transformed to become a place to be. Figure 7-7 visualizes, at street view, the kind of transformations that the International Boulevard corridor might undergo, using Photoshop. Of course, this is a simple rendering that has not stood the test of rigorous financial analysis, and it is safe to say International Boulevard will not look like

Figure 7-6. Fruitvale station's place identity. Ground-floor retail and terraced buildings embrace the Latino heritage of the Fruitvale neighborhood. (Photo by Kaid Benfield.)

Figure 7-7. Visualizing the transformation of International Boulevard, Fruitvale station's main commercial street. As input to a community engagement process, images show how *(top)* the current, drab-looking car-oriented main street might be transformed into *(bottom)* a more pedestrian-oriented district through a combination of storefront improvements, landscaping (including a green median strip), and midrise infill housing. Over the longer term, a streetcar and bikeway might share International Boulevard, complete with mature shade trees. (Source: Fruitvale Unity Council.)

this 30 years from now. However, on-the-street cross-sectional images do serve the purpose of stimulating discussions and debate on how the neighborhood might change over time. They are an effective tool of community engagement and help elevate the importance of place-making in the minds of local residents and merchants. Their contribution lies in enhancing the process, not necessarily the final product, of TOD planning.

Part of Fruitvale's place-making transformation has been making it one of the most bicycle-friendly transit stations in the United States. A substantial amount of cycling infrastructure has been built around the Fruitvale station in the past decade and a half, with the kilometers of bike lanes and protected paths within a mile radius of the station having increased eightfold between 1998 and 2008. Within the village and near the station entrance lies a 200-space high-quality attended bike station, providing secure parking, repair services, and short-term bike rentals. These investments have clearly paid off. In 2008, one in ten access trips to Fruitvale station was by bicycle, up from less than 5 percent 10 years earlier. This is one of the highest bicycle modal splits outside a university campus setting in the United States.[26]

The Pearl District, Portland, Oregon: Streetcar-Oriented Development

The Pearl is a former warehouse district, just north of downtown Portland, which over the past two decades has been transformed into a chic, vibrant, streetcar-served neighborhood. Streetcars are yesteryear's technology, using century-old refurbished trains that run in mixed traffic, stopping frequently and sharing streets with pedestrians and cyclists. Most function as central-city circulators, connecting destinations that are beyond a 5-minute walk. Their slower speeds fit nicely with the cadence of an active pedestrian cityscape. Because they run in city streets and are cheaper and less intrusive to build than metros, streetcars can be built quickly and with fewer disruptions.[27] As a number of European cities have witnessed, "streetcars represent a paradigm change in the way cities and transit agencies think and plan for transit: they are about redevelopment as much as they are about transportation, so land use planning plays a critical role."[28]

In Portland, the streetcar was the transportation horse that led the urban redevelopment cart. Driving the program was a vision to infuse life into and exploit the development potential of a long-languishing former warehouse and railyard district. Mixed-use, infill development at high densities with very high-quality streetscaping and landscaping enhancements was the vision that drove the investment program. In return for the landowner of a strategically located 40-acre parcel increasing densities from 15 to 125 units per acre, the city and private-sector partners invested in a streetcar that sought to mimic the successes of tramway-driven inner-city regeneration in places such as Munich and Melbourne. This was a risky proposition because in the early 1990s, when the investment decision was made, there was no precedent for such urban regeneration in the United States. Portland's strong commitment to smart growth at the time, such as forming an urban growth boundary and investing in light-rail transit system, no doubt contributed to the success of the Pearl District. But so did a pent-up demand for high-quality, in-city living in a neighborhood with character, tradition, a small-block walkable landscape, and some of the edgy qualities that come with converted loft space and high-ceiling former warehouses. The city capitalized on this combination of community assets and emerging market interests by investing heavily in streetscape enhancements, such as sidewalk upgrades, landscaping and greening of pocket parks, street furniture, refurbishment of street lamps, and building façade upgrades, giving the Pearl a unique identity far from suburbia (figure 7-8). By all accounts, the 2.4-mile streetcar starter line, which opened in 2001, coupled with ancillary streetscape enhancements, accelerated the influx of private-sector capital into the neighborhood.

Today, the Pearl District is Portland's densest and arguably most popular neighborhood. By 2008, more than ten thousand housing units had been built, a quarter of which were affordable. The city's 20-year housing goal was met within 7 years on one-tenth the projected land area. In 2006, the streetcar was extended to a second large vacant tract, the South Waterfront, where another ambitious redevelopment effort was under way, lengthening the system to 4 miles. Nearly 5 million square feet of commercial floor space has been added within two blocks of the streetcar corridor. The combination of improved access and high-quality urban development has unleashed a strong market demand to exploit development opportunities along the corridor. Development has clearly gravitated to city blocks off the rail line. During its first decade, properties closest to the streetcar were developed at 90 percent of their permissible densities, compared with 43 percent of allowable densities for parcels three or more blocks away.[29] Before the investment, the reverse was true. All in all, Portland's streetcar is credited with spawning $2.3 billion in private investment in the Pearl District. Those moving into the district use the streetcar to get around. In 2008, 58 percent of Pearl District residents reported using modes other than driving to get to work.[30] By developing space in the district that encourages the movement of people instead of cars, the Pearl District has become an attractive, high-demand place to live. Midrise housing in a highly accessible central-city location combined with very high-quality urban streetscapes dotted with parks and plazas has proven to be a winning formula. The Pearl District's success has prompted some sixty U.S. cities to follow Portland's lead, planning their own streetcars as a hoped-for catalyst to urban regeneration.[31]

The Beaverton Round, Portland, Oregon: TOD's Market Limits

Not all of metro Portland's endeavors to create attractive, functional districts around rail stations have been successful. The Round was an ambitious initiative to build a major hub around a light-rail station in the town of Beaverton on Portland's west side, focused on

Figure 7-8. Rail-oriented place-making in the Pearl District. The district's masterplan orchestrated myriad independent, small-lot infill projects, typically upper-level lofts and ground-floor retail, along the streetcar corridor. (Photos by *[top]* Eckert and Eckert and *[bottom]* Lynda Jeffers.)

a signature building and prominent civic space. The project borrowed a page from Scandinavian designs of people-oriented suburban rail hubs. However, unbridled enthusiasm to create a vibrant, viable rail-oriented center could not overcome the realities of weak market demand.[32]

The project was dubbed "The Round" after the opening of a crescent-shaped building that surrounds a large, European-style plaza anchored by a light-rail stop (figure 7-9). It was envisioned as an echo of the burgeoning condo scene in downtown Portland, including office and retail space, upscale restaurants, and a movie theater. Its design embraced New Urbanist principles: a transit orientation, a commons, and a pedestrian-friendly street grid. It also included a multilevel parking garage within view of the station, which detracted from the project's visual appeal.

From the beginning, the project had a number of strikes against it that, despite the best of design and place-making intentions, could not be overcome. The station lies in the heart of a car-dependent, low-density suburb. The site itself has the stigma of a former light industrial and sewage treatment facility. Nearby are used-car lots and abandoned freight rail tracks. More vibrant is a close-by commercial corridor serviced by a main highway, but the Beaverton Round is physically isolated from it. Lack of exposure to a major arterial and the project's isolated feel chased new businesses away. Many would-be condominium buyers were deterred by the neighboring automobile dealerships and empty building sites. Also, the absence of direct secure parking dissuaded high-end retail and office tenants from locating at the Round (figure 7-10).

Figure 7-9. Beaverton Round. (Photo by *The Oregonian*.)

Figure 7-10. Disconnected buildings and parking expanses envelop the Beaverton Round. (Photo by *The Oregonian*.)

What exists today is fraction of envisaged development. Planners thought that car sales lots, abandoned agriculture sites, and "underperforming asphalt" could be overcome through an iconic building and a regional light-rail stop, eventually attracting high-end residential and commercial tenants. They did not. Further undermining the project were the high costs of brownfield site remediation. Poor subsoils required costly building foundations, limiting the footprint and placement of buildings. As discovered at the Round, once builders start excavating grounds of former industrial sites, the cost of removing and upgrading pipes, decontaminating soils, and dealing with other surprises can substantially inflate the cost of well-intended redevelopment projects.

The lesson from Beaverton Round is that despite the best of place-making intentions, TOD cannot overcome a weak local real estate market. Nor can it magically turn around a place with a tarnished image. Initial predictions about the ability of this submarket to support European-style TOD were way off the mark. The upscale condo scene of the Pearl District, which planners hoped to recreate in Beaverton, did not work in a suburban enclave with poor access and a poor image, rail services notwithstanding. Suburban TODs on former industrial sites are unchartered waters. In such settings planners are well advised to err on the side of caution.

Hong Kong: Rail Development, Place-Making, and Profiteering

If place-oriented TOD has value, this should be reflected in real estate markets. The robust, teeming-with-life enclave of Hong Kong is one of the best places to see whether this is so.

Any visitor to Hong Kong instantly recognizes that public transit is the lifeblood of the city. Hong Kong boasts a rich offering of transit services, including a high-capacity railway network, surface street trams, ferries, and an assortment of buses and minibuses. In late 2007, the city's main passenger rail operator, MTR Corporation, merged with the former Kowloon–Canton Railway Corporation, forming a 168-kilometer network of high-capacity, grade-separated services in Hong Kong island, the Kowloon peninsula, the Northern Territories (to the Chinese border), and, through a recent extension, to Hong Kong's new international airport. The system continues to expand as Hong Kong continues to grow outward. More than 90 percent of motorized trips in Hong Kong are by public transit, the highest market share anywhere.[33]

Hong Kong is one of the few places in the world where public transport makes a profit, courtesy of MTR's Rail + Property (R+P) program. R+P is one of the purest examples of transit value capture. Given the high premium placed on access to fast, efficient, and reliable public transport services in a dense, congested city such as Hong Kong, the price of land near railway stations is generally higher than elsewhere, sometimes by several orders of magnitude. MTR has used its ability to obtain the development rights for land around stations at a favorable price to recoup the cost of investing in rail transit and turn a profit.

MTR and R+P

As a private corporation that sells shares on the Hong Kong stock market, MTR operates on commercial principles, financing and operating railway services that not only are self-supporting but also yield a net return on investment. Effectively, the fully loaded costs of public transport investments, operations, and maintenance are covered by supplementing fare and other revenues with income from ancillary real estate development, such as the sale of development rights, joint venturing with private real estate developers, and running retail outlets in and around subway stations.

Throughout the 1980s and 1990s, the Hong Kong Special Administrative Region (HKSAR) government was the sole owner of MTR. In 2000, 23 percent of MTR's shares were offered to private investors on the stock exchange. The presence of private shareholders exerted a strong market discipline on MTR, prompting the company managers to become more entrepreneurial and business-minded. However, HKSAR's majority shareholder status ensured that MTR weighed the broader public interest in its day-to-day decisions, including the promotion of TOD.

The privileged position accorded to MTR by HKSAR has allowed it to reap huge windfalls from selling development rights. MTR purchases development rights from HKSAR at a "before rail" price and sells these rights to a selected developer (among a list of qualified bidders) at an "after rail" price. The differences between land values as greenfield versus rail-served sites can be gargantuan in a land-constrained place such as Hong Kong, generating enough to cover the cost of railway investments and then some.

R+P and TOD

In the early 2000s, growing concerns about quality of life and Hong Kong's global competitiveness prodded local officials to adopt a policy of integrating high-quality infrastructure investments and land development. Hong Kong has long had tall towers surrounding and above railway stations, but density alone does not make for high-quality places. Attractive urban landscapes and pleasant yet functional walking environments were often missing in and around stations.

The first generation of R+P projects built by MTR were hardly pedestrian-friendly TODs. Most featured indistinguishable apartment towers that dumped pedestrians onto busy streets and offered little guidance on finding a subway entrance. Growing public discontent over sterile station area environments and the sagging real estate market performance of older buildings prompted MTR officials to pay more attention to principles of good town planning. Perhaps most notable was the establishment of an urban design and planning division within the corporation, charged with pursuing land development strategies that met corporate financial objectives while also promoting local land use objectives and better walking environments. R+P projects from the early 1980s responded to rather than anticipated development. By the turn of the century, the reverse was true. In keeping with the Hong Kong government's Regional Development Strategy to shape urban growth through railway investments and enhance pedestrian environments, recent railway investments and their associated R+P projects have been in advance of market demand.

Recently built MTR stations and their associated R+P projects embrace the Scandinavian model of TOD design, seeking to impart a sense of place and function as community hubs, albeit at much higher densities. They do this in large part by creating a sizable public space outside the station embellished by public art. Tung Chung station is one such example. The station and its adjacent civic square is today the hub of Tung Chung new town. The community sees itself as a landmark gateway to Hong Kong's international airport. Compared with earlier R+P projects, Tung Chung is designed at more of a human scale, featuring bright night lights, openness (much appreciated in a hyperdense city), vivid and coordinated urban designs, and through active pedestrian movements, the kind of natural surveillance that gives people a sense of comfort and ease (figure 7-11). An urban design audit found newer R+P projects like Tung Chung scored much higher than early-generation high-rise projects in terms of connectivity, comfort, aesthetics, public amenities, legibility, and natural surveillance.[34]

If R+P projects built as pedestrian-friendly TODs are beneficial, this should be reflected in ridership statistics and real estate market performance. A statistical analysis found that each additional household built within 500 meters of an MTR station added 1.75 transit trips per weekday.[35] If designed to incorporate place-making elements (e.g., grade-separated skyways; mixed land uses, including retail shops, along pedestrian corridors;

Figure 7-11. Tung Chung Station area. Occupying a 21.7-hectare parcel, Tung Chung was conceptualized and built along the lines of a masterplanned new town, comprising predominantly residential housing intermixed with retail shops, offices, and a hotel next to the station. (Photo by MTR Corporation.)

architectural integration; and provision of public amenities such as pocket parks and water art), each new housing unit added 2.84 daily rail trips. This relationship has not gone unnoticed among MTR's management: Transit-oriented designs and high-quality pedestrian environments can increase farebox income and generate walk-on traffic, boosting sales at MTR-owned shops in and around railway stations.

Equally important have been the price premiums recorded for R+P housing projects designed according to TOD principles. A notable example is the Hang Hau MTR station, built as a "New Town Intown" along the Tseung Kwan O brownfield redevelopment corridor. There, a strong emphasis was given to place-making. Owner-occupied apartments are directly tied to a nicely landscaped garden and private clubhouse that sits above the station. Residents also have direct elevator connections to the station concourse and lower-level shopping mall. A phalanx of second-level footbridges links the shopping mall and station to the surrounding neighborhood. Hang Hau's R+P project has a comfortable, human-scale feel and a design that not only instills a sense of place but also protects the financial investments of tenants. These benefits have been capitalized into land prices. A recent hedonic price model study that controlled for building types and distance to subway entrances found that Hang Hau's condominiums built under the R+P model with transit-oriented designs enjoyed average rent premiums of 22 percent.[36] Overall, the analysis found price premiums ranging from US$12 to US$36 per square foot of gross floor area for housing estates built atop or adjacent to MTR stations. It is for such reasons that high-quality urban designs and pedestrian environments are now *de rigueur* at all new R+P projects.

With Hong Kong's return to mainland China, one might have expected programs such as R+P to have gravitated to mega-metropolises such as Beijing, Shanghai, and Guangzhou. Planet Earth certainly would benefit. As discussed in chapter 9, however, this has not been the case.

Connecting Places in Other TOD Place Types

This section reviews experiences with TODs of a particular type. These are specialized TODs where planners, engineers, and designers have had to wrestle with the challenges of designing for place, mobility, and connectivity. Three specialized TOD place types are discussed: green TODs, kid-friendly TODs, and adaptive reuse TODs.

Green TODs

An ultra–environmentally friendly version of TOD, green TOD, is taking form in several cities.[37] Green TOD is a marriage of TOD and green urbanism. The combination can create synergies that yield environmental benefits beyond the sum of what TOD and green urbanism offer individually. TOD works on shrinking a city's environmental footprint by reducing vehicle miles traveled (VMT), a direct correlate of energy consumption and tailpipe emissions. VMT is reduced not only by auto-to-transit modal shifts but also by replacing trips to off-site destinations that would have been by car with on-site walking and cycling enabled by the mix of uses. Green urbanism reduces energy use, emissions, water pollution, and waste from stationary sources, in the form of green architecture and sustainable community designs.[38] With green urbanism, pocket parks and community gardens replace surface parking. Renewable energy might come from solar and wind and from biofuels created from organic waste and wastewater sludge. Insulation, triple-glazed windows, airtight construction, bioswales, recycling and reuse of materials, land reuse, and low-impact building materials further shrink the footprint of green TOD. Mixed land uses are a particularly important feature of green TODs, offering economies of scope (e.g., there is far more waste heat from commercial uses than there is demand for commercial hot water; however, nearby residential uses allow a higher portion of commercial waste heat to be reused). In combination, the co-benefits of TOD and green urbanism can deliver energy self-sufficiency, zero-waste living, and sustainable mobility. The reductions in annual CO_2 emissions per capita among those residing in green TODs relative to conventional development patterns are estimated at 24 to 29 percent.[39]

One of the best-known green TODs is Hammarby Sjöstad, a brownfield redevelopment in the city of Stockholm.[40] Hammarby Sjöstad marked an abrupt shift in Stockholm's urban planning practice. After decades of building new towns on peripheral greenfield sites, Hammarby Sjöstad is one of several "new towns in town" created after Stockholm's 1999 City Plan set forth a vision to "Build the City Inwards." Consisting of some 160 hectares of brownfield redevelopment, Hammarby Sjöstad is Stockholm's largest urban regeneration project to date. Table 7-1 outlines Hammarby Sjöstad's green TOD features.

Green Transportation

A tramway (*Tvärbanan*) runs through the heart of Hammarby Sjöstad along a 3-kilometer boulevard. Taller buildings (mostly six to eight stories) cluster along the transit spine, and building heights taper with distance from the rail-served corridor. Rail stations are well

Table 7-1. Green TOD attributes of Hammarby Sjöstad.

	Green transportation		Green urbanism	
Built environment	**Infrastructure**	**Programs and policies**	**Energy**	**Open space, water, and stormwater**
• Brownfield • Infill • Former army barracks • High density along light-rail boulevard • TOD: mixed use with ground-floor retail	• Tvärbanan light rail line: 3 stops in district • Other transit: – Bus lines – Ferry service • Bike lanes and bike and pedestrian bridges: – Ample bike parking at every building • Car sharing • Near congestion toll boundary • Pedestrian-friendly design, complete streets, traffic calming	• Transit Boulevard is focus of activity and commerce • Grid streets increase connectivity and calm traffic • Convenient bike parking and storage at every building • Congestion pricing for car use into core city	• Waste converted to energy: – Food waste and wastewater sludge converted to biogas and used for heating – Combustible waste burned for energy and heat – Paper recycled • Combined heat and power plant: – Heat recaptured for reuse • Low-energy construction and energy-saving measures: – Efficient appliances – Maximum glazing and insulation	• Stormwater treatment – Rainwater collection – Maximum permeable surfaces – Purify runoff through soil filtration • Ample open space: – Inner courtyards – Parks – Playgrounds – Green median – Borders large nature reserve with ski slopes • Preservation of existing trees and open space • Reduced water flow faucets and low-flush toilets

designed and fully weather protected, and they provide real-time arrival information. Parks, walkways, and green spaces are also prominent throughout Hammarby Sjöstad. Where possible, the natural landscape has been preserved. Bike lanes run along major boulevards, ample bike parking can be found at every building, and bike and pedestrian bridges cross waterways. Design features that are integral to TOD, such as buildings that go up to the sidewalk line (i.e., no setbacks), offer comfortable and secure walking corridors with clear sightlines. Such practices also bring destinations together and through side friction end up slowing traffic.

Car sharing and limited parking have led to fairly low car ownership rates among Hammarby Sjöstad residents. Also, the neighborhood sits just outside Stockholm' congestion toll boundary, which adds a further incentive to use public transport, walk, or bike when heading to the central city.

Green Urbanism

Hammarby Sjöstad's green urbanism is found in energy production, waste and water management, and building designs. The highest energy efficiency standards are used. A district heating network provides 80 percent of residents' heating needs, substantially reducing energy loss in the heating system. Eighty percent of heat energy comes from renewable sources. The use of district cooling reduces carbon dioxide emissions in Stockholm by about 50,000 tons annually. After heat has been extracted from the warm, purified wastewater, the remaining cold water is used for district cooling, such as replacing energy-guzzling air conditioning systems in office buildings.

The ecological feature that has received the most attention is Hammarby Sjöstad's fully integrated closed-loop eco-cycle model. The system recycles waste and maximizes the reuse of waste energy and materials for heating, transportation, cooking, and electricity. Waste is also converted into energy for district heating and cooling, in the form of biogas created from treated wastewater (produced in the wastewater treatment plant from digestion of organic waste sludge) and the incineration of combustible waste. In addition, biogas is used to run local buses, and biogas cookers are installed in about a thousand apartments. Solar panels provide 50 percent of the hot water needs for many buildings during summer months.

Impacts

According to the initial assessment when Hammarby Sjöstad was roughly half built out, it had already achieved a 32 to 39 percent reduction in overall emissions and pollution (air, soil, and water), a 28 to 42 percent reduction in nonrenewable energy use, and a 33 to 38 percent reduction in ground-level ozone relative to comparison communities with similar household incomes. Buildings and transportation accounted for most of the reduced environmental impacts.[41] Environmental benefits from transportation have

accrued from Hammarby Sjöstad's high share of nonmotorized trips and low car ownership levels. Studies show that residents' carbon footprint from transportation in 2002 was
much lower than comparison communities: 438 versus 913 kilograms of CO_2 equivalent
per apartment per year.[42] Because of comparative low car ownership rates and high public
transit usage, more recent data suggest that average overall transport-related emissions
for residents of Hammarby Sjöstad are less than half that of the average Stockholm resident and less than a third of that of the typical Swede.[43] These percentages will probably
increase with time as Stockholm aims to become carbon neutral and totally fossil free by
mid-century.

Another barometer of Hammarby Sjöstad's environmental benefits is the healthy local
economy (e.g., a higher median household income and lower unemployment rate relative to the city as a whole).[44] Also, land prices and rents have risen more rapidly since
2000 than in most other parts of the Stockholm region. Today, Hammarby Sjöstad is considered to be a desirable and thus more expensive place to live relative to the inner city
and other "new towns in town."

Kid-Friendly TODs

Conventional wisdom holds that TODs are most attractive to households in the early and
late stages of the adult life cycles, that is, young professionals, childless couples, retirees,
and empty-nesters. They are considered less attractive to families with children. However,
several European communities show that TODs can be kid-friendly.[45] These can be created
by replacing surface parking with communal gardens, playgrounds, tot-lots, and open
space.

Shrinking parking's footprint reduces heat island effects and water pollution from
oil-stained runoff into streams. It also helps recharge groundwater, allowing greener and
healthier gardens and play areas. Such car-restricted settings are not only safer for kids
to play; they are more secure because of "natural surveillance," the ability of residents to
keep an eye on who is using community spaces. Several European kid-friendly TODs are
briefly noted here:

- *GWL-Terrain, Amsterdam.* As a car-restricted project in a liberal city known for can-
  nabis shops and its red-light district, one might assume GWL-Terrain caters to bohe-
  mians and counterculturalists. With its gardens, green spaces, playgrounds, and
  good tram access to Amsterdam's many cultural offerings, GWL-Terrain is quite
  family oriented: 42 percent of households have children under 18 years of age, more
  than in surrounding neighborhoods and well above the 24 percent for Amsterdam
  as a whole.[46] Only 20 percent of families own a car.

- *Rieselfeld and Vauban districts, Freiburg, Germany.* On the outskirts of arguably Germany's greenest city, Freiberg, these two eco-communities feature ample play areas and bike paths, narrow shared "play streets" that slow traffic, and tram spines that run through their interiors. More than 40 percent of households in both communities have children, and cycling and transit make up the majority of nonwalking trips.[47] Shrinkage of parking's footprint has freed up land for interior gardens and playgrounds in Rieselfeld (figure 7-12).

TOD as Adaptive Reuse: Experiences from Dallas

Adaptive reuse of former industrial sites, railyards, and warehouses is yet another emerging TOD place type. The Pearl District case cited earlier is one example. Another is Mockingbird Station in Dallas, Texas, a mixed-use urban chic village built on former industrial land and disused asphalt parking 4 miles north of downtown Dallas.[48] The development links directly to the Mockingbird light-rail station via a pedestrian bridge (figure 7-13). Mockingbird sits on land once given over to a telephone wiring factory and several smaller industrial uses. The assemblage of offices, shops, restaurants, and lofts near the station has created a 24/7 place. Many residents patronize the generous retail and entertainment offerings at the Mockingbird Station, keeping the project active well into the evening.

Figure 7-12. Kid-friendly TOD in Rieselfeld, Germany. Gardens and play areas replace surface parking. (Photo by Klaus Siegl.)

Figure 7-13. Mockingbird Station, Dallas. (Source: Dallas Area Rapid Transit.)

Recalling trips to New York City and Europe during his youth, developer Ken Hughes consciously sought to tap into the transit system to bring the ambience and energy of other worldly places to Dallas. Remarked Hughes, "If you look at the chemistry in London, Paris, Mexico City or wherever there's mass transit, you find kinetic activity created by transit stations. A little bit of that will happen here with the trains."[49] At Mockingbird Station, place-making was toward the top of the list of project design considerations.

Another example of adaptive reuse TOD in the Dallas Metroplex is the Plano station on Dallas's exurban fringes. Plano lies some 40 minutes north of downtown Dallas on the Dallas Area Rapid Transit (DART) Red Line. During the boom times of the 1980s, millions of square feet of campus-style office space was built throughout Plano. In reaction to the city's increasingly car-choked streets, Plano's city council approved a vision plan in the late 1990s. The plan's overriding goal was to create a compact town center with a unique identity focused on the DART light-rail station, embracing its historical past and focusing on creating a highly walkable, human-scale environment. The city introduced a historic tax exemption to encourage the restoration of older structures and introduced form-based codes. Anchoring the rebirth of downtown Plano is Eastside Village, a moderately dense mixed-use project fronting directly onto DART's light-rail station plaza. As revealed by the before-and-after changes in the Plano station area (figure 7-14), the project does a

Figure 7-14. Adaptive reuse and transformation of central Plano. Tree-lined, ground-floor retail opens onto the light-rail stop. The "Dallas Donut" design relegates the interior parking structure to a secondary role. (Source: Dallas Area Rapid Transit.)

wonderful job of incorporating a parking structure without being spatially overwhelmed by it. The bottom photo of figure 7-14 shows a three- and four-story building that wraps around three sides of a multilevel parking structure, which can be accessed only from the rear alley. In what has been called the Dallas Donut design, parking is relegated to a tertiary mobility role, behind rail transit and foot traffic. Today, more than a thousand residential units lie within a quarter-mile of Plano's rail stop, some in historic buildings, others in mixed-use complexes.[50] The once sleepy downtown today has the persona of a 24/7 place.

A third example of successful adaptive reuse of former industrial land is the Cedars Station on the south line of Dallas's light-rail system. The Southside is a ten-story, mixed-use "live and work" center that reused an abandoned Sears Roebuck & Co. Catalogue Merchandise Center built in 1913. With more than 1.4 million square feet, the project includes lofts, retail space (e.g., coffee shop, small grocery, dry cleaner), offices, and live performance space. The loft units are occupied primarily by young professional couples and empty nesters attracted to the district's arts focus. The project's commercial space continues to expand.

Close

Transit corridors are natural habitats for enhancing access and place-making. Stations and their surroundings are ideal catchments for concentrating residential and commercial growth, and under the right conditions they can serve as community hubs. Because all transit trips involve travel by foot to some degree, high-quality walking environments are imperative for any successful TOD. By definition, transit-oriented development must also be pedestrian-oriented development.

As discussed in this chapter, the challenges of creating attractive and successful TODs go well beyond simply stacking up building heights within several blocks of transit stops. Introducing an effective planning process that allows communities to concentrate on a limited number of stations with the highest TOD potential is particularly important. As has been the case in Portland, Oregon, and as applied on a global stage by ITDP in its *TOD Standard*, TOD typologies can be an effective tool for articulating the unique design, connectivity, and mobility elements most appropriate for particular TOD types. Under the right conditions, moreover, experiences in places such as Hong Kong and Hammarby Sjöstad show that good transit-oriented designs can increase land values and stimulate local economies. Thus, sustainable urbanism and sustainable finance can be wholly compatible objectives and outcomes, leading to the kind of "better economies" discussed in chapter 4.

Given that most future urban population growth over the next two decades will be in developing countries, the opportunities for successfully linking urban development and public transport in the Global South are unprecedented. Much of this growth will occur in medium-size cities below half a million inhabitants, places that are more likely to be able to afford and thus build BRT systems rather than metros. A bus-based form of small-scale TOD interlaced with high-quality infrastructure for pedestrians and cyclists may be appropriate in many emerging cities. More examples of successful BRT–land use integration, as in the well-chronicled experience of Curitiba, Brazil, are very much needed. Compact development is a cardinal feature of TOD, but because many developing cities are already dense, a number of authors point out that in both BRT and urban rail nodes, high-quality walkable and mixed-use environments are particularly lacking.[51] Chapter 9 reflects on these challenges.

8

Road Contraction

We opted for the somewhat broad term *contraction* in this chapter's title because it best captures what this chapter is about: shrinking the footprint of channel-ways given over to private cars and trucks and reassigning this space to other, less disruptive, more people-oriented uses, such as greenways, pedestrian zones, bike lanes, and public parks. More common terms are *traffic calming* and *road dieting*, although such measures are less about reclaiming land and more about slowing traffic flows to the pace of cyclists and pedestrians, or thereabouts. Even more extreme measures have been introduced to rein in the amount of pavement given over to cars, notably the demolition of elevated freeways, replaced by boulevards, greenways, and linear parks. Each is a different form of pulling back in recognition that the past half-century of transportation policies and investments in many corners of the world have been tilted heavily in favor of auto-mobility, at the expense of community quality and place-making. *Contraction*, we believe, is an apt term to describe a host of actions, from intersection neckdowns to freeway teardowns, aimed at reordering mobility priorities in favor of more sustainable modes and giving as much attention to place-making as to movement. Contraction is a form of land reclamation, which, as discussed in this chapter, involves reassigning land for place-making and green mobility purposes.

A safe, active pedestrian environment is a cardinal feature of a vibrant, livable neighborhood. So is the absence of a barrier or obstruction that limits the ability to socialize and interact with friends and neighbors. By descaling transportation infrastructure and creating new pedestrian zones and crossings as well as fine-grained networks of bike paths and sidewalks, road contractions enhance green forms of connectivity. They also increase physical activity and help build social capital. They give rise to a more human-scale city.

143

Traffic Calming

Over the past half-century, many European cities have sought to tame, slow the speeds, and reduce dependency on the private car.[1] Traffic calming was pioneered by Dutch planners and engineers who introduced speed humps, realigned roads, necked-down intersections, and planted trees and flowerpots in the middle of streets to slow traffic. It is one of the first and arguably one of the purest forms of promoting livability and place-making in the urban transportation sector, as discussed in chapter 2. With traffic calming, the street becomes as an extension of a neighborhood's livable space—a place to walk, chat, socialize, and play. Automobile passage becomes secondary. The desires of residents take precedence over movement (especially cars driven by nonresidents). Applied almost exclusively to local street systems—either access roads in neighborhoods or narrow passageways in centuries-old downtowns—traffic calming also deflects through-traffic and redirects flows to wider, higher -speed facilities. In so doing, it also helps reduce accidents.[2]

Some European communities have opted to calm traffic using cellular neighborhood designs that require motorists to follow roundabout routes while providing direct connections to cyclists and pedestrians traveling from one cell to another. Central Gothenburg, Sweden, was one of the first places to block through-traffic with cellular designs, forcing traffic onto an inner ring roads instead. A more recent example is Houten, the Netherlands, a masterplanned community south of Utrecht, designed and built to prioritize travel by bicycle and walking. Houten's physical layout resembles a butterfly, with a ring road encircling sixteen residential cells, each no more than 2 kilometers from the central train station (figure 8-1).[3] Green (bike and pedestrian) corridors permeate Houten's interior, providing high connectivity and, courtesy of tunnels, bridges, and prioritization schemes, often uninterrupted flows. Motorists, on the other hand, must take a ring road when driving from one residential district to another. Entrance to many cycle paths is blocked by retractable bollards, so cars are physically unable to enter these pathways unless they are equipped to lower bollards. The environmental and safety impacts of this cellular, green mobility scheme are impressive: More than half of trips by Houten residents are by walking or cycling, car use is 25 percent lower than in similar-size Dutch cities, traffic accidents are one-third the national average, and half of all shopping trips are less than 1 kilometer in distance.[4]

Car-Free Districts

An even bolder urban design and traffic management strategy has been the outright banning of cars from the cores of traditional neighborhoods and districts, complemented by the upgrading and beautification of pedestrian spaces. This practice has become common in many older European cities whose narrow and winding inner-city street were never designed for motorized traffic. Car-free historical districts today thrive in Athens, Greece;

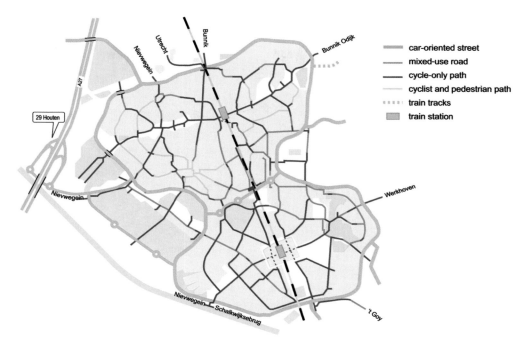

Figure 8-1. Street layout and cellular design of Houten, the Netherlands. (Source: Municipality of Houten.)

Seville, Spain; Lübeck and Bremen, Germany; Bologna and Sienna, Italy; and Bruges, Belgium, as well as substantial portions of university towns such as Gröningen and Delft, the Netherlands; Oxford and Cambridge, England; and Freiburg and Münster, Germany.[5] Collapsible bollards have proven particularly effective at controlling entry; they physically bar cars from car-free zones yet allow residents, taxis, emergency vehicles, and delivery trucks free entry. However, physical barriers are giving way to modern technology. In Cambridge, England, license plate recognition cameras recently replaced bollards for controlling entry to the city's historical core (figure 8-2).

Extended pedestrian-only shopping streets and promenades have also gained popularity in Europe, such as Copenhagen's Strøget, Lisbon's Baixa, and Gamla Stan in old-town Stockholm. Multiblock car-free streets and enhanced pedestrian zones can also be found in cities of the developing world, including Curitiba (twenty city blocks), Buenos Aires (twelve blocks of Florida Street and several car-free waterfront redevelopment projects), Guadalajara (fifteen downtown streets), and Beirut (much of the historical core). Even a handful of newly built or redeveloped residential communities that are car-restricted exist, such as Vauban and Rieselfeld outside of Freiburg, Amsterdam's GWL Terrein brownfield redevelopment, Vienna's Mustersiedling Floridsdorf housing project, Munich's Kolumbusplatz neighborhood, Slateford Green in central Edinburgh, the Stellwerk 60 project

Figure 8-2. Cameras monitor bus, taxi, and bicycle access into the historical core of Cambridge, England. (Photo by Steve Denman.)

in Cologne, and Masdar City outside of Abu Dhabi. In Vauban, a 40-hectare suburban community of five thousand inhabitants briefly mentioned in the previous chapter, most streets have no cars and most housing units have no driveway or garage. Only 2.2 out of every 10 Vauban residents own a car, compared with 4.3 of 10 in nearby Freiburg (billed as Germany's greenest city).[6] Upon moving to Vauban, moreover, 57 percent of adult residents got rid of a car.[7]

Barcelona is currently limiting vehicle access to emergency vehicles throughout the built-up residential districts in the city's traditional core. Under the *superilles*, or super-block, initiative, nonlocal through-traffic must pass the exterior of neighborhoods, along wider commercial streets (figure 8-3). Entry by residents' cars, delivery trucks, and emergency vehicles is limited to a few access points and controlled by retractable bollards, with priority given to pedestrians, followed by cyclists. Traffic calming treatments, including pocket parks planted in former street intersections, force service vehicles and residents' cars to a slow crawl. Barcelona's superblock scheme aims to disrupt the tendency of

▌SUPERBLOCKS MODEL

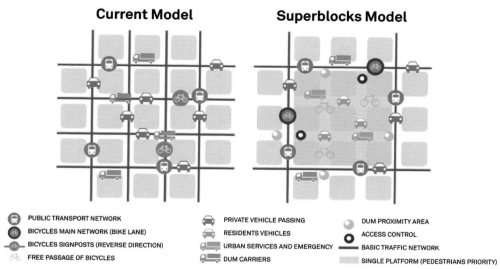

Current Model   **Superblocks Model**

PUBLIC TRANSPORT NETWORK	PRIVATE VEHICLE PASSING · DUM PROXIMITY AREA
BICYCLES MAIN NETWORK (BIKE LANE)	RESIDENTS VEHICLES · ACCESS CONTROL
BICYCLES SIGNPOSTS (REVERSE DIRECTION)	URBAN SERVICES AND EMERGENCY · BASIC TRAFFIC NETWORK
FREE PASSAGE OF BICYCLES	DUM CARRIERS · SINGLE PLATFORM (PEDESTRIANS PRIORITY)

Figure 8-3. Comparison of Barcelona's superblock model with the current model of evenly dispersed traffic. (Source: Agencia de Ecologia Urbana de Barcelona.)

rectilinear grids (as displayed in figure 2-3 in chapter 2) to evenly disperse traffic throughout a road network. With through-traffic deflected to wider exterior streets, interior residential streets become safer and more livable. Within superblocks, traffic speeds have fallen below 10 kilometers per hour. One sign that residents like car-restricted districts is they are regularly organizing events. They're also pressuring Barcelona officials to add trees, benches, and playgrounds. By 2018, the city hopes to turn half of its residential roads into pedestrian-friendly spaces. Barcelona's superblocks are a good example of small-scale urban recalibration, reflected in the city's description of the scheme: "a way of organizing the city which reverses the dominance of vehicles in the distribution of public space and gives priority to people, improving environmental conditions and people's quality of life."[8]

Despite some initial uneasiness by merchants, residents, and politicians, global experiences with creating car-free districts, auto-restricted neighborhoods, and pedestrian-only streets have generally been positive, as long as high-quality and frequent transit services are in place to absorb displaced car traffic. A study of pedestrianized zones and car-free districts of German cities recorded appreciable increases in pedestrian flows, transit ridership, land values, and retail sales transactions as well as property conversions to more intensive land uses, matched by fewer traffic accidents and fatalities.[9] An international assessment of more than one hundred cases of road capacity reductions (e.g., car-free zones, pedestrian street conversions, and street and bridge closures) found an average overall reduction in motorized traffic of 25 percent, even after controlling for possible increased travel on parallel routes. This "evaporated" traffic represented a combination of people forsaking low-value, discretionary trips and opting for alternative modes, including transit riding, walking, and cycling.[10]

Road Dieting

A road diet is the transportation field's equivalent to "tightening the belt": reducing the number or width of travel lanes. The freed-up space is used to add or widen footpaths, cycle lanes, or even tram tracks in the middle of the road. The aim is not so much to divert or ban traffic but rather to slow it down, closer to the cadence of pedestrians and cyclists, and promote green modes. Road dieting is tied to the Complete Streets movement, which aims to provide adequate, safe, and convenient passageway to all forms of mobility, motorized or not.

The city of San Francisco has been a leader in the road dieting movement, having completed more than forty projects since the late 1970s.[11] One of the city's main north–south arterials, Valencia Street, was reduced from four to two travel lanes in 1999, with a center turn lane and bike lanes added in place of the former travel lanes.[12] Bicycle traffic has since increased significantly, and average car speeds have fallen. Traffic engineers feared that accident rates would rise over time, but this has not happened on Valencia Street or along many other road-dieted corridors. A matched-pair before-and-after study of thirty road diet projects in eight U.S. cities found narrowed roadways had 6 percent fewer accidents than otherwise similar control sites.[13]

The city of Chattanooga, Tennessee, has introduced one of the more notable road-dieting schemes to date in an effort to reconnect its downtown to the riverfront. Planners sought to change the image and functionality of Riverfront Parkway from a high-speed thoroughfare to a more pedestrian-friendly, slower-paced corridor. Completed in 2005, the parkway was transformed from a five-lane, limited-access facility into a two-lane surface street, featuring continuous sidewalks, a 4-meter-wide riverfront promenade, and pedestrian access to major visitor attractions (figure 8-4). Proponents hoped the project would help revitalize downtown Chattanooga, which appears to have occurred. Local sources credit the Riverfront Parkway conversion with helping to attract millions of dollars of investment in the immediate downtown area, making the once moribund riverfront one of Chattanooga's premier addresses.[14] A variety of new, mostly high-end residential and commercial developments have been constructed over the past decade, lined along the narrowed, walking-friendly parkway. "Before the redesign, the facility felt like a highway, but now it feels like a road through a park," remarked Karen Hundt, director

Figure 8-4. Road dieting of Riverfront Parkway in Chattanooga, Tennessee, improving access between the river and downtown. (Source: *[top]* U.S. Department of Transportation, Federal Highway Administration; *[bottom]* City of Chattanooga, Chattanooga Planning & Design Studio.)

of the Chattanooga–Hamilton County Regional Planning Agency's Planning and Design Studio, which contributed financially to the project.[15] Advocates view the slimmed-down Riverfront Parkway as a sea change in local planning policies, demonstrating the city's new emphasis on livability and place-making, even if it is at the expense of slowing through traffic.

Green Connectors

Although they do not necessarily reduce road capacity, green connectors are a form of land reclamation in that they redistribute scarce urban real estate to eco-friendly modes. In Europe and Latin America, green connectors have taken the form of perpendicular and protected bike paths and footpaths that directly link surrounding residential areas to rail and bus rapid transit (BRT) stops.[16] In urban and suburban districts of Copenhagen, Bogotá, and other world-class transit cities, networks of footpaths provide direct connections within 5-minute walksheds of transit hubs, and bikeway connectors fan even farther out. Green connectors have also been created in car-free or car-restricted districts. Even in the car-dependent suburbs of the United States, green connectors exist in the form of cut-throughs that link cul-de-sac bulbs, creating more direct, permeable walking routes.

Green connectors are being built to improve access to more than transit stops and isolated cul-de-sacs. Hamburg, Germany, has begun building a network of car-free "park connectors" between all of the city's major parks, community gardens, and playgrounds. The resulting green network, scheduled to be completed by 2030, is to cover 40 percent of the city, enabling commutes across the city entirely by bicycle or on foot.[17] Besides improving fitness and reducing CO_2 emissions, by limiting the city's impermeable surface area the network of green spaces will keep the city cooler and mitigate flooding during periods of heavy rainfall.

Zurich, Switzerland, is likewise building an integrated network of in-city green connectors, one that links not only parklands and open space but also transit hubs. Figure 8-5 is a schema of the system. Over the years, Zurich has methodically added links to the network of regional walkways that connect parks and "green lands," historical cultural conservation areas, open spaces, landmarks, major squares, and public facilities. These in turn are linked via perpendicular connectors to major destinations, including railway stations, shopping centers, movie theaters, and opera houses. Within the walksheds of transit hubs and public centers is a second level of community walkways. Tramways and dedicated bus lanes connect these hubs, forming a regional network that provides continuous footpaths for those seeking long, leisurely walks and good transit connections for those wanting to quickly reach other parts of the city.

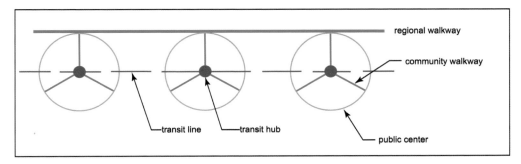

Figure 8-5. Schema of Zurich, Switzerland's network of green connectors. Regional walkways connect green areas and footpaths connect to transit lines, transit hubs, and other key destinations.

Roadway Deconstruction and Reassignments

The most radical form of road contraction has been the outright removal of elevated freeways and motorways. In the United States, city leaders in Portland, San Francisco, Seattle, Milwaukee, and Boston have opted to tear down longstanding elevated freeway structures and replace them with linear parkways or less obtrusive, more human-scale surface boulevards. A number of other U.S. cities aim to follow suit. For the past decade, the Congress for New Urbanism has maintained a Web site on "freeways without futures," currently identifying ten destined for upending.[18] Freeway teardowns are among the boldest, most visible examples of urban recalibration: from a focus on auto-mobility to a focus on livability, from an emphasis on expediting the movement of well-paid suburbanites commuting to central cities to improving the quality of central city living and working.

The contraction of road space and dismemberment of road-oriented infrastructure has gained international momentum as well. Stockholm's disassembly of a maze of roadway infrastructure in its downtown waterfront, replaced by pedestrian bridges and promenades, is one such example. So is Rio de Janeiro's teardown of an imposing viaduct that separated downtown Rio from the waterfront, replaced by a pedestrian plaza and tramway, all in time for the 2016 Summer Olympics (shown in chapter 1). Arguably the boldest initiatives to reclaim land and reduce the automobile's ecological footprint so far have been in Seoul, South Korea, to which we turn next.

Urban Regeneration in Seoul

Over the past decade and a half, South Korea's capital and principal city, Seoul, has embarked on an ambitious program of urban land reclamation and regeneration. To make Seoul attractive to outside investors and increase the city's competitiveness and attractiveness relative to other East Asia megacities, the city has aggressively invested in public transit improvements while also shrinking the ecological footprint of the private car by reclaiming urban space consumed by roads and highways. Seoul's case experiences are chronicled in this section.

Land Reclamation in Seoul

In the 1980s and 1990s, Seoul built twenty-six new towns on its periphery, most separated from the urban core by a protective greenbelt. New towns were a product of the central government's "Two Million Homes Construction Plan," aimed at increasing housing supplies in step with the consumption demands of the nation's burgeoning middle class. Rather than dormitory communities, however, they were to be full-fledged, self-contained, complete communities where residents could live, work, shop, and play. Over the past quarter century, however, the bulk of greater Seoul's job growth occurred in the central city, giving rise to a tidal pattern of new-town workers in-commuting in the morning and out-commuting in the evening. Traffic congestion and air quality materially worsened as a result. By the turn of the century, the idea of reurbanizing Seoul's central areas as "new towns in town" began to surface.

The person who led the charge of reinvesting in and reenergizing the central city was Myung-Bak Lee. In 2001, Lee ran for mayor of Seoul, partly on a platform of regenerating the urban core to create a more sustainable yet productive city. Lee campaigned on the premise that Seoul could achieve a better balance between function and the environment by reordering public priorities so as to emphasize quality of place. Before becoming mayor, Lee founded and led the Hyundai Group, South Korea's largest builder of public works and infrastructure projects. He earned the nickname "Bulldozer" Lee, partly because of the company's legacy of constructing massive roadways throughout the country but also because he reputedly took apart a bulldozer to study its mechanisms to help figure out ways to keep it from breaking down.

Lee won a decisive victory for Seoul's mayoral seat, and upon assuming office in early 2002 he moved quickly on his campaign promises. His vision for Seoul's future urban transportation called for not only expanding public transit services but also reclaiming urban space consumed by roads and highways—notably space used to funnel new-town inhabitants in and out of the central city. The network of elevated freeways that converged on central Seoul carried high costs: the severing of longstanding neighborhoods, the formation of barriers and visual blight, the casting of shadows, and increased noise, fumes, and vibrations affecting surrounding areas. Although freeways provided important mobility benefits, Lee recognized that these have to be weighed against their nuisance effects, particularly in today's amenity-conscious workplace.

Myung-Bak Lee's visions for Seoul's future were shaped by what was happening in several Latin American cities at the time. Embracing the views of urban visionaries such as Jaime Lerner of Curitiba, Brazil, and Enrique Penalosa of Bogotá, Colombia, both of whom staked their political careers on curbing the presence of cars in their own central cities, Mayor Lee defended the roadway removal projects on the grounds that "we want to make a city where people come first, not cars."[19] The transformation of space for cars to space for people represented, in the Lee's words, "a new paradigm for urban management in the new century."[20]

The removal of a 6-kilometer elevated freeway in the heart of Seoul, Cheong Gye Cheon (CGC), followed by the daylighting of an urban stream and opening of a pedestrian-friendly greenway, was Lee's signature public works project (figure 8-6).[21] The elevated motorway had corroded from decades of lying atop the culverted stream and needed to be rebuilt or removed altogether.[22] Lee chose the removal option. Change was swift. By February 2003, a plan for the freeway removal was completed, and 5 months later, the freeway had been completely dismantled. Some 2 years later, in September 2005, the restored CGC stream and linear greenway were opened to the public.[23] The entire cost of the freeway demolition and stream restoration was US$313 million. By comparison, the US$15 billion "Big Dig" freeway burial megaproject in Boston took a quarter century to complete.

The restoration of the CGC stream has been more than the greening of central-city Seoul. For many local residents, it has marked a rediscovery of the city's past. Hidden by the freeway were a number of long-forgotten treasures, including twenty-two historical footbridges that crossed the stream and myriad stone carvings and relics. Today, the CGC stream and greenway is Seoul's second most popular tourist draw. On weekends and summer evenings, thousands of residents and tourists can be seen strolling along the flowing stream's banks, enjoying a small slice of tranquility in an otherwise dense, bustling city.

Though not as large or as costly, another symbolically important road contraction project was the conversion of a prominent 1.3-hectare surface street intersection to an oval-shaped park in front of Seoul's city hall, the nerve center of the city (figure 8-7). The huge swath of real estate devoted to car maneuvers in front of City Hall, an architectural icon and one of the busiest locations in the city, created a pedestrian-hostile environment. Many residents en route to City Hall had to take a circuitous route and dodge weaving cars when trying to cross the road. The former traffic circle is today a popular leisure spot, directly connected to City Hall and used for public celebrations, cultural performances, and student demonstrations. During the winter, a large outdoor ice rink occupies the oval. Once populated by fast-moving cars, the doorsteps to City Hall are now populated with people throughout the day.

Seoul's commitment to reclaiming land from cars and creating a more pedestrian-friendly city continues today. Under the "Walk-Friendly Seoul" program, the four-lane Gwangjingyo Road has been trimmed to two lanes, and a number of car-free districts have been created, including much of Hongik University, helping it earn the title of "one of the coolest neighborhoods" in 2016.[24] Seoul is also repurposing motorways. The recently

Figure 8-6. Transformation of Cheong Gye Cheon from *(top)* an elevated freeway (2002) to *(bottom)* an urban greenway (2003). (Photos by Na young wan, Seoul Metropolitan Government.)

Figure 8-7. Conversion of traffic intersection *(top)* **to an oval park** *(bottom)* **in front of Seoul City Hall.** (Photos by Na young wan, Seoul Metropolitan Government.)

opened Skygarden features a half mile of open-air public space 55 feet above city streets along an abandoned highway, reminiscent of New York's High Line (reviewed in chapter 5). Skygarden's reassignment of pavement from cars to people has brought cafés, exhibitions, trampolines, and even a footbath to the condemned former overpass. More than 200 species of trees, shrubs, and flowers now adorn an elevated passageway once reserved for cars, trucks, and buses.

Improved Transit Connectivity in Seoul

The withdrawal of road capacity in the world's second largest megalopolis, where car ownership rates are rocketing, is unlikely to improve urban living. To Mayor Lee's credit, he understood that public transportation had to be substantially expanded and upgraded to absorb the traffic (169,000 daily cars in the case of the CGC freeway) displaced by large-scale reductions in roadway capacity. This was done partly through the extension of Seoul's subway Line 7 (28 kilometers in length) and the opening of Line 6 (35 kilometers in length). As important was the 2004 opening of seven new lines of exclusive median-lane buses (stretching 84 kilometers, later expanded to 162 kilometers) and 294 kilometers of dedicated curbside bus lanes. In all, 74 kilometers of road lanes were expropriated to accommodate Seoul's BRT network between 2002 and 2004, at the time of the motorway land grabs. In addition, many regular bus routes were reconfigured to better feed into the city's extensive subway system, and an integrated fare and transfer system between buses and the metrorail network was introduced.[25]

Seoul's BRT investments have reaped mobility dividends. Along BRT corridors, within 1 year bus operating speeds increased from an average of 11 to more than 21 kilometers per hour, even in passenger car lanes.[26] Moreover, BRT buses carry more than six times as many passengers per hour as buses operating on regular, mixed-traffic lanes. And because they are less subject to the vagaries of ambient traffic flows, buses operating in dedicated lanes have become more reliable: The travel-time variation of Seoul's BRT buses is, on average, one-fifth that of buses operating on nonexclusive lanes.[27] In addition, protective lanes have reduced accidents, down 27 percent 1 year after BRT services were introduced. Because of these service enhancements and safety improvements, ridership on BRT buses increased 60 percent faster than on non-BRT buses during the first 3 years of operations.[28]

More was done than transit service expansion to increase connectivity in the midst of central-city place-making. A real-time traffic information system with message boards and in-vehicle navigation aids was introduced to guide traffic flows and alert motorists to downstream hotspots. Several one-way arterial couplets were also created, and curbside parking was substantially curtailed to help expedite traffic flows. More draconian was the introduction of a license plate scheme that, based on the last number on their plates, requires motorists to leave their cars at home every 10 days.

Capitalizing the Benefits of Greenways

Chapter 4, "Better Economies," discussed evidence on the benefits of greenery and open space on land prices. Seoul's experiences further confirm these benefits. Studies by the Seoul Development Institute found that the CGC conversion to greenway increased property values.[29] From 2003 to 2005, office rents went up by an average of 10 percent, and land prices jumped by nearly 40 percent within the CGC impact zone (approximately 2 kilometers in each direction from the corridor). The number of businesses and mixed-use buildings within the zone also rose. So did mean condominium prices.

A more recent study gauged the spatial reach of Seoul's motorway-to-greenway conversion.[30] Land value premiums were found for commercial parcels within 500 meters of the corridor for both the former freeway and present-day urban greenway (figure 8-8). However, premiums were noticeably higher for parcels within the 500 meters of the urban greenway entrance points than the former freeway on-ramps. For residential properties, housing was found to be worth less within 3 kilometers of the elevated freeway, reflecting a dis-amenity, but the opposite held once the corridor was transformed to a greenway: Homes within 2 kilometers were worth as much as 8 percent more. Clearly, Seoul's unique freeway disinvestment and greenway investment scheme conferred net benefits to both residential and nonresidential property owners.

From the standpoint of land market performance, one could argue that an urban amenity, specifically quality of urban space, was more highly valued in central Seoul than a significant component of urban infrastructure, namely a freeway. That is, quality of place has won out over auto-mobility as a desirable urban attribute.

Is the theory that urban amenities such as greenways attract highly sought-after "creative class workers"—who, according to the likes of Richard Florida and Ed Glaeser, drive economic growth and increase global competitiveness among twenty-first-century cities—borne out by Seoul's experiences? Research led by Chang-Deok Kang, chair of the

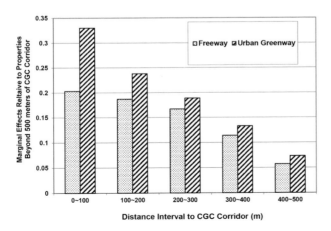

Figure 8-8. Marginal effects of the CGC freeway and urban greenway on nonresidential property values by distance intervals, 2001–2006. (Source: Chang-Doek Kang and Robert Cervero, "From Elevated Freeway to Urban Greenway: Land Value Impacts of Seoul, Korea's CGC Project," *Urban Studies* 46, no. 13 (2009): 2786).

urban planning program at Chung-Ang University in Seoul, suggests it is.[31] Using location quotients[32] to gauge the degree of spatial clustering, figure 8-9 indicates that creative class workers—those in science, math, engineering, education, finance, business, law, architecture, media, design, and similar high-value, knowledge-based fields—were more likely to be concentrated along the greenway than the motorway corridor. Relative to land more than 1 kilometer beyond the corridors, the location quotients of creative class workers for commercial parcels within 100 meters of greenway entrance points were 1.5 times higher, compared with 1.25 times higher for parcels that were within 100 meters of former freeway on-ramps. And although there tended to be less concentration of creative class workers for the 100- to 1,000-meter zone of freeway on-ramps, the opposite held for the greenway: Location quotients were up to 50 percent higher for parcels within 100 to 200 meters of the greenway (than otherwise similar parcels 1 kilometer or farther away, with clustering dissipating with distance from pedestrian entry points).

Seoul's motorway-to-greenway conversion also conferred environmental benefits. For one, air pollution levels fell. Concentrations of fine-grained particulate matter along the CGC corridor were 13 percent higher than Seoul's regional average before the conversion; afterwards, they were 4 percent below the region's average.[33] Nitrogen dioxide concentrations, a precursor to the formation of photochemical smog, went from 2 percent above the regional average when the freeway was in operation to 17 percent below when the greenway was in place.

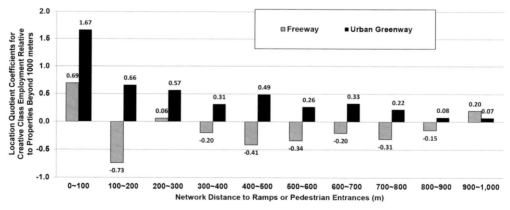

Figure 8-9. Impacts of greenway versus motorway on creative class employment. Marginal differences in location quotients for buffer zones (horizontal axis) relative to parcels beyond 1,000 meters (1 kilometer) of ramps or pedestrian entrances. (Source: Chang-Deok Kang, "Land Market Impacts and Firm Geography in a Green and Transit-Oriented City: The Case of Seoul, Korea" [PhD diss., Berkeley: Fischer Center for Real Estate and Urban Economics, University of California, 2009]; Robert Cervero and Chang-Deok Kang, "From Elevated Freeway to Linear Park: Land Price Impacts of Seoul, Korea's CGC Project," VWP-2008-7 [Berkeley: Institute of Transportation Studies, UC Berkeley Center for Future Urban Transportation, 2008]).

Many urban centers suffer a heat island effect, with temperatures higher than surrounding suburban and rural areas because of greater surface area coverage, and Seoul is no
exception. The cooling benefits of the CGC transformation were revealed by a heat island
study that found that ambient temperatures along the central-city stream and greenway
were 3.3° and 5.9° centigrade lower than along a parallel surface arterial five blocks away.[34]

The evidence to date suggests that Seoul's program of land reclamation and roadway contraction has been a bona fide success. Land prices have risen and traffic conditions have not materially changed, owing in good part to vastly expanded public transit
services that absorbed some of the former car traffic. Myung-Bak Lee's commitment to
sustainable urbanism paid off in personal ways. In 2007, Lee was chosen as the "Hero of
Environment" in *Time* magazine along with former U.S. vice president Al Gore. The CGC
stream restoration catapulted Lee to national prominence, and some local observers credit
this with helping him win South Korea's presidency in 2007.

San Francisco's Freeway-to-Boulevard Conversions

San Francisco was a pioneer in America's freeway revolt movement of the 1960s, with
grassroots activists halting the planned construction of two mammoth double-decker
freeways: the fully extended Embarcadero Freeway, which was to link the Golden Gate
Bridge to the Bay Bridge, and the Central Freeway in the heart of the city.[35] Still, portions of these elevated freeways were completed before the public backlash halted further
expansion. Both served as critical arteries for funneling motorists in and out of the city
but were also blamed for severing and disrupting neighborhoods.

On October 17, 1989, the 7.1-magnitude Loma Prieta earthquake struck the San Francisco Bay Area. Both the Embarcadero and Central freeways were crippled but still standing. Earthquake damage forced city officials to address whether to sink funds into building new facilities and seismically retrofitting existing ones or replacing structures with
slower-moving at-grade facilities while opening up access to waterfronts and removing
physical obstructions. Demolition was shown to be more cost-effective and, furthermore,
offered an opportunity for economic revitalization. In the case of San Francisco's moribund eastside waterfront, a local columnist noted the place-making potential: "Damage
to the Embarcadero Freeway from the Loma Prieta quake revealed a landscape of striking
views and singular opportunities for great public places along the waterfront—a gritty
and largely hidden industrial zone to which the city had turned its back."[36] Embarcadero
Boulevard took the demolished elevated freeway's place and was completed in mid-2000.
Before-and-after pictures reveal the dramatic change to San Francisco's waterfront (figure
8-10). The corridor formerly occupied by a double-decked freeway had been transformed
into a multilane boulevard flanked by a promenade of wide sidewalks, ribbons of street
lights, mature palm trees, historic streetcars, waterfront plazas, and the world's largest
piece of public art.[37]

Figure 8-10. Transformation from the Embarcadero Freeway *(top)* to the streetcar-friendly Embarcadero Boulevard *(bottom)*. (Photos by *[top] Better Cities & Towns; [bottom]* PikappaǀDreamtimes.com.)

The transformation of San Francisco's former Central Freeway to a multiway boulevard was no less spectacular. Replacing the double-decker structure was a 133-foot-wide Parisian-inspired boulevard with four central through-lanes flanked by two peripheral lanes for local traffic and parking.[38] A central median and side strips provided safe haven for pedestrians and cyclists, an important consideration given that many motorists would have previously driven the freeway at faster speeds. Figure 8-11 shows the Central Freeway corridor's before-and-after transformation.

Neighborhood Impacts

In the case of the Embarcadero district, surrounding neighborhoods were found to have generally fared better economically from the freeway-to-boulevard conversion than otherwise similar ones farther from the corridor, in terms of housing construction, job growth, and land price increases.[39] San Francisco unquestionably has a much nicer eastern waterfront than in the past. This conversion was a catalyst to a host of private investments that revitalized the city's east side, including the renovation of Pier 1 (now offices) and the Ferry Building (a market hall and offices) and construction of the new Pacific Bell baseball park.[40] Several blocks inland, once industrial areas south of Market Street quickly became thriving, high-density mixed-use neighborhoods. By one account, "The emergence of the South of Market (SoMa) area—and, in particular, the rise of 'Multimedia Gulch' as the center of the dot.com revolution—certainly was affected by the removal of the earthquake-damaged freeway ramps on nearby blocks."[41]

In the former Central Freeway corridor, the removal of an eyesore also triggered private reinvestment in the area and, as feared by some, also gentrified the neighborhood. As whites moved into the neighborhood, blacks moved out. Restaurants, bars, and entertainment venues that appeal to the creative class replaced mercantile type stores that existed before the boulevard conversion. To the city's credit, it anticipated and responded to this gentrification, mandating that new investors contribute to an escrow fund to help finance below-market-rate housing.

Traffic and Safety Impacts

Many transportation officials and business leaders opposed removal of the Embarcadero and Central Freeways on the grounds that traffic congestion and car–pedestrian accident levels would increase. One year after the 1989 Loma Prieta earthquake, annual vehicular injury accidents increased by 24 percent from prequake levels; however, postquake pedestrian-related accidents fell by 3 percent.[42] By the late 1990s, San Francisco had the highest rate of pedestrian injuries and fatalities of any California city.[43] Critics claimed this was a consequence of freeway removal, notably intermixing formerly grade-separated traffic with pedestrians. The city has since introduced a series of pedestrian and traffic

Figure 8-11. Transformation from Central Freeway *(top)* to Octavia Boulevard *(bottom)*. (Photos by *[top] San Francisco Chronicle*/Michael Macor and *[bottom]* Elizabeth Macdonald.)

calming improvements, including the road dieting schemes mentioned earlier, to reverse these figures.

There was a lot of hyperbole about the traffic nightmares that would be caused by freeway removals. When the California Department of Transportation closed the middle section of the Central Freeway in 1996, the director of operations predicted there would be bumper-to-bumper traffic for 45 miles east across the Bay Bridge and south into the San Francisco peninsula.[44] State traffic planners warned that morning commutes would increase by as much as 2 hours.

The traffic nightmares never materialized. People adjusted when, where, and how they traveled or even if they traveled. Steps were also taken to improve surface street flows. Besides expanding transit services, as in Seoul, San Francisco's traffic engineers installed a dynamic signal system that allowed "green waves" of traffic that formerly moved on elevated freeways to move swiftly along city streets used also by pedestrians and cyclists. A survey mailed to 8,000 drivers whose license plates had been recorded on the two freeways before closures revealed that 66 percent had shifted to another freeway, 11 percent used city streets for their entire trips, 2.2 percent switched to public transit, and 2.8 percent said they no longer made the trip previously made on the freeway.[45] The survey also found that 19.8 percent of survey respondents stated they made fewer trips since the freeway closure. Most were discretionary trips, such as for recreation.

Just as new road construction induces travel, road contractions reduce it. Some 6 months after the September 2005 opening of Octavia Boulevard, the former 93,100 vehicles recorded on the Central Freeway in 1995 had dropped by 52 percent, to 44,900 vehicles. Today, Octavia Boulevard and the network of streets that link to it operate at capacity during peak hours but rarely if ever reach gridlock.[46] The traffic-carrying ability of well-designed boulevards partly explains the absence of traffic bedlam along San Francisco's former freeway corridors. A multiway boulevard is capable of handling large volumes of fast-moving through-traffic (upwards of six thousand cars per direction per hour) and slower local traffic within the same right-of-way but on separate yet closely connected roadways.[47]

Close

A consistent thread among the road contraction and land reclamation projects reviewed in this chapter is the redefinition and reprioritization of the role of public infrastructure and community living. Long considered a public asset, land-hungry freeways and roadway interchanges can over time become a public liability. Civic leaders are increasingly turning to a different kind of public asset to grow local economies: public amenities, urban parks, and other civic functions that enhance aesthetics, quality of life, and connection to place. In an increasingly competitive, knowledge-based global marketplace, improved civic spaces and expansion of the arts and cultural entertainment offerings appeal to highly sought professional-class workers. These need not be just for elites, however. Greenways and public spaces can and should become important community gathering places, open to people from all walks of life, as has been the case with Seoul's CGC. Social diversity is critical to inclusive connectivity and place-making, be it for building social capital, promoting physical activity, or providing more people with the option of green mobility.

Road contraction and expropriation projects could well be harbingers of a new era, wherein indiscriminate large-scale infrastructure construction and a blind devotion to mobility-based planning are no longer acceptable. The footprint of the urban transport sector—freeways, interchanges, surface roads, and parking but also disused railyards and freight terminals—is immense, consuming as much as half of all land area in highly motorized cities (and thus separating activities from each other, creating greater demands for motorized transportation and roadway infrastructure). Whatever freeways and mega-scale infrastructure projects are built in coming years will have to be strategically sited and carefully designed to pass a stricter litmus test of contributing to larger urban development and place-focused objectives of the cities and neighborhoods they serve. Experiences in Seoul, San Francisco, and European cities suggest that providing high-quality public transport services, multiway boulevards, and green connectors decreases the need for high-capacity elevated freeway structures. To the extent that past infrastructure investments have been heavily skewed to favor carbon-intensive, private mobility, such initiatives bring balance to the practice of urban planning and urban design. This, we contend, is a signature feature of successfully connecting places and achieving sustainable urban futures.

As reviewed earlier, European cities have led the way in creating car-free and car-restricted districts. While cities in the United States, Canada, and Australia focus on accommodating the growth in car travel, in much of Europe the challenge has been to cope with rising motorization in an urban fabric of narrow lanes and tight land constraints.[48] This has spawned the "3 S" movement in some of Europe's more progressive cities, a commitment to designing cities for *short*-distance travel, by *slower* modes (enabled by short-distance travel), exploiting *smart* technologies. Smart technologies need not be the exclusive domain of self-driving robocars and sophisticated real-time traffic control networks but should also encompass radio-controlled retractable bollards and license plate recognition cameras for restricting car movements, bike-sharing schemes, and demand-activated signal prioritization to cyclists and pedestrians. Although such measures might be small in and of themselves, collectively they can make a big difference in improving the balance between the place and mobility functions of a city.

PART III

Looking Forward

The final three chapters of this book consider what planning beyond mobility means in a world of rapid geographic, technological, social, and demographic change. More people now live in cities than in the countryside and, increasingly, they live in dense and fast-growing cities in Asia, Latin America, and Africa. Meanwhile, new and emerging technologies, such as smartphones and self-driving vehicles, are changing how and where people live, travel, relax, and shop. These and other trends, such as aging societies and the shared economy, will have profound impacts on the future of the sustainable city and how urban recalibration might lead to better social, environmental, and economic outcomes.

Chapter 9 focuses on the ground zero of population growth: cities in the Global South. The United Nations predicts the world will add another 1.5 billion urban residents over the next two decades. Most will live in the fast-growing, dense suburbs of Asian, African, and Latin American cities rather than the more walkable and transit-friendly centers. Providing clear skies, clean water, high-quality housing, safe streets, and adequate access to jobs and public services in these cities will be a daunting challenge, but it is essential to charting a course to a more sustainable urban future. High walking rates, dense neighborhoods, and an organic mix of land uses make many of these cities ideal places to promote and advance sustainable urban growth. However, repeating the mistakes of a mobility-focused approach to building cities, outlined in the first section of the book, would be ecologically and socially disastrous.

New technologies—particularly self-driving vehicles—offer an opportunity to make a clean break with unsustainable transportation practices in both the Global North and Global South. Chapter 10 examines how technology will begin to change the relationship between mobility and place and might reduce the harm caused by local pollution and traffic collisions. Although new technologies might increase how much people move in a given day, they also create opportunities to improve people's day-to-day experience and enjoyment of the city.

In chapter 11 we reflect on the opportunities and challenges posed by the combination of powerful megatrends, such as aging societies and collaborative consumption, and technological advances. Just as the interaction between mobility and place determines accessibility, it is the interaction between emerging trends that will shape how cities grow and whether their neighborhoods and residents thrive. Finally, we conclude with a call for more holistic measures of cities' success and a discussion of the need for more inclusive cities that are sustainable, pleasant, and economically productive but also provide opportunities for all residents, regardless of income, race, or social class. For a city to be truly livable and accessible, it must meet the needs of its most vulnerable citizens, not just its most affluent.

9

The Global South

The United Nations Conference on Housing and Sustainable Urban Development met in Quito, Ecuador, in October 2016 to launch a new global commitment to sustainable urban development. Habitat III, as the conference is called, resulted in the adoption of the New Urban Agenda, which prioritizes the relationship between urbanization and sustainable development and promotes a global vision of just, safe, healthy, accessible, affordable, resilient, and sustainable cities for all. These objectives fit well with the call for planning beyond mobility. However, as the New Urban Agenda emphasizes, the challenges of sustainable urban development in the Global South can be daunting. High poverty rates and poor access to jobs and education hinder economic and social opportunities. Achieving a better balance between mobility and place might seem less important in places where there is not enough investment in mobility or place, not to mention education or other infrastructure. Nevertheless, poor design around new transportation infrastructure increases travel times, decreases safety, and encourages a shift to private cars. By ignoring the safety and comfort of pedestrians and cyclists, local governments not only treat poorer residents like second-class citizens but virtually guarantee that they will switch to cars and motorcycles as they get wealthier.

Over the next 20 years, the United Nations Population Division estimates that the world will add another 1.5 billion urban residents—more than the total projected 1.4 billion global population increase.[1] Nearly all this growth will occur in cities of less developed countries in Asia, Africa, and Latin America (figure 9-1). Balancing mobility and place in the cities of the Global South—the ground zero of future urban growth—is essential to developing sustainable communities, environments, and economies.

Low ($1,045 or less)
Lower middle ($1,046–$4,125)   High ($12,736 or more)
Upper middle ($4,126–$12,735)   No data

Figure 9-1. Map of low-, middle-, and high-income countries. Statistics presented throughout this chapter refer to low- and middle-income countries. (Source: World Bank World Development Indicator Maps.)

There is a great deal of diversity across the cities of the Global South, from Asian megacities to small, fast-growing regional hubs in Africa. The extent of the variation complicates generalizations about the urban Global South or even categorization into city types based on size, growth patterns, form, or geography. Three billion people, roughly 40 percent of the world's population, live in these thousands of cities. That there is substantial variation is hardly surprising. Nevertheless, presenting trends by city type and categorizing by urban form not only illuminate some of these differences but also provide a framework for discussing mobility and place in the Global South. Because the dominant transportation technology plays such an important role in how cities form and how residents experience the city, we also consider whether most travel occurs by transit, foot, or motorcycle.

Throughout the Global South, the car—for all its benefits to individual consumers—poses serious threats to communities, the environment, and even the economy. From 2009 to 2010, the total fleet of registered cars increased by 8.7 percent in Asia and 8.4 percent in Latin America, compared with 0.2 percent in the United States and 1.2 percent in Western Europe.[2] In 2009, China surpassed the United States as the world's largest car market.[3] The growth in private cars contributes substantially to what may be the two greatest challenges to creating better communities in the Global South: poor local air quality and unsafe streets. These are not just minor inconveniences but public health crises. As discussed in chapters 2 and 3, poor local air quality and traffic collisions are two of the planet's leading killers and have disproportionate effects in the Global South. Improving cities in the Global South requires not just constraining private car ownership and use but, more importantly, providing attractive and convenient public transportation, pedestrian spaces, and bicycle networks in a wide variety of cities and neighborhoods. It will also require a focus on reducing the harm caused by cars, trucks, and motorcycles, which will continue to play an important role in urban transportation systems.

In addition to its relationship to local and global emissions, increased fuel consumption from rapid urbanization and motorization can strain many budgets and contribute to social unrest. Current and former gas-exporting nations often subsidize fuel. This not only regressively benefits the wealthiest households, which consume the most fuel, it distorts the overall economy to be more fuel-intensive and encourages cross-border smuggling of subsidized fuel. Even after a country switches from being a net oil exporter to a net importer, subsidies are difficult to remove. In Indonesia, it took more than a decade as a net oil importer and the election of a popular and progressive president to end longstanding fuel subsidies. Egypt's fuel subsidies have survived a popular uprising, a military coup, and a decade of net oil imports.

Poor access to jobs and high rates of inequality also create substantial challenges. Although economic and educational opportunities have helped drive the past half century of urbanization, millions are unemployed or underemployed. In many cities, the majority of households rely on jobs in the informal economy with uncertain wages and little or no health or other insurance. This can limit residents' access to other parts of the formal economy, such as small business loans, home mortgages, or education loans. Without formal health insurance, a single sickness or injury can wipe out a family's savings or investment opportunities. Women and youth are particularly likely to be underemployed or unemployed and rely heavily on the informal sector.

Finally, although perhaps trivial when compared with public health and job opportunities, place-making also matters. Diverse, high-quality, and interesting neighborhoods attract not only residents but also jobs, tourists, and shoppers. Many new and fast-growing neighborhoods lack the distinctiveness that makes for great place and is common in many older parts of cities. Better connections to transportation amenities such as metro stations, urban greenways, and arterials can help create a distinct sense of place where local shops and markets thrive. Too often urban arterials emphasize throughput of private cars and public buses at the expense of neighborhood quality. The great urban thoroughfares of the world are known for the bustling pedestrian activities around them, not the number of vehicles moved per hour during rush hour.

In this chapter, we provide a broad overview of some of the types of cities in the Global South and describe the scale of the challenge of producing more sustainable social, environmental, and economic outcomes. We then emphasize these challenges through the lens of improving neighborhoods in the fast-growing suburbs of the Global South. In cities that lack adequate housing or infrastructure, a better balance between mobility and place can feel like a minor issue or even a distraction. However, neither slum upgrading, planned informal expansion, nor publicly subsidized mortgage markets have done enough to integrate transportation investments with suburban growth. Furthermore, the tendency to view new road and transit investments strictly in terms of mobility has hampered sustainable development in the Global South. In the last section of the chapter, we provide examples of the challenges, missed opportunities, and potential benefits of using high-capacity transit investments to shape urban form and improve local neighborhood conditions. Transit, more than other transportation technology, has the potential to dramatically reshape form and improve urban conditions in the Global South.

Transit Cities

There is a common saying in public transportation planning that mass transit needs mass. For a public bus to make sense from an economic and environmental perspective, there must be enough people going along the bus corridor to fill bus seats. High-capacity systems such as subways, light rail, and bus rapid transit (BRT) need even more passengers and thus an even greater mass of people living around their stations. For the most part, cities of the Global South have mass, in terms of density as well as size. In Mexico City, for example, even the most remote suburban neighborhoods are dense enough on average to support high-capacity subways and metros.[4] In fact, many suburban neighborhoods are as dense as or denser than typical downtown neighborhoods.

There is no shortage of large, dense, and fast-growing cities in the Global South. In fact, some of the fastest population growth is happening in the largest cities, particularly the lowest-income ones, which are doubling in population every 5 years (table 9-1). Nearly 350 million new residents will live in cities with more than 5 million residents by 2030. Cities with 1 to 5 million residents, which are certainly large enough to support high-quality mass transit systems, are projected to add another 250 million residents. In total, 45 percent of urban residents of the Global South will live in cities with a million or more residents by 2030. These places are generally ideal locations for developing and strengthening transit use. Of course, population density is just one form of density. A 2017 World Bank report argues that one of the greatest challenges of African cities is that high population densities are not matched by a density of jobs, built form, or urban amenities.[5]

Even smaller cities often rely heavily on transit. Across Mexico's 100 largest cities, residents rely on transit for 43 percent of commutes to work. In the smallest third of these cities, which have between 75,000 and 200,000 residents, 37 percent of workers commute by transit.[6] As in many other parts of the world, residents rely primarily on

Table 9-1. Population (millions) in low- and middle-income cities by city size.

Income group	City size	2000	2015	2030	AAGR (%)	Total (%), 2030
Upper-middle (includes China)	5 million or more	165	315	453	5.8	11.6
Lower-middle (includes India)	5 million or more	117	202	345	6.5	8.8
Low	5 million or more	16	34	109	18.8	2.8
Subtotal	**5 million or more**	**299**	**551**	**907**	**6.8**	**23.2**
Upper-middle	1 to 5 million	234	351	468	3.3	12.0
Lower-middle	1 to 5 million	127	210	318	5.0	8.1
Low	1 to 5 million	34	62	83	4.9	2.1
Subtotal	**1 to 5 million**	**395**	**624**	**869**	**4.0**	**22.3**
Upper-middle	0.3 to 1 million	183	281	354	3.1	9.1
Lower-middle	0.3 to 1 million	98	142	210	3.8	5.4
Low	0.3 to 1 million	22	37	69	7.3	1.8
Subtotal	**0.3 to 1 million**	**303**	**459**	**632**	**3.6**	**16.2**
Upper-middle	Fewer than 0.3 million	484	629	683	1.4	17.5
Lower-middle	Fewer than 0.3 million	362	486	605	2.2	15.5
Low	Fewer than 0.3 million	88	145	207	4.5	5.3
Subtotal	**Fewer than 0.3 million**	**934**	**1,260**	**1,495**	**2.0**	**38.3**
Total	**All sizes**	**1,931**	**2,894**	**3,903**	**3.4**	**100.0**

Source: United Nations Population Division World Urbanization Prospects, the 2014 Revision.
Note: AAGR is the linear average annual growth rate.

privately provided transit in minivans and minibuses, with varying levels of service quality and official regulation (figure 9-2). Researchers often refer to these services collectively as informal transit or paratransit, and locals use local names such as *angkots*, *matatus*, or *peseros*, which describe specific vehicle types and services. Although frequently criticized for low vehicle standards and high emissions, these informal transit services are the workhorse of public transportation in the Global South. For the 1.25 billion residents of low- and middle-income countries with fewer than 300,000 residents, they are generally the only available form of public transportation and a major source of employment.

Even in large, dense cities with great metros or high-capacity bus systems, informal transit remains an important part of the transportation landscape. Across a score of large African cities, 36 to 100 percent of public transit travel is on informal paratransit. In

Figure 9-2. An *angkot* plying its trade in Solo, Indonesia. *Angkot* is a portmanteau for the Bahasa words for "city" and "transportation." (Photo by Dennie Ramon.)

two-thirds of these cities, more than 80 percent of public transit is on informal paratransit.[7] In Mexico City and Bogotá, 50 percent and 43 percent of motorized trips involve some form of paratransit.

Nonmotorized Cities

For all the emphasis on cars and transit, walking remains the most globally important mode of transportation. Nearly everyone walks, even if it's just to get from the front door to a car parked on the street. Although walking rates are high from small villages to megacities, rates are particularly high in small, compact cities with low household incomes and walkable historic cores. These cities are particularly common in Africa and South Asia but also in wealthier parts of Latin America and East Asia. Globally, almost 40 percent of all trips are made by foot, and the figure is close to 90 percent in many smaller and poorer cities.[8] In 2030, well over a third of the urban residents of low- and middle-income countries will live in cities with fewer than 300,000 people. Most will rely heavily on walking and other nonmotorized modes of transportation. Even the largest cities can have high rates of walking. In Dhaka, the Bangladeshi capital of 17 million and the world's densest city, more than half of trips are by foot, bicycle, or rickshaw.[9] In Bogotá, a wealthy and large city, residents make 43 percent of all trips by foot.[10] Density and a healthy mix of houses, shops, and businesses make walking an attractive alternative even in peripheral neighborhoods of massive metropolitan areas.

Because walking produces almost no local or global pollution, creates no traffic fatalities, costs residents only the food needed to power their legs, has proven health benefits, and requires low infrastructure investments relative to highways or transit, maintaining high walking rates is critically important in the Global South. The biggest disadvantage of relying on walking, of course, is the slow speeds. As households earn more income, members often shift to motorized forms of transportation such as cars, transit, or motorcycles that allow them to access more of the city. Unfortunately, as a result many cities and countries neglect pedestrian infrastructure under the assumption that residents will switch to motorized modes if and when they can afford them.

Bicycles offer another opportunity to increase access to various parts of the city without increasing pollution, infrastructure costs, or traffic fatalities. Many cities in the Global South rely heavily on bicycles. As incomes have increased and the costs of cars and motorcycles decreased, however, bicycle use has decreased in many parts of the world. In Beijing, for example, bicycle mode share fell sharply, from 54 percent in 1986 to 23 percent in 2007.[11] Nevertheless, rising incomes do not necessitate a decrease in bicycle use. Cities such as Amsterdam and Copenhagen prove that a city can be modern, wealthy, globally connected, and bicycle reliant. Authors John Pucher and Ralph Buehler argue that the Netherlands, Denmark, and Germany took active steps to make cycling convenient, comfortable, and safe.[12] As a result, women and older adults are just as likely to bike as young men, who dominate cycling in the United States and Great Britain. This is particularly important in poorer cities of the Global South, where working-age men are generally abler to access motorized transportation.[13] Cities such as Bogotá and Buenos Aires have seen increased cycling rates as a result of investments in cycle tracks and bicycle paths.

Motorcycle Cities

In many cities, motorcycles, mopeds, and other motorized two-wheelers have come to dominate the transportation system. Asia currently has about three-quarters of the global two-wheeler fleet, and motorcycles are the primary mode of transportation in large cities such as Taipei, Ho Chi Minh City, and Hanoi. Small to medium-sized Asian cities, which tend to have narrow streets, limited parking spaces, poor transit, and short trip distances, are particularly reliant on motorized two-wheelers.[14] Solo, an Indonesian city of 500,000 to 600,000 residents, is an example of one such city. Between 2009 and 2013, the number of registered motorcycles more than doubled from 208,000 to 424,000—nearly one for every for every man, woman, and child.[15] As in other Indonesian cities, rising incomes, inexpensive motorcycles, easy credit, and low fuel prices (subsidized before 2015) helped

Figure 9-3. Motorcyclists in Solo, Indonesia. (Photo by Dennie Ramon.)

encourage a rapid increase in motorcycle ownership and use (figure 9-3). Millions of others live in cities like Solo, where transit service is poor, transit use is low, and the cost and convenience of motorcycles have made them the mode of choice. The number of people living in Asian cities with 300,000 to 1 million residents is expected to double from 550 million in 2015 to just over 1 billion in 2030 (table 9-1). The size, number, and importance of motorcycle cities are increasing rapidly.

Outside Asia, motorcycle ownership and use have also been growing in a number of Latin American and African cities.[16] Motorcycle taxis are an important component of the transportation system in African cities such as Douala, Lagos, and Ouagadougou. In Jakarta, motorcycle owners can use the smartphone application Go-Jek to provide taxi services in a similar way to car owners with Uber or Lyft. Motorcycle use is sometimes thought to follow a Kuznets curve, where use increases with income up until a certain income level before decreasing as more households switch to driving cars. In the 1960s, many poorer European countries had larger motorcycle fleets than car fleets, much like in Asia today.[17] Because motorcycles consume roadway and parking spaces more efficiently than cars, a similar shift from motorcycles to cars in Asian cities will come at a high social and economic cost. Nevertheless, more needs to be done to reduce the harm that motorcycles cause through local pollution and the degradation of public space and pedestrian safety. Motorcycles often infringe on public spaces, overtaking sidewalks and blocking pedestrians, as well as emitting toxic fumes and producing substantial noise pollution.

Designing for a Planet of Suburbs

As the global urban population has increased, so has the process of suburbanization. Most metropolitan areas are expanding geographically more quickly than the population is growing. Although developing cities are, on average, three times denser than cities in the developed world, densities have been declining by about 1 percent to 2 percent annually.[18] Based on experiences in wealthier countries, the rise in gross domestic product (GDP) per capita, and the rapid increase in vehicle fleets, it is easy to assume that as urban residents of the Global South are getting wealthier, they are choosing to live in larger homes on larger lots in suburban areas and rely more heavily on cars. Yet the average suburban expansion in a developing city bears little physical or socioeconomic resemblance to the typical American or European suburb. Although there are many examples of high-income gated suburban communities, developing world suburbs are generally poor and densely populated. In Mexico City—which is wealthier, more suburbanized, and more reliant on private cars than most developing cities—car ownership and suburbanization are not moving hand in hand.[19] Instead, wealthier households opt to own cars and live in central locations with good accessibility, and poorer households tend to live further from the urban center and rely on transit, particularly for longer trips such as commutes to jobs in the urban center. This is the polar opposite of most American cities.

The suburbanization of cities in the Global South presents additional challenges to planning and designing people-oriented cities. First and foremost, suburban neighborhoods often lack or have limited basic infrastructure such as piped water, sewage, or paved roads. High-quality suburban transit service is rare, and accessibility to major job centers, hospitals, and schools is often poor. Although neighborhoods that experience these conditions—sometimes referred to as informal settlements, slums, *favelas*, shanty towns, or *bidonvilles*—often exist in central areas of the city, they are most prevalent on the periphery where accessibility to jobs and services is generally low. Where they occur closer to the center, it is often a result of urban expansion. For example, Dharavi, sometimes referred to as the world's largest slum, began on the northern periphery of Mumbai. As Mumbai has expanded northward from a compact peninsular city of 3 million in 1950 to a dense and sprawling megacity of 21 million in 2015, Dharavi has come to occupy something close to metropolitan Mumbai's geographic and population center.

Second, suburbs in the Global South often concentrate poverty and contribute to socioeconomic segregation. In addition to access to hard infrastructure, access to less tangible socioeconomic opportunities is important. More segregated and concentrated poverty are associated with lower incomes, higher unemployment, lower education, higher crime rates, and worse health outcomes.[20]

Third, residents often lack formal title to property. A lack of formal title—or multiple, conflicting titles—makes housing tenure insecure, discourages property owners from investing, hinders the resale of houses or businesses, and prevents homeowners from leveraging the value of their home or accessing the formal banking system. Compare that to the United States, where the national outstanding mortgage debt is about $110,000 per household—more than twice the typical household's income.[21] Although many government agencies try to encourage access to formal titles, land use regulations are sometimes so out of touch with the reality on the ground as to make this impossible. For example, minimum lot sizes in Nairobi, Kenya, are 500 square meters, but population densities in its largest slum, Kibera, are as high as 2,000 per hectare. Without violating the lot size regulations and without including any space for roads or open space, households would have to include 100 members to achieve that density.[22]

Improving Suburban Conditions

Planning for better communities, environments, and economies in the fast-growing suburbs that dominate the urban landscape in the Global South presents some notable challenges. A lack of basic infrastructure has led to an emphasis on providing greater access to land title, water, and sewer systems using three overarching approaches discussed in this section. Despite some successful programs and policies, however, little has been done to improve the integration of transportation and surrounding land uses or the quality of the pedestrian environment. Without improvements, suburban residents will inevitably turn to private cars and motorcycles, as incomes allow. The net result will be higher levels of pollution, higher traffic fatality rates, and less money to spend on other household goods. Although the context is vastly different from the suburban office complexes such as Tysons or Hacienda Business Park described in chapter 6, the need for better planning is greater, and the stakes are higher.

Suburban Upgrading

The first overarching approach is to upgrade existing settlements, particularly informal ones, in what is sometime referred to as slum upgrading or informal upgrading. In places such as Rio de Janeiro, Brazil, the number and proportion of residents living in informal settlements (*favelas*) has grown rapidly with the urban population. By the 1990s, a quarter of Rio's urban population—more than a million residents—lived in hundreds of *favelas* throughout the city.[23] Slum Dwellers International, a transnational network of community-based nongovernment institutions with a focus on housing and urban poverty, describes upgrading as "any intervention that improves the physical conditions of a settlement, which in turn enhances the lives of its inhabitants."[24] Many, such as the Favela Bairro program in Rio de Janeiro and Urban Upgrading Project for Vietnam, are large-scale public investments supported by international lending agencies such as the World Bank and the Inter-American Development Bank to provide basic infrastructure, such as piped water and paved roads, in conjunction with legal title and sometimes softer infrastructure such as micro-lending and community centers. Rio's Favela Bairro, one of the most popular and imitated upgrading programs,[25] has brought new water connections, sewage, trash collection, paved roads, open space, social services, and more secure tenure to hundreds of thousands of residents since the first phase in 1994.[26] Similarly, the Urban Upgrading Project for Vietnam improved local infrastructure for millions of residents in the target cities of Nam Dinh, Hai Phong, Ho Chi Minh, and Can Tho.[27] The project also emphasized stormwater management and flood control by adding 500 kilometers of drains, dredging lakes and canals, building 240 kilometers of roadway that double as stormwater berms, and relocating households from homes that were particularly vulnerable to flooding or ecologically harmful.

How successful are these large-scale upgrading programs at achieving the aims of this book? The Inter-American Development Bank conducted an ex-post evaluation to compare upgraded neighborhoods with similar neighborhoods that had not benefited from Favela Bairro.[28] Although the program improved access to infrastructure and increased property values between 40 and 75 percent, it failed to improve employment rates or access times to transit. Informal settlements on mountainsides are particularly difficult places to provide high-quality transit and require innovative transportation solutions like Medellín's Metrocable, discussed later in this chapter. Unlike in Rio de Janeiro, residents in Vietnamese cities rely more heavily on motorcycles than on public transportation. Given flat, low-lying terrain, road paving makes motorcycle trips faster and more convenient. Thus Vietnam's upgrading projects increased regional and local accessibility. Microloans, along with road paving and flood protection, also helped entrepreneurs expand their businesses and thus contributed to the economic development of commercial corridors and nonresidential destinations.

Planning for Suburbs

The second approach is to provide land title, basic infrastructure, and other services to fast-growing urban areas, generally in the suburbs, before settlement occurs. This approach has particular appeal because informal settlements often lack sufficient space for high-quality public transportation and remain popular in contemporary discussions of how to address urban growth in the Global South.[29] One of the earliest and best-documented cases—probably because of the involvement of thirteen internationally recognized architects—Proyecto Experimental de Vivienda (PREVI) sought to develop a national model to address Peru's rapid urbanization and growing housing crisis in the late 1960s.[30] Although

PREVI, a partnership between the Peruvian government and United Nations Development Program, failed to create a national model and only led to 1,500 new dwelling units on Lima's periphery, it did help popularize an approach that proliferated widely through programs such as the World Bank's Sites and Services program.

Between 1972 and 1990, the World Bank participated in more than one hundred Sites and Services projects, and other aid institutions, such as the United Nations Development Program, were involved in many more.[31] Initiated with an $8 million World Bank loan in 1972, *Parcelles Assainies* ("Sanitized Plots" in English) was one of the first and largest World Bank Sites and Services projects.[32] Like many African capitals, Dakar, Senegal, has grown rapidly since independence, from about 350,000 residents in 1960 to 3.5 million today. The initial plan called for fourteen thousand 150-square-meter lots with piped water, sanitation, unpaved roads, and limited services. With an estimated ten residents per plot and an ambitious 6-year timeframe, the project would have housed nearly a quarter of Dakar's metropolitan population at the time. Residents would pay back a low-interest loan that financed these upfront investments. Although the project started slowly, the settlement grew rapidly and housed between 350,000 and 500,000 residents by 2006.[33] According to the Ministry of Urbanism's 2001 urban plan, Parcelles Assainies accommodated 15 percent of the metropolitan housing stock on just 6 percent of the urban land area.[34]

Although Parcelles Assainies and PREVI have received considerable attention, each has had its set of challenges. PREVI never achieved anything close to the scale needed to address housing problems in Lima, Peru, or the Global South more generally. Furthermore, the neighborhood is little different from surrounding informal settlements that grew organically over time in terms of the quality of place or access to infrastructure.[35] In Parcelles Assainies, the provision of basic services did not keep pace with settlement's rapid growth. In 2001, just 12 percent of households had sewer connections, 90 percent had electricity, and 75 percent had drinking water—although these connections are twice the rates of 1980 and better than those in Pikine, a vast informal settlement just east of Parcelles Assainies where the government relocated residents of more central slums in the 1950s and 1960s.[36]

Although slightly closer to central Dakar than Pikine, Parcelles Assainies was built on the northern periphery of the Dakar peninsula with little attention paid to local or metropolitan transportation connections. The narrow streets in northern Dakar are densely packed with minibuses, taxis, freight vehicles, and a few private cars. Congestion is endemic, travel times are long, and pollution levels are high. Thus, although Parcelles Assainies provided a large number of housing units with higher quality than surrounding neighborhoods, the challenges of improving accessibility to jobs, services, and urban amenities remain largely unresolved. Creating a safe, reasonably attractive public realm for pedestrians should take more of a priority in efforts to plan for sustainable suburban growth.

Enabling Mortgage Markets

The third approach has been to enable mortgage markets and encourage the private sector to provide new housing in fast-growing suburbs. For the World Bank, this is part of a larger shift from financing individual projects to reforming the housing sector to develop formal mortgage markets and encourage private sector involvement in low-cost housing production.[37] In 1981, the World Bank ended its Senegalese Sites and Services program and, in 1988, lent the Senegalese government $46 million to strengthen the capacity of the Senegalese National Housing Bank and support the construction and sales of titled and serviced lots.[38] The National Housing Bank is involved in lending to builders and homebuyers for the commercial housing developments and empty lots that line the main road heading east out of Dakar (figure 9-4). Special loan products support purchases by informal workers and by the many migrant workers living abroad, particularly in Europe.[39] Although most housing production in Dakar is still informal, the formal production of housing is a growing and notable feature of the suburban landscape.

Nowhere has the shift to formal mortgage markets been more notable than in Mexico, where private developers acquire large peripheral lots, build new housing speculatively, and sell completed homes in massive developments to households that qualify for publicly subsidized mortgages.[40] Sometime between 2000 and 2010, the annual production of commercially built homes surpassed the number of new informal units.[41] Public

Figure 9-4. Housing units under construction off of the main road out of Dakar. (Photo by Erick Guerra.)

policies—including the legalization of sales of communally owned farmland, a simplifica-tion of housing construction regulations, and active political engagement with private developers—facilitated the shift in housing production.[42] During this housing transition, public agencies provided nearly three-quarters of all housing loans by value—and even more by volume.[43] The effects on the ground are startling. Developments of tens of thou-sands of densely packed 25- to 50-square-meter row houses (figure 9-5) have transformed many suburban municipalities over the course of a decade or two.

Although commercially produced and publicly subsidized housing has helped hun-dreds of thousands middle- and lower-middle-income households acquire housing with basic infrastructure in countries such as Mexico and Senegal, the suburban housing transition has struggled to produce sustainable and well-designed neighborhoods. The new developments tend to be single-use, with limited community infrastructure such as schools or parks, socioeconomically segregated and located on the periphery, where devel-opers can acquire large tracts of land. Despite the low car ownership rates of residents, the settlements are designed around cars, with ample parking, limited transit infrastruc-ture, and an intentional separation from neighboring street networks and bus stops. Even when settlements are located near high-capacity transit, like the development pictured

Figure 9-5. Publicly subsidized commercial housing development in Santa Rosa, Queretaro. Narrow, single-story row homes like these are typical of low-cost commercial hous-ing developments in Mexico. (Photo by Erick Guerra.)

in figure 9-9 later in this chapter, no attention is given to connecting residents to the transit services they use. As a result, households in commercial housing developments in suburban Mexico are about 60 percent more likely to own a car than similar households in neighboring informal settlements. They also drive two to four times more per day.[44]

Organic Place-Making

Despite some notable challenges, suburban neighborhoods in the Global South have some advantages over suburban neighborhoods in the Global North. There is enough density to support local retail, transit, and small businesses. Along with unenforced or limited land use regulation, this density supports a good mix of housing, shops, and businesses, even in neighborhoods that began primarily as residential. Dharavi, for example, has become famous for its small-scale manufacturing. Finally, although high-quality transit service is often lacking, local residents and drivers' associations provide taxi and transit services by motorcycle, car, minivan, or bus. Where there is a demand for food, transportation services, or local businesses, informal providers generally emerge.

Even in commercially produced housing developments, residents recreate their surroundings to make them more walkable, better connected, and more suited to daily life without a car. Many homeowners convert all or part of their units to commercial uses. Small convenience stores are most common and most visible, but converted units include a range of local services such as pharmacies, health clinics, dentists, veterinarians, Internet cafés, restaurants, and photocopy centers. Commercial conversions on arterial streets are the norm rather than the exception.

In Mexico City's suburbs, residents have reconnected local streets to the rest of the grid. For example, the developer Urbi built the 2-kilometer road that defines the western edge of Las Villas Santa Bárbara and Las Palmas, two contiguous commercial developments with fifteen thousand housing units in Ixtapaluca.[45] Divided by a fenced median, it runs parallel to a municipal road for its length. The road passes thirty-five perpendicular roads in the informal settlement to the west without a single planned physical connection. Over time, however, residents have knocked down fences, dug shallow trenches, and even built full-fledged new intersections to make new connections for pedestrians and vehicles. The most finished of these access points resemble the unpaved gravel roads of the informal settlement, not the paved formal roads of the commercial development. Just as residents see to it that housing estates are dotted with retail and convenience shops, they go the extra length to ensure roads provide access and connectivity.

Designing for a Transit Metropolis

At the 2012 Rio+ 20 Conference, the World Bank, Inter-American Development Bank, African Development Bank, and other international aid agencies announced a "game-changing" commitment to sustainable transport, pledging substantial financial support over the next decade for this purpose, with the lion's share slated for public transport.[46] A recent World Bank publication, *Transforming Cities with Transit*, argues for treating new investments in high-end transit systems as more than projects to move people through space.[47] They are potentially powerful city-shaping ones as well. More than any other type of investment, public transit has the greatest potential to shape urbanization and encourage more sustainable settlement patterns in the Global South.

Governments and development agencies have taken up the challenge and invested significantly in high-capacity transit in many Asian, Latin American, and African cities. Beijing's subway system grew from just two lines in 2000 to one of the world's largest metro systems today. Each year, a dozen new BRT lines open in cities around the world. Concerns about economic competitiveness, congestion, sprawl, pollution, and accessibility for the poor and middle class motivate these investments. As measured by the number of kilometers built or the number of passengers transported, these investments have been a great success. As measured by the creation of great places, the integration with metropolitan form, or the ability to shape urban growth, the record is far less successful.

In *The Transit Metropolis: A Global Inquiry*, one of this book's authors, Robert Cervero, opens by stating, "A transit metropolis is a region where a workable fit exists between transit services and urban form. In some cases, this means compact, mixed-use development well suited to rail services, and in others it means flexible, fleetfooted bus services well suited to spread-out development. What matters is that transit and the city co-exist in harmony."[48] We argue throughout the cases and examples in this section that a better integration between transit and the city in the Global South is needed, not just at the metropolitan scale but also at the local scale. Too often new transit investments are treated simply as infrastructure to move people, rather than a framework for growth and a part of the urban landscape. This is understandable given the great mobility needs. However, an emphasis on place-making, integrated land use, and local design would improve transit investments' ability to shape the kinds of sustainable cities that will thrive in the coming decades, even as incomes rise and car ownership increases.

Transit and TOD Challenges in China

In the world of sustainable transportation and urbanism, China is the 800-pound gorilla. With some ten thousand new automobile registrations added to the streets of China each day, creating Chinese cities with a strong transit orientation is of global importance. North America, Europe, and Australia can do everything right in advancing sustainable futures. However, whatever progress they make in reducing greenhouse gases and fuel consumption will be quickly eclipsed if China continues to mimic American-style patterns of suburbanization, car ownership, and travel.[49]

Studies reveal that urban morphologies strongly influence travel in China. The change from organically evolved, mixed-use enclaves—where many people lived, worked, and shopped in the same area—to car-oriented large-block suburbs has dramatically enlarged the environmental footprint of Chinese households. A study of nine hundred households that either voluntarily moved or were relocated from traditional mixed-use, highly walkable neighborhoods in Shanghai's urban core to isolated, superblock, and gated housing units on the periphery showed that travel patterns were strongly affected. Dramatic shifts from nonmotorized to motorized travel and journeys of far longer duration resulted in an estimated 50 percent increase in surveyed households' vehicle kilometers traveled.[50]

To date, good transit-oriented designs are more the exception than the rule in Chinese cities. To a large extent, transit investments and urban development are weakly linked in Chinese cities.[51] The clash between stations as focal areas for development and as jumping on–off points for accessing regional trains has undermined efforts to nurture functional transit-oriented development (TOD). This is seen in the failure to articulate urban densities (e.g., tapering building heights with distances from stations), the siting of stations in isolated superblocks, poor pedestrian access, and a lack of mixed land uses.[52] Large blocks, wide boulevards, and segregated land uses have isolated many Chinese rail stations and created pedestrian-hostile environments. The end results are less than impressive. From Beijing's main train station, the number of jobs that could be reached by foot within 20 minutes in 2005 was 157,200. For London's main station, King's Cross, the figure was 352,800 and for New York City, with its fine-grained grid and embroidered pattern of land uses, the figure for Grand Central Station was more than 1.7 million jobs.[53] Even with the rapid increase in the number of stations, little has been done to encourage transit-focused growth or pleasant pedestrian environments in Beijing and other Chinese cities.

In China, rail has been a magnet for growth, albeit fragmented. Beijing's steady expansion of metro rail services has been accompanied by a real estate boom. Housing projects have followed Beijing's rail networks, but jobs and businesses have not.[54] Many new communities developed along rail corridors have become veritable bedroom communities. Skewed commuting patterns have resulted. A study of three residential new towns in Beijing's rail-served northern suburbs found as many as nine times the number of rail passengers heading inbound in the morning peak as heading outbound.[55] Moreover, poor integration of station designs with surrounding development has led to chaotic pedestrian circulation patterns and long passenger queues at suburban stations such as Xizhimen on Beijing's Line 2.[56]

The absence of station-area master planning has also led to substandard development. A case in point is Beijing's Sihui interchange station on Lines 1 and 8 between the 3rd and 4th ring roads.[57] There, a massive concrete slab was built over the 40-hectare depot site next to the station, enabling the Beijing City Underground Railway Company to lease 700,000 square meters of air rights to developers. However, no design or development standards were set as part of the lease agreement. To economize on the cost of a thousand-plus apartments built atop the site, only one footbridge was built to the Sihui subway station. Overcrowded sidewalks and queues at the station entrance resulted, severely detracting from the station environment and lowering land prices. The poor-quality environment surrounding the Sihui station underscores the importance of a master planning entity that oversees project development and ensures a functional relationship between the public and private realms of station settings.

Urban design and place-making considerations are beginning to gain importance in Chinese cities. In all-out campaigns to reduce traffic congestion and air pollution, a number of Chinese cities have embraced TOD in recent years and at the regional scale declared themselves as future transit metropolises. Transit-supportive design guidelines recently released by the city of Chongqing stress the importance of breaking up superblocks with fine-grained rectilinear grids to create more permeable streetscapes and intersperse land uses so that many are within a walkable distance (figure 9-6). Beijing and Shenzhen have adopted TOD as a guiding design principle in their most recent long-range masterplans.[58] Rail and land use integration is also being pursued for financial purposes. In 2013, Hong Kong's MTR broke ground on its first R+P project in China: 1,700 apartments and a shopping mall above a metro station in Shenzhen (see chapter 7 for an overview of Hong Kong's R+P projects). Future residents will have all-weather pedestrian access to Longsheng metro station on the Longhua Line. Although China's heavily regulated land markets constrain the ability to fully recapture value from rail investments, the physical integration of private development and public transit through the R+P model could serve as a TOD prototype for other Chinese cities.[59]

Place-making transformations are also occurring at Chinese TODs. An example is the Luohu transit hub in Shenzhen. As a large intermodal transfer station for metropolitan and intercity fast trains, Luohu was scaled and designed for purposes of logistical efficiency. Figure 9-7 shows the station's main entrance and exit ways, previously an intercept point for train customers to connect to awaiting buses, taxis, and cars. Today, these functions have been replaced by a heavily landscaped, people-oriented outdoor plaza and relocated to the periphery and a below-level intermodal connection point. Customers entering and exiting the Luohu station are now treated to an airy and largely conflict-free walking environment that blends the station concourse and the immediate surroundings. Luohu station could very well be a harbinger of place-making principles usurping logistical ones at key stations of China's continually expanding urban rail network.

Bus Rapid Transit

Of all contemporary urban transportation policies, BRT is perhaps the most celebrated. Since Bogotá's TransMilenio demonstrated that—with sufficient frequency, right-of-way, lane priority, and boarding facilities—BRT could match the performance of all but the

DISCOURAGED:
Arterial-dominant Superblock network

- *Prioritizes cars over people*
- *Discourages pedestrian activity*

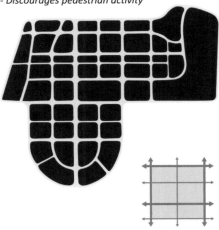

Superblock Grid

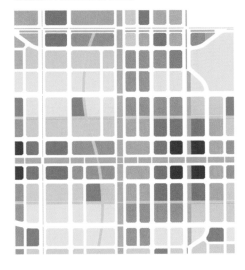

RECOMMENDED:
Urban Network of smaller blocks

- *Prioritizes people over cars*
- *Supports pedestrian and economic activity*

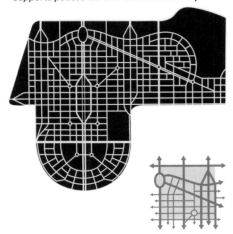

Urban Network Grid

Figure 9-6. Breaking up the superblock: TOD guidelines for Chongqing, China. The left image recommends a fine-grained grid network that increases connectivity for pedestrians; the right image shows that smaller blocks allow a more intimate mixing of land uses, such as neighborhood shops. (Source: Calthorpe and Associates, Transit Oriented Districts Plan, Liangji-ang New District, Chongqing Planning Bureau, 2013.)

Figure 9-7. Shenzhen's Luohu Station was transformed from a logistical node to a pedestrian-activated rail-served place. In place of pedestrians, swarms of taxis, cars, and buses previously occupied the space in front of the station. (Photo by Chris Yunker, Flickr Creative Commons.)

most-used high-capacity rail systems,[60] the number of BRT lines around the world has grown exponentially.[61] The combination of short construction periods and low investment costs has made BRT particularly popular in the Global South, where transit demand is often high but investment funds are often scarce. Latin American cities such as Bogotá, São Paulo, and Santiago led the way in building high-end BRT in the early 2000s (even earlier in the case of Curitiba). China, which has been adding BRT lane-kilometers at a faster pace than anywhere else over the past 8 years, is similarly building high-end systems, such as in Guangzhou and Xiamen.

As with rail systems in China, however, an emphasis on mobility over place-making has limited the effectiveness of many global BRT investments. In this section we examine the challenge of balancing the mobility and place-making roles of BRT for two of the largest systems built to date: Bogotá's TransMilenio and Ahmedabad's Janmarg. We then look at two recent BRT investments in Guangzhou, China, and Solo, Indonesia. In Guangzhou, the integration of the transit investment with urban greenways and surrounding land uses shows BRT at its best in Asia. In Solo, the low ridership and poor system performance show the challenges of developing BRT in the world's fast-growing motorcycle cities.

The TransMilenio Experience (Bogotá, Colombia)

Although Bogotá's TransMilenio is a widely celebrated BRT investment, able to carry some forty-five thousand passengers per direction per hour and earning the Institute for Transportation and Development Policy's Gold Standard, reshaping urban form and land use patterns was not a primary objective in its design. Building the system quickly and increasing affordable transport for the poor was. Placement of BRT lines in mostly economically stagnant zones that were largely built out has suppressed land development. So has the siting of BRT stations in busy roadway medians, limiting joint development opportunities and creating unattractive pedestrian environs around stations. Minimal proactive station area planning and a dearth of incentives for private property owners to redevelop parcels have also tempered TOD activities.

Between 2004 and 2010, the mean floor area ratio of residential and commercial development increased by 7 percent throughout the city of Bogotá, compared with 5 percent within 1,000 meters of stations along the initial 42-kilometer system.[62] In fact, more densification occurred along surface bus routes that feed into suburban TransMilenio stations than around BRT stops. Matched pair comparisons of changes in building footprints between 1998 and 2011 for 1-kilometer radii around BRT stations and otherwise similar control areas further revealed weak effects on urban growth. For all but end-of-line stations, more new construction occurred beyond than within 1,000 meters of stations.

Bogotá's experiences square with those of prior transit investments, namely that transit cannot overcome weak local real estate markets.[63] Station siting also matters. Placing stops in the medians of active roadways inevitably means a poor-quality pedestrian access environment and thus little commercial development near the stations themselves. TransMilenio's design gave little weight to the pedestrian experience. The visually prominent skywalks that connect to BRT stops create lengthy, circuitous walks, can be noisy (resonating like steel drums during peak traffic conditions, by some accounts), and are difficult for older adults, the disabled, and semiambulatory people to negotiate.

Bogotá's experiences further show that planning matters. Neither the city nor neighborhood districts (where detailed land use planning is regulated and implemented) prepared station area plans to orchestrate private development, change zoning (including increasing permissible densities), introduce complementary improvements (such as streetscape enhancements) to entice private investments, or take any other proactive steps to leverage new development.

Experiences in Ahmedabad, India

In the 2009, Ahmedabad opened India's first and what remains the country's largest BRT network. Called Janmarg ("People's Way"), the 45-kilometer system was built to relieve mounting traffic congestion in India's fifth largest city. The ingredients were there for BRT to shape future urban growth: rapid growth and motorization coupled with worsening traffic congestion.[64] To date, however, few notable changes have occurred near Janmarg stations.

As in Bogotá, Janmarg was envisaged and designed as a mobility investment, not a city-shaping one. Janmarg lines were and are being selected to serve the city's fastest-growing areas, more so than in the case of Bogotá, but little attention has been given to integrating BRT stops with surrounding neighborhoods or increasing the share of future populations and workers near BRT. Janmarg was designed mainly to keep costs low. Little thought was given to urban development possibilities. No land use or TOD plans have been prepared for any Janmarg stations. What land development is occurring has been left solely to private market forces.

So far, Ahmedabad officials have opted to maintain uniform densities throughout the city, regardless of how close parcels are to transit corridors. This has been done to disperse trips and thus decongest the city. It has also been done for sociocultural reasons, namely to avoid creating a privileged class of land owners whose newfound wealth is created through government fiat. However, keeping densities uniform also shifts growth to the periphery, in a more auto-oriented configuration. In the near term, the city may experience less traffic congestion because of density caps, but over the long term, the resulting auto-oriented urban form could backfire, creating more traffic congestion and air pollution for the region as a whole.

Several design shortcomings must be overcome if Ahmedabad's BRT is to shape urban growth. Janmarg was designed as a closed system, requiring users to access stations sited in the medians of roadways by foot, bicycle, car, two-wheeler, three-wheeler, or surface street buses. However, little attention has been given to perpendicular connectors to BRT stops. No secondary feeder systems provide safe and efficient pedestrian, bikeway, and transit connections to mainline services. Although a substantial network of cycle tracks was built in conjunction with Janmarg, for the most part bike paths run parallel rather than perpendicular to the busway, functioning more as competitive than complementary systems. Moreover, there is no bicycle parking at stations. What few pedestrian-ways exist near Janmarg stops are often occupied by motorcycles and fast-moving three-wheel vehicles.

BRT–Land Use Integration in Guangzhou

Guangzhou's highly praised BRT system contrasts notably with the poor-quality transit station designs of many other Chinese cities. In addition to increasing bus speeds and the share of residents traveling by transit, Guangzhou earns kudos for care given to the connections between surrounding developments and BRT platforms, in contrast to places such as Ahmedabad, where pedestrian access has been a secondary consideration (figure 9-8). Guangzhou's BRT features seamless pedestrian connections through gently sloped footbridges and same-level integration with the second floors of adjoining commercial buildings. Because of the combination of high-quality BRT services and pedestrian connections to stations, high-rise commercial development is gravitating to Guangzhou's BRT corridor, increasing real estate prices by 30 percent during the first 2 years of BRT operations.[65]

Guangzhou also worked to integrate its BRT system with the urban villages it has absorbed as the city's population doubled from 6 million to 12 million over the past 25 years. These highly dense urban villages, once on the fringe, now exist cheek by jowl with new midrise and high-rise developments but often lack key urban infrastructure or formal land rights. The Guangzhou BRT system improves connections for two dozen of these populous informal neighborhoods, improving not just accessibility for residents but also the performance of the transit system. The Tangxiacun station at Tangxia Village, a settlement of 350,000 primarily migrant worker residents, has become one of the world's busiest BRT stations, with eight thousand boardings per hour during peak hours.[66]

BRT in Indonesia

Indonesian cities have been aggressive in building BRT systems in recent years. Only China, a country with five times more residents, has added BRT to more cities than Indonesia since 2000.[67] Indonesia's first system, TransJakarta, launched in Jakarta in 2004,

Figure 9-8. Bus Rapid Transit in Guangzhou (left) and Ahmedabad (right). Guangzhou's BRT design works to accommodate and integrate pedestrians. Ahmedabad's BRT stations lie midblock with limited pedestrian access points and few protections against moving traffic, including motorcycles and motorized three-wheelers. (Photos by (*left*) ITDP China; (*right*) ITDP India.)

has struggled to play a major mobility role, in part due to a minimalist design (e.g., no passing lanes), operational problems (e.g., widespread bus bunching), and failure to integrate private paratransit services as feeders. Although it is the world's longest BRT system, daily BRT ridership has stagnated at around 350,000 passengers, and peak capacity is one-twelfth that of Bogotá's TransMilenio. This is partly because TransJakarta simply does not serve the majority of informal settlements, residential subdivisions, activity centers, and other major trip generators spread throughout the metropolis. Informal minibuses do.

The track record of Indonesia's other BRT systems is even poorer. Of the nineteen global BRT systems that opened in 2010 and 2011, the three with the lowest ridership were in Indonesia (Palembang, Solo, and Gorontalo).[68] With an average of thirty-nine weekday riders per BRT kilometer, the three Indonesian systems have less than a quarter of the average ridership of conventional U.S. bus systems (authors' calculation using the National Transit Database). The systems lack many important features of BRT, such as dedicated travel lanes, and thus offer almost no savings in cost and travel times over existing minibuses. Moreover, the systems are not competitive with motorcycles or motorcycle taxis, which provide much faster point-to-point travel at almost the same price.

Recognizing the need to make transit more competitive, the capital district of Jakarta and one of the major minibus companies, Kopaja, are piloting a project to allow minibus drivers to use BRT lanes for longer, point-to-point trips that are not particularly well served by TransJakarta. Minibus drivers are also becoming formalized employees of the public system, undergoing training, receiving a salary (as opposed paying a fixed amount to the minibus company and keeping profits above this as earnings), and wearing a TransJakarta uniform. Although the jury is still out on how successful Jakarta's foray into private minibus–public BRT integration will be, Kopaja minibus owners and drivers, TransJakarta, and transportation officials are optimistic about the future. As of mid-2017, more than three hundred Kopaja minibuses were operating on TransJakarta's dedicated busways, three times as many as one year earlier.

Suburban Transit Investments

Even where transit thrives, integrates well into the urban fabric, and helps shape growth, a great challenge remains: the difficulty of expanding high-quality transit into the fast-growing and often transit-dependent periphery. In Mumbai, which has a substantial suburban rail network, living near a rail station is associated with less travel by motorcycle and car.[69] Although the suburban rail lines have helped shape Mumbai's growth, travel by rail is long and arduously crowded, and many suburban households live far from rail stations. Several problems make suburban transit investments even more challenging than urban ones. First, suburban investments are generally playing catch-up, providing service into dense suburban neighborhoods instead of shaping growth. Second, the terrain in the suburbs is often mountainous or otherwise difficult to build on. Third, suburban investments often cross multiple jurisdictional boundaries, which make planning and investment more politically and financially complicated. And finally, purely based on geography and geometry, suburban lines generally need more kilometers of trackway to connect to the rest of the city. Even when suburban lines are built, the investments almost invariably favor mobility over place. Mexico City's suburban investments are a case in point.

As in other cities in the Global South, Mexico City's population has grown primarily in suburban neighborhoods. Since the first metro line opened in 1969, more than 80 percent of population growth has been suburban, but just 11 out of 192 metro stations are in the suburbs. Nevertheless, suburban residents, who account for 56 percent of the metropolitan population, use transit more frequently than those in the city proper—65 percent of motorized travel compared with 60 percent. Mexico City largely failed to use the metro to help shape urban growth, and as in Bogotá and Ahmedabad, stations are rarely well integrated into the urban fabric. Just 3 percent of metropolitan trips relied exclusively on walking and the metro. More than two-thirds of all metro trips also involved a ride on a privately operated minibus or minivan. Another 14 percent linked to public buses, light rail, and other vehicular modes. As a result of high suburban ridership, average daily boardings are particularly high at end-of-the-line stations, where suburban residents access the high-capacity transit system.

Instead of increasing suburban transit, the most notable transit investments of the past decade have been six BRT lines, which also provide service primarily in the city center, and Line 12, which increases metro service from east to west along the southern central part of the city proper. At the turn of the millennium, one metro line, Line B, opened and significantly expanded high-capacity transit into the large, densely populated, and relatively poor suburban municipality of Ecatepec. The investment increased population density around suburban stations and improved transit service for local residents but had little or no influence on downtown development, regional growth patterns, congestion, or car ownership.[70] Most new metro passengers previously used road-based transit. The terminal station also connects to a recently opened suburban BRT line, the Mexibus, which provides high-capacity transit service farther into the suburbs along the center lanes of a six-lane highway. Although ridership is high, integration with surrounding neighborhoods is extremely poor. In order to access high density commercial housing developments next to the stations, residents have to cross two lanes (three including the bus lane) of highway traffic and cross a poorly lit ditch and freight rail line along a narrow and cracked cement path (figure 9-9). A suburban train line opened into the northwest in 2008, but a full-distance fare costs three times more than the metro. Combined with a metro trip, a commuter in the northwestern suburbs would spend 60 percent of the daily minimum wage to get to and from work on the suburban train.

Figure 9-9. The Mexibus BRT in suburban Mexico City is poorly integrated with nearby residential neighborhoods. (Photos by Erick Guerra.)

Ciudad Azteca: A Different Kind of TOD

Despite the failure to integrate into the urban fabric, several suburban transfer stations have become models for TOD in Mexico City, although the style and form differ substantially from the projects described in chapter 5. Ciudad Azteca is Line B's terminal and busiest station, with more than 5.5 million passengers boarding in a single month.[71] It is also Mexico City's first intermodal transfer center (CETRAM), a privately owned and operated real estate development that facilitates transit connections between the metro, the Mexibus BRT, taxis, several interregional bus lines, and more than fifty private minivan routes that serve other destinations throughout the State of Mexico.

In addition to charging fees to transit and taxi operators to use its enclosed transfer facilities, the developer PRODI also built a shopping mall, cinema, and a low-cost hospital connected to the metro station. The hospital, in particular, has been financially successful and attracts patients from underserved suburban communities. Although a cinema, shopping mall, and massive transfer center may not evoke traditional notions of TOD accessibility, the development caters to the needs of suburban commuters transferring to terminal metro stations. Ciudad Azteca has also become a destination in itself and improved residents' access not just to recreation and shopping but also to health services. The transfer center, which opened in 2009, 10 years after the station, has become a model for suburban TOD and is being replicated around the city.

Medellín Metrocable

Located in a valley, Medellín, Colombia's informal settlements grew rapidly up steep hills and mountainsides as the metropolitan population increased tenfold from 1950 to 2015.

As in Dakar and Rio de Janeiro, residents often face long and expensive trips on privately provided transportation to access the center of the city. With the first Line K opening in 2004, Medellín's Metrocable formed part of a comprehensive strategy to improve conditions in Popular and Santa Cruz, two of the poorest and most densely populated suburban municipalities in Colombia's second largest city. The Metrocable uses an aerial gondola system to bring passengers up and down the steep hillside. Around the stations, the municipal government also invested in schools, libraries, open space, pedestrian paths, and social housing. Station integration and design were important features of the investment rather than afterthoughts. Two additional lines opened in 2008 and 2010—one part of another comprehensive package of investments in a poor suburban neighborhood, the other to provide public transit access to a large, regional park.

In 2005, most households around the Line K were categorized as low income or very low income, and only 6 percent of trips involved a personal car or motorcycle. Most residents walked or took the bus. In areas around stations, travel times and travel expenditures decreased relative to similar neighborhoods, and in the most distant stations, travel times to the metro have been cut from an hour to 15 minutes at certain times of day.[72] Unless a person lives fairly close to a station, however, it is often faster to take an informal bus, which is more likely to have a nearby stop.[73] Walking and buses remain the two most important modes even in the neighborhoods around Metrocable stations, which are most useful for travel to the city center.[74]

The Metrocable design has two additional attractive features. First, the small cable cars and automated system allow very rapid frequency, with passengers rarely having to wait more than a few minutes. Second, at just over $10 million per kilometer of investment, the system costs are comparable to those of a high-quality BRT system, and the local government and private sector financed the project without external support.[75]

In terms of the financing, station integration, and improved accessibility, the Medellín Metrocable demonstrates how local governments can use transit investments as catalysts and support for other suburban upgrading initiatives. In this respect, the Medellín experience has lessons to offer for programs such as PREVI, Favela Bairro, and Parcelles Assainies. However, it also reinforces the challenges of improving mobility and placemaking in the fast-growing suburbs of the Global South. Medellín's hillsides remain poor, and residents continue to spend substantial time, energy, and money to get from the periphery to the more centrally located neighborhoods where the jobs, hospitals, cultural amenities, and educational opportunities remain concentrated. It is also unclear how replicable the system will be. In Rio de Janeiro, local residents widely criticized a now-defunct government program to build cable cars into *favelas* for costing too much and failing to meet local transportation needs.

Close

Balancing mobility and place-making in the fast-growing cities of the Global South is no small task. Many of the world's fastest-growing neighborhoods not only have inadequate transportation infrastructure but also lack basic infrastructure such as piped water, waste management, and reliable electricity supply. Local governments often do not have the financial and technical capacity to invest in basic infrastructure, never mind world-class transit systems. Even where transit investments have improved mobility substantially, they rarely integrate well into urban fabrics or create senses of place. At a metropolitan scale, transit investments have done too little to shape urban growth. Instead, informal paratransit or personal motorcycles provide mobility for long-distance trips in most of the Global South's fast-growing suburbs. As a result, settlements are often uniformly dense and sprawling. Both mobility and place-making suffer.

Despite these challenges, several characteristics make integrated transportation and land use planning promising in the Global South. First, even the most remote neighborhoods are generally dense enough to support regular transit services, shops, and a wide range of services. Although travel to major job centers is often long and expensive, local clinics, restaurants, and convenience stores are generally just a short walk away. Even in neighborhoods that began primarily as residential, a mix of uses open and thrive over time. Second, walking rates and transit use remain high, despite sometimes poor and even unsafe conditions. Rather than a call to inaction, this suggests that improvements to transit and nonmotorized infrastructure can play a substantial role not only in improving contemporary conditions but also in discouraging a shift to private cars and motorcycles in the future. The case of plummeting bicycling rates in Chinese cities demonstrates how quickly the tide can change, if planners and policymakers do not work hard to provide adequate space and convenient connections to pedestrians or cyclists. The rapid rise in motorcycle use and decline in public transit use in cities such as Ho Chi Minh City and Jakarta tell a similar story.

Third, there are big opportunities for social and economic gains. For example, despite high walking rates and transit use, fatality rates are high in many Latin American, Asian, and African cities. Shifts in public policy, traffic enforcement, and infrastructure design have the potential to substantially reduce the number of people who die each year. Building rapid thoroughfares for the minority who drive with elevated or no crossings for the majority who walk has created a social, economic, and public health disaster. Reducing traffic injuries and fatalities should be a key goal of transportation and land use planning in the Global South.

Fourth and finally, technological advances in robotics and computing power have the potential drastically to alter transportation systems and their relationship to land use. We discuss the probable and potential impacts of driverless cars, virtual reality, three-dimensional printing, and drones on mobility and place-making in the following chapter. Some of these technologies may allow cities in the Global South to skip a generation of transportation technology, in particular the privately owned, personal motorized vehicle with an internal combustion engine. In telephony, cell phones were a similar leapfrog technology that had disproportionate benefits for poorer countries and cities that never established landlines. A World Bank study found that an additional ten cell phones per hundred households contributed to almost one percentage point in GDP per capita in the Global South.[76] Building on the new technology, places such as Kenya have become world leaders in providing mobile banking services and mobile-based currency. New transportation technologies may similarly have the biggest impacts in the Global South. Given high population density, low accessibility, and an entrepreneurial approach to transportation services, cities in the Global South may also lead the way in developing new transportation systems to meet the challenges of providing better accessibility for their fast-growing suburban areas.

10

Emerging Technologies

The digital revolution is giving way to a robotics revolution that is likely to touch nearly every aspect of human life. Scientists and enthusiasts are working to perfect the three-dimensional printing of meat, machine guns, and nearly everything in between. Medical advances are leading to longer, more active lives. Virtual reality goggles are not only changing how people consume videogames and movies but could change how they conduct meetings and communicate with loved ones. Auto manufacturers, technology giants, and startups are working to perfect the technologies that will allow cars, trucks, and buses to drive themselves safely on city streets in the coming decades. Many of these technological innovations will shape not just how people travel but how much they travel, where they choose to live and work, and what kinds of cities they inhabit.

This chapter explores what planning and designing cities beyond mobility means in a world of rapid technological change. Technologies such as smartphone-enabled ride-sharing services have already had significant impacts on cities and transportation systems. Self-driving cars could fundamentally alter how people travel—whether by car or transit—and have substantial spillover effects on urban form and the quality of local neighborhoods and downtowns. If cars drive themselves, furthermore, this will probably reduce the amount of urban space dedicated to parking and may even change how people pay for car travel. Advances in freight delivery and communication technologies will continue to influence how people shop and communicate, with implications for the balance between mobility and place.

Emerging technologies have the potential to encourage or hinder the growth of people-oriented cities. Throughout this chapter, we discuss new technologies' relationship to mobility and place with a tempered optimism. Although many new technologies could continue the current trajectory of favoring mobility over place, technological innovation offers a rare opportunity to break with the historical dependencies of a transportation and land use system that consumes excessive amounts of fossil fuels, urban land, and financial resources. The typical car sits idle 23 hours per day. When it is used, three out of four seats are often empty. For many trips, cars are vastly overpowered and oversized, relying on a two-ton steel cage to shuttle around a 150-pound person. With more than twice as many parking spaces as vehicles, most parking also sits idle, consuming land that could otherwise be used for housing, offices, or open space. New technologies present important and perhaps unprecedented opportunities to rebalance cities to focus more on people and places and less on mobility.

Ride-Hailing and Shared-Ride Services

The past decade has witnessed an explosive growth in new forms of urban mobility, ones that fill the vast spectrum between expensive, exclusive-ride taxi services and highly standardized, fixed-route, fixed-schedule bus services. Using smartphone technologies and riding the wave of increased collaborative consumption, a rich assortment of mobility providers today plies the streets of cities worldwide, from ride-hail services such as Uber and Lyft to various forms of microtransit, including private commuter minibuses, dynamic vanpools and carpools, and taxi-like ride-share services (e.g., UberPool and Lyft Line). New-age micromobility is hardly a developed-cities phenomenon: In Jakarta, a motorcycle taxi service called GoJek that uses smartphone apps for ride requests and payments has exploded onto the scene, as has BluJek, which offers motorcycle taxi services for women, operated by women. For consumers, new-age mobility services have been mostly good news, enriching their mobility choices by providing heretofore unprecedented levels of, in economist-talk, service and price points. Recent research on ride-hail services in San Francisco found that what appeals to customers most is convenience and time savings. Among the chief reasons people took Uber and Lyft were ease of payment and ride requests using smartphones plus short average wait times (compared with taxis).[1] To no surprise, this was particularly so among Millennials.

Although ride hailing could weaken the role of transit in cities (as was suggested in the San Francisco study), to the degree that Uber and Lyft users begin sharing rides in return for a break in fares, it could transform mass transit as we know it, elevating the mobility role of dynamic ridesharing worldwide. Shared ride hailing has become the fastest-growing market for companies such as Uber and Lyft. UberPool currently operates in more than thirty U.S. cities, claiming more than half of all Uber journeys in some.[2] In Los Angeles and San Francisco, more than 100,000 trips per week are by Uber Pool. In both cities, shared ride-hail services are flourishing, sometimes functioning as station cars, a form of micromobility envisaged to get passengers to and from stations on California's urban rail systems two decades ago,[3] with 14 percent of UberPool trips in Los Angeles and 10 percent in San Francisco starting or ending at rail transit stations.[4] The American Public Transportation Association, a lobbying organization for U.S. transit interests, has formally endorsed shared ride-hail services. Their view is that dynamic ridesharing enlarges the circus tent of collective ride travelers and complements traditional public transit. In Bogotá, Colombia, Uber serves districts unserved by the TransMilenio bus rapid transit (BRT) system, in addition to functioning as a perpendicular feeder to BRT stops.

What could be truly transformative, catapulting shared ride-hail services into the big leagues of urban mobility and advancing the adaptive transit model more than anything, is the mapping of and organizing services around hotspots (i.e., frequent passenger pickup and dropoff points). In return for walking a few blocks to a hotspot, customers get a break in fares. Hotspots convert the much more complicated ride matching of many-to-many trips to a much more tractable pattern of matching a few origins and a few destinations. It is infinitesimally easier for onboard computers to work out a traveling salesman algorithm to pick up multiple passengers along a route if people load and disembark at hotspots rather than their individual street addresses. This would also reduce the current problem of shared taxi passengers waiting at someone's house for another passenger to descend and enter the vehicle. As new technologies allow cars to drive themselves, the potential of ride-hailing and shared-ride services will only increase.

Driverless Cars: The Elephant in the Room

No new technology has captured the imagination and interest of futurists, architects, planners, and policymakers like driverless cars. Not only do driverless cars and other automated vehicles have the potential to reduce traffic fatalities, extend personal mobility to millions, and alter the way that most people travel, they could also fundamentally transform cities. In the United States, self-driving cars could reduce the amount of space dedicated to parking and roadways, improve the quality and coverage of transit services, reduce car ownership, and encourage more walking and biking. In cities in the Global South, where a minority of people drive, automated technologies could drastically improve the quality, speed, and efficiency of transit, particularly road-based transit in minivans and minibuses. As shown in chapter 9, the benefits of reducing transportation-related fatalities and injuries are greatest in the Global South.

Optimists envision a future where driverless cars lead to a revolution in shared urban mobility and inevitably reduce the harm our current transportation systems cause to the environment, people, and cities. In this optimistic vision, most people will not own cars but instead will rely on services provided by fleets of automated taxis and transit vehicles. Why own a car when you can summon one to pick you up while avoiding the worries of parking, insurance, or maintenance? Consumers will choose between single-occupant vehicles and larger shared vehicles, based on price, travel times, and personal preferences. Because people will now pay for vehicle travel per mile driven, instead of with lumpy vehicle and insurance payments, they will also be more likely to consider saving money by walking or biking. By reducing the need for urban parking spaces, furthermore, cities and towns will be able to dedicate substantially more space to making urban areas pleasant and safe for pedestrians and cyclists.

However, there are also reasons for pessimism. Although we would like nothing more than for a new transportation technology to lead unequivocally to the better environments, better economies, and better communities that we argue for in this book, driverless cars present several threats to sustainable urbanization. If, indeed, self-driving cars reduce the perceived and actual costs of driving, people will drive substantially more. If this happens, vehicle automation will be just one more in a long series of technologies that makes driving more comfortable and convenient. Households will tend to own their own vehicles, send them on errands, and even have them circle to avoid paying for parking in dense neighborhoods. Many cars may become full-time mobile offices, whisking people between meetings throughout the day and increasing the share of commuters who move regularly between metropolitan regions.

Self-driving cars will also expand personal mobility for the one-third of the Americans without drivers' licenses and the one-tenth of households without cars due to age, disability, low income, or preference. Expanded access to cars may be particularly valuable to the nation's older adults, many of whom live in and would like to remain in car-dependent communities. This increased access to private mobility will no doubt produce substantial benefits for consumers. These benefits will come in the form of increased mobility and at the expense of place, however. Even if self-driving cars double existing capacity, this capacity will fill quickly, and dispersed development will consume more land and erode the sustainability benefits from increased efficiency. Regional travel modelers in the United States have thus far predicted that self-driving cars will increase the total amount of driving by 5 to 25 percent.[5] In addition to driving longer distances, travelers may be even more disconnected from social interactions and public spaces. Passengers will move from private door to private door and never even have to look at the space they are moving through, instead consuming media through Internet-connected devices and consoles. This is not a successful recipe for building great places or social capital.

Tremendous uncertainty dogs efforts to predict how driverless cars will change cities or influence the many relationships between mobility and place. Because new technologies are expensive, and the average passenger car is more than 11 years old,[6] there will also probably be time to assess and influence the way self-driving cars affect cities and place. We remain cautiously optimistic that driverless cars, more than any new technology, will enable a new and better balance between mobility and place. After providing a brief summary of the current state of automated vehicle technologies, we discuss four ways that driverless cars are likely to disrupt the current relationship between mobility and place and could help spark a much-needed reordering of current urban priorities.

The State of Driverless Cars

Despite a long interest in the potential for and benefits of self-driving vehicles,[7] only recently has the confluence of rapid improvements in computer processing, satellite positioning, and laser sensing made this long-held dream a reality. In 2004, no research team's self-driving car managed to complete even a tenth of the Defense Advanced Research Projects Agency's 150-mile obstacle course designed to challenge autonomous vehicles and spur new technological innovations. A year later, five teams completed the challenge. Current systems rely on the Global Positioning System, cameras, and other sensors, particularly lidar (like radar but with lasers instead of radio), to detect a vehicle's location and the location of surrounding vehicles, people, and obstacles to remain safely in the center of a highway lane or move around on city streets (figure 10-1). Between zero and full autonomy is a range of functional controls such as adaptive center lane cruise control,

Figure 10-1. Carnegie Mellon Tartan Racing's winner of the 2007 Defense Advanced Research Projects Agency challenge. The image shows the range of sensors used on an automated vehicle. (Source: Carnegie Mellon Tartan Racing.)

which can take over the driving task on highways but requires the driver to remain attentive and ready to take over the task of driving at short notice.

Most major car manufacturers already market and sell high-end vehicles with features such as automated braking, self-parking, lane departure warning, and variable-speed cruise control. Most, along with technology firms, are also racing to develop fully autonomous vehicles. Nissan announced that it plans to mass market cars with automated steering, braking, and acceleration by 2020. Ford Motor Companies has set a goal of producing fully autonomous cars by 2021.[8] Google has logged more than 2 million miles of driving in its autonomous vehicles and developed a prototype car with no brake pedal, accelerator, or steering wheel.[9] Uber has begun testing self-driving taxis in Pittsburgh, Pennsylvania, although testing engineers remain behind the wheel to monitor the system and ensure safety. Daimler is testing an autonomous eighteen-wheeler prototype on public roads in Nevada.[10] Many transit agencies and airports already have decades of experience operating driverless trains on fixed guideways,[11] and the European Union–funded City-Mobil2, French company EZ10, the Delft Technological University, Delphi Automotive in partnership with the Singapore Land Transportation Authority, and the many others are already testing driverless minibuses on public streets and private campuses.[12]

Although technological hurdles remain—particularly in regard to poor weather, low-cost remote sensing, and changing road conditions—fully autonomous vehicles that have the potential to reshape transportation and cities will be commercially available and driving themselves on city streets and highways in the next 5 to 20 years. These will dramatically influence traffic safety, the amount of space dedicated to mobility, the quantity and quality of transit, and the way that consumers pay for mobility.

Safety

By removing humans and human error from the driving task, self-driving vehicles are likely to reduce traffic collisions substantially.[13] This puts autonomous vehicles in a long line of technological improvements that have made driving ever safer. Over the past 20 years in the United States, the number of traffic fatalities per capita and per mile driven have decreased by 50 and 60 percent, respectively. Unlike with other safety improvements, however, self-driving cars may also reduce the number and perhaps proportion of pedestrian fatalities, which have remained stubbornly flat or risen in the United States and many other countries despite an otherwise improving safety record. In 2015 and 2016, the number of pedestrians killed in traffic collisions increased and reached the highest level in two decades. The precise cause of the rise is unknown, but drivers distracted by cell phones is a likely culprit.

In addition to removing human error, driverless cars will tend to be conservative, law-abiding, and polite drivers. A computer system will never get annoyed, experience road rage, or intentionally threaten or harm another road user. This is particularly important in urban areas, where drivers frequently speed, run stop signs, honk at pedestrians, and fail to yield at crosswalks, behaviors that make walking less safe and less pleasant. If pedestrians know and trust autonomous vehicles to interact safely and politely, they will be much more comfortable using unmarked crosswalks and even jaywalking.[14] Thus driverless cars will make walking faster, more pleasant, and more common in dense urban areas, where aggressive driving often keeps pedestrians off the streets.

Changing this dynamic relationship between drivers and pedestrians could have a transformative effect over time as dense, urban streets become ever more pedestrian-oriented. Bicyclists may also benefit. Perceived safety risk is the number one deterrent to bicycle use, and reliably safe and predictable self-driving vehicles would vastly improve cycling conditions, even in cities with little or no cycling infrastructure. Thus driverless cars may have important, unanticipated, and beneficial side effects for pedestrians and cyclists. These benefits will have to be programmed into autonomous vehicles, however. Although popular newspaper articles have focused on unusual ethical dilemmas a car might face in specific circumstances—such as the choice between driving off the side of a cliff or running over a group of school children—far more important will be the overarching programming decisions about how fast vehicles may drive in urban settings, how conservatively they behave around pedestrians, and whether they follow all rules of the road, such as coming to a complete stop at a stop sign. The National Association of City Transportation Officials, an organization representing the largest American cities, has recommended that automated vehicles be limited to 25 miles per hour in urban settings as a safeguard to pedestrians and cyclists.[15]

Expanding Transit Options

Automated vehicle technologies may also dramatically reduce the cost of providing transit, particularly in smaller vehicles such as cars and minibuses. The cost of hiring drivers makes it prohibitively expensive for most transit agencies to run smaller vehicles with more frequent service, a practice that would otherwise be attractive to passengers. Indeed, transit may be one of the first sectors where vehicle automation thrives. Many transit agencies and airports already have decades of experience operating driverless trains on fixed guideways, the European Union–funded CityMobil2 (figure 10-2) has already begun testing driverless transit on public street, campuses such as Carnegie Mellon's are already developing self-driving shuttles, and French startup EasyMile has built a twelve-passenger driverless shuttle to provide transit in Paris.[16] Some metropolitan planners in the United States are hopeful driverless vehicles can facilitate the provision of flexible and frequent transit service in smaller vehicles that can compete with the speed and convenience of private cars or provide last-mile service in lower-density suburban neighborhoods.[17]

Figure 10-2. CityMobil2 bus operating on public right of way. (Photo by Technalia, Flickr creative commons.)

In the United States and Europe, automated vehicle technologies may also lead to a rapid reentry of the private sector into the business of providing transit services. Before the 1960s, private companies provided nearly all bus and rail services in American cities. Only as the services became unprofitable and began closing did the public sector take on the role as the primary provider of transit. In Europe, private firms are still common but receive subsidies to provide service. If new technologies substantially reduce the costs of providing transit service and the ability to increase the value of transit (e.g., by making it better able to move passengers from door to door instead of station to station), the private sector could rapidly expand its provision of transit services. Already, companies such as Chariot and Uber have entered the market, providing cell phone–enabled luxury bus services along popular transit routes in major cities and pooled taxi services. Large employers, such as Google and Apple, provide bus services for their many employees who live in San Francisco and Oakland but commute to the Silicon Valley. Whether driverless cars increase or decrease the total amount of driving will depend largely on the extent to which large technology and vehicle manufacturers provide shared ride services or sell self-driving vehicles to individual consumers.

In cities in the Global South, the potential gains from automated transit are probably even larger. As discussed in the previous section, substantial numbers of urban residents in the Global South rely on privately provided transit in minivans or minibuses for daily motorized travel, even in cities with metros or BRT networks. If automation can reduce the cost and improve the service of these vehicles, this could slow or even halt the rapid growth in private car ownership and use. Most optimistically, automated transit might provide a leapfrog technology that helps emerging countries increase personal mobility without environmentally, socially, and economically costly investments in new roads, transit infrastructure, parking, and lower-density settlement patterns. As with cell phones and telephony, vehicle automation could help residents skip an entire generation of the predominant mobility technology. If new technologies can help disconnect increased mobility from decreased quality of place, then residents of middle-income cities that are transit reliant—such as those in China, Latin America, and India—will benefit substantially in the near future. Despite the need for faster, safer, and more reliable transit, however, the poorest cities in the Global South will probably be among the last places to adopt expensive new labor-saving technologies because wages are low and investment dollars are scarce.

A Parking Revolution

Whether automated vehicles spark a transformation in transit and shared urban mobility, parking in cities will change. This is no small impact. In his book *The High Cost of Free Parking*, Donald Shoup calls parking policy perhaps the greatest disaster in American city planning and estimates that the total cost of all parking in the United States is as high as or higher than the total value of the private car fleet.[18] Others have estimated that adding parking to the life-cycle emissions calculations of private cars increases emissions by 25 to 90 percent for many local pollutants and greenhouse gases.[19] Parking is also one of the largest consumers of urban land (see figure 6-4).[20] Even in dense cities, substantial space is given away to park private vehicles, at the expense of more housing, shops, offices, open space, and other public amenities. Much of this space sits unused at any given time, and the number of parking spaces may exceed the number of vehicles by as much as eight spaces per car in some cities.[21]

Even if driverless cars have little effect on car ownership or driving rates, the effect on parking and its relationship to other land uses will be substantial. Rather than circling for an open space in difficult-to-park neighborhoods—an estimated quarter to half of all traffic in popular commercial neighborhoods[22]—travelers will exit cars at the front door of their destinations. In turn, private cars will probably identify and move to the least expensive places to park within a short pickup time of the owner. Shared vehicles will park only when passenger demand is low and may—like bus, rail, and truck fleets—be stored in large warehouses or open lots in low-value parts of cities. Even in easy-to-park places such as suburban office parks or shopping malls, automated cars will drop passengers near the main entrances before moving on to the next passenger or searching for a low-cost and convenient parking space.

In short, parking—one of the largest land consumers and a substantial impediment to planning for people and places—will be largely decoupled from other land uses. Entire lanes of on-street parking might now be easily reused for widened sidewalks, urban cycle tracks, open space, or even commercial uses such as food trucks. In addition to reclaiming space from parking, this decoupling will facilitate the reuse and historic preservation of older buildings where parking availability may be lower than the market supports or current regulations allow.

Getting the Price of Car Travel Right

Vehicle automation may also help revolutionize how people and societies pay for roadways and travel. Although transportation experts often disagree on specific policies, few disagree that the cost of car travel, including parking, is substantially underpriced. Chapters 2, 3, and 4 describe some of the high costs automobiles impose in terms of traffic congestion, environmental pollution, traffic fatalities, and degraded public space. In the current system, where the public sector provides roadways, private companies sell vehicles and fuel, and the general public consumes transportation services, appropriately pricing the transportation system has been challenging and elusive. To date only a handful of cities, such as Singapore and London, charge motorists to enter the most congested parts of the cities. Although these programs have been successful, current congestion-charging technologies—based on video cameras in London and electronic gantries in Singapore—are fairly expensive and clunky to administer. Where taxes are imposed more generally, such as with fuel taxes, revenues are used to expand roadways, not to offset the environmental, economic, or social costs imposed on others.

Driverless cars have the potential to lead to a more appropriate pricing of car travel and to shift more of the costs of driving to the margin, as trips are made, instead of lumpy payments for insurance, storage, repairs, or vehicle purchases. Because driverless cars will have built-in technologies that know where and at what time a car consumes road space, it will also be technically fairly simple to charge for road space where and when it is consumed. If these charges happen at the margin, as with a toll, drivers will become more cognizant about avoiding congested parts of the city during congested times of day and about the pollution they impose on others. The latter is particularly important because poorer households, which tend to drive the least, often bear the highest pollution costs.[23] Technology and automotive companies will begin to offer a variety of pricing packages to consumers. Many consumers will continue to prefer to pay for automobility with monthly or annual lump-sum payments. Others, however, will choose to pay for each trip individually and choose between walking, driving, transit, and biking based on price, travel time, and convenience. This will be particularly common in cities. Finally, driver-less technologies may lead to a shift in vehicle ownership patterns, with more vehicles owned by large companies such as Ford, Toyota, Uber, and Lyft. Politically and logistically, it is far simpler to tax a small number of companies for the costs they impose on society than it is to tax the public at large. Thus automated vehicles will make congestion pricing not only cheaper, easier, and more flexible to administer but also more publicly palatable.

Freight Movement in Cities

In addition to transforming passenger movements, new technologies are changing and will continue to change how goods are produced, moved, and consumed in cities. These changes could substantially influence the balance between mobility and place. Already, three-dimensional printing is leading to a revival in small manufacturing, much of it based in cities. If the technology continues apace, it could bring substantial amounts of manufacturing closer to the location of consumers. This would have transformative impacts on global freight flows, affecting not only Asian manufacturing hubs but also port cities such as Newark, Los Angeles, and Baltimore. On one hand, this would lower the amount of trucking and associated pollution in affected cities. On the other hand, it could lead to substantial economic restructuring that harms cities with a high economic reliance on port activities.

Within cities, freight and logistics companies will probably be among the first to adopt new technologies. Already in 2014, more than $1 trillion in retail goods were purchased online, 6 percent of retail sales worldwide. Online shopping continues to trend upward. The nature of urban goods movement is changing accordingly, from truckloads of mer-chandise hauled to brick-and-mortar stores to parcels and packages carried to purchasers' front doors. With Millennials leading the way in online purchases and increasingly living in urban centers, these trends have created new logistical challenges, notably more and more delivery trucks converging on and traveling in central neighborhoods and compact urban districts. Big e-commerce players, such as Amazon, have opened freight warehouse consolidation–distribution centers on the peripheries and in the exurbs of numerous U.S. cities. Many are also developing technologies and plans to deliver smaller packages with automated drones.

More immediately, logistics companies are using algorithms to reduce the amount of travel on congested central-city streets to reduce the costs of parcel delivery. Still, new, somewhat unprecedented problems continue to crop up, such as increased noise, fumes, and traffic disruption in residential neighborhoods and worsening pavement damage from steady flows of FedEx, UPS, DHL, and other package delivery carriers. These carriers treat parking tickets in urban areas as another cost of business. The arrival of more and more delivery trucks has prompted some to insist that staging areas, curbside spaces, and even passageways be provided for these carriers, in keeping with complete streets principles. Parcel trucks are legitimate users of street space, and like cyclists and pedestrians, it is argued, they need to be accommodated. Some even call for wider roads and thicker pavements to accommodate rising numbers of parcel delivery trucks. To do so, however, would embrace mobility over place by designing communities to accommodate movements (in this case, of parcel trucks), possibly at the expense of neighborhood quality, safety, and livability. Consistent with the themes of this book, a reordering of priorities would mean planning and designing neighborhoods for people and places rather than packages, parcels, and parcel trucks. A people- and place-focused strategy might call for the siting of dropoff/pickup bins (perhaps near neighborhood bus stops) or the conversion of vacant stores in outdated local shopping plazas or even abandoned school buildings into parcel pickup areas, which could reduce the number of delivery trucks driving around neighborhoods. Although we remain hopeful about new freight delivery technologies, these have the potential to harm as well as improve place. Thousands of automated delivery drones may reduce truck travel in cities and make it easier to order goods more quickly, but they will almost certainly have some unanticipated and unpleasant effects on urban quality of life.

Communication Technologies

With the proliferation of mass automobility and telephony in the 1960s, planning scholar Melvin Webber argued that proximity and place were losing value and, as a result, people would abandon cities for what he called the Non-Place Urban Realm.[24] Others predicted that the Internet and advances in teleconferencing would reduce the need for travel or face-to-face meetings. Much the opposite has occurred. As technology has connected people, face-to-face meetings have retained and even grown in importance. Millennials are choosing cell phones over cars. And cities such as New York, Philadelphia, and Boston have increased in population for the first time since Webber's prediction. Even as parents and the press worry about the impact of video games on children's physical activities and mental health, the world's most popular game of 2016, Pokémon Go, has brought millions out into public spaces and parks and appears to be influencing how much children walk, get outside, and socialize.[25] Dating apps have revolutionized the way that young people meet and increased the desirability of living in big cities with larger pools of prospective partners and convenient places to meet and socialize in person.

A great deal of uncertainty surrounds how people and firms will respond to substantial advances in virtual or augmented reality technologies. Almost certainly, they will help increase the share of workers who work from home, a share that has increased steadily from 2 percent to about 4 percent since the U.S. Census started keeping track in 1980. However, past trends suggest that as communication provides a substitute for mobility, people choose to live closer together instead of farther apart. If this trend continues, it suggests that cities and regions that emphasize place over mobility will be most attractive to new residents.

The Realm of Possibility

In 1917, it would have been hard to imagine how new technologies were going to affect cities and travel over the next century. The world was at war in Europe. Airplanes were novelties. Although mass motorization had started in the United States, electric streetcars were on the rise and dominated urban transportation systems.[26] Modern medicine and sanitation had improved dramatically, but city officials had to try to balance public health along with place and mobility. For every prediction that futurists got right, they got a dozen wrong. In 2017, advances in computing power are sparking rapid advances in communications, robotics, medicine, sensing, energy production, and manufacturing. These will have profound, though highly uncertain, impacts on human settlements, transportation systems, and travel behavior.

The rapid nature of these advances—just 5 years ago driverless cars felt like a futurist fantasy to most outside of the industry and many within—is shortening the horizon of uncertainty. As the head of Carnegie Mellon's Robotics Lab, ground zero of much of the recent innovation in automated vehicle technologies, put it in a recent interview, "I've been doing robotics for two decades, and if you look at the progress made between 1995 to 2005, in the past couple years we've seen more progress than in that whole decade."[27] To put the pace of innovation in context, it took more than a century to advance from the first automobile to the mass-produced Ford Model T and another half century before the car's influence on settlement patterns, travel behavior, and the environment were starting to be acknowledged. A hundred years of past technological innovation may now be compressed into a decade or two (Apple sold its first iPhone just 10 years ago). Put another way, our consideration of how new technology will influence mobility and place should perhaps be accorded the same level of uncertainty as H. G. Wells's *Anticipations* of how the mechanical progress at the end of the nineteenth century would influence the twentieth century. Some predictions will be right. Others will be wrong. Most will be right in some ways but wrong in others.

When technology changes quickly, so does its influence on and relationship to society. The realm of possibility is far wider than what we can hope to cover in this chapter.

Within this realm of possibility, moreover, is the possibility that new technologies will have only a marginal influence on travel behavior or settlement patterns. Nevertheless, we argue that a renewed focus on place is in order. New technologies will probably create numerous opportunities to better balance mobility and place but also to continue the modern trajectory of increasing mobility at the expense of place. If the history of the private car and urban highways is any guide, taking advantage of these opportunities will require a committed focus on place, rather than an uncritical embrace of new technology.

11

Toward Sustainable Urban Futures

This book advances the idea of moving beyond mobility as a platform for achieving more sustainable urban futures. The first chapter adopted the term *urban recalibration* as a framework for doing so. Rather than sweeping reforms or a Kuhnian paradigm shift, urban recalibration calls for a series of calculated steps aimed at a strategic longer-range vision of a city's future, advancing principles of people-oriented development and place-making every bit as much as private car mobility, if not more. Rather than driving down sustainability metrics such as vehicle miles traveled (VMT) per capita in one fell swoop through dramatic changes, it entails a series of 1 to 2 percent recalibration "victories"—intersection by intersection, neighborhood by neighborhood—that cumulatively move beyond the historically almost singular focus on mobility, making for better communities, better environments, and better economies. With urban recalibration, change is more evolutionary than revolutionary.

We concede that the ideas advanced in this book are not necessarily new. However, assembling the latest thinking and research in a single volume, and reflecting on contemporary challenges such as information technologies and developing cities, we hope, materially helps in moving us beyond mobility. The seeds of recalibrating the planning of cities and downsizing the role of mobility can be found in early commentaries on new-age technologies and their implications for cities and travel. In 1995, this book's first author wrote a commentary titled "Why Go Anywhere" that laid out core principles of *Beyond Mobility* in the sesquicentennial anniversary of *Scientific American*:

> *The past 150 years has been a self-perpetuating cycle of urban transportation advances and decentralization. . . . One sensible and compelling alternative (to intelligent transportation technologies) would be to reduce the need to travel in the first place through . . . appropriately designed communities that put most destinations within walking or bicycle-riding distance, and telecommunications, computers and other technologies that let many people work from their homes or from facilities nearby. . . . The difference between advancing these costly transportation technologies as opposed to designing new kinds of sustainable communities is the difference between automobility and accessibility. Enhancing automobility—the ability to get from place to place in the convenience of one's own car—is and has been the dominant paradigm guiding transportation investments throughout this century. Accessibility, in contrast, is about creating places that reduce the need to travel and, in so doing, conserve resources, protect the environment and promote social justice. Have technology, will travel; have sustainable communities, will prosper.*[1]

Density and Design

Implicit in a lot of this book's discussions is the densification of cities. Denser cities have been associated with lower per capita transport energy consumption and VMT, although the consensus view is that it's what often accompanies density (e.g., mixed land uses that shorten distances, higher-quality transit services, expensive parking) that influences travel, not building heights or block massing.[2] Location also matters. Almost any development in a central location will generate fewer car trips than the best-designed, compact mixed-use project in a remote location.[3] Public policies can be just as important, particularly in combination with compact, pedestrian-friendly development. A 2006 pilot test of VMT charges in Portland, Oregon, for example, found a larger decline in VMT among those living in dense, mixed-use neighborhoods than those living elsewhere.[4]

The relationship between urban densities, traffic congestion, and quality of life is rather perplexing. In high-income countries, the densest cities are often among the most traffic choked. Based on data from millions of TomTom navigation device users, the company ranks dense yet popular tourist destinations such as Rome, London, Paris, San Francisco, New York, and Sydney as among the world's most congested high-income cities.[5] Even in such eminently walkable cities with world-class transit, as long as automobiles (including taxis) are prevalent, high population densities translate into high traffic densities and thus congestion.

Yet traffic snarls do not always equate with poor quality of living. Take Vancouver, British Columbia, for example. In 2013, greater Vancouver was ranked by TomTom as North America's most congested metro area. Yet the Economist Intelligence Unit ranked Vancouver the most livable city in the world in 2011, and even in its latest (2016) listing, Vancouver was ranked third worldwide and tops among North American cities.[6] Being stuck in traffic is something everyone abhors and for many reflects a deteriorating quality of life. Yet experiences in places such as Vancouver (the only North American city without a grade-separated freeway) prompt us to question the very idea of congestion as a negative externality. There is "good" congestion and "bad" congestion, just as there's good and bad cholesterol. In Vancouver, good congestion reflects a vibrant, highly animated, mixed-use, pedestrian-friendly city, one that has refrained from overinvesting in motorways and directed sizable resources to green modes and urban place-making. There is also bad congestion, particularly outside the Vancouver proper, where many suburbs and exurbs are as car dependent as those south of the forty-ninth parallel. However, in well-designed cities such as Vancouver, many travelers have respectable options to avoid congestion, such as cycling to work, taking transit, or living in a mixed-use community (although wealthy folks admittedly are better able to do so than others). In short, traffic congestion is not all bad; it goes with the territory of being in a dense, compact city and can spawn and reinforce walkable, mixed-use neighborhoods.

Several key aspects of urban density are important to weigh in advancing sustainable urban futures. First, the relationship between travel and density is nonlinear, notably following an exponential decay function. What this means is that the biggest declines in car use and VMT per capita occur when going from the very low densities of large-lot suburban housing to the densities of two- to three-story walkup apartments and town-homes found in traditional neighborhoods. High-rise and even midrise, Hong Kong–style buildings are not necessary for substantially driving down VMT.[7] Second, how densities are organized matters. The suburbs of Stockholm, for instance, have "articulated densities" concentrated along urban rail corridors, akin to "necklaces of pearls."[8] This contrasts with the suburbs of Los Angeles, whose blended densities are actually higher than those of Stockholm, but rather than focusing on transit corridors, they tend to be spread along main arteries and local streets.[9] Stockholm averages much higher transit ridership rates than Los Angeles partly as a result.[10] Last but not least, urban design matters.[11] Studies show that urban amenities and high-quality designs—ones that create comfortable, memorable, and legible urban spaces—soften peoples' perceptions of density.[12] With high-quality urban designs and place-making, urban densities can be bumped up, higher than might normally be accepted, so as to make public transit investments and operations cost-effective.[13] And as described throughout this book, a host of side benefits accrue from compact growth, be they a stronger attachment of residents to their neighborhoods, the feeling of security that comes from more eyes on the street, or active living.

Megatrends and Urban Futures

The preceding chapter discussed a host of unfolding technological advances that pose significant challenges in charting sustainable urban futures. In addition to speed-enhancing technologies such as autonomous vehicles, several powerful megatrends also need to be weighed in recalibrating the planning and design of twenty-first-century cities. Several of these are discussed below.

Aging Societies

The fastest-growing age group worldwide is people 60 years of age and older, who currently make up about 12 percent of global population, up from 8 percent in 1950.[14] Growing at a rate of 3.26 percent annually, those 60 years and over will make up nearly a quarter of the world's population by 2050, except in the poorest continent, Africa. Societal aging is most pronounced in East Asian countries such as Japan and Taiwan, where the shapes of population pyramids have dramatically flipped over the past half century, from bottom-heavy pyramids to top-heavy torsos. In advanced economies, graying societies are a product of declining birth rates (owing in part to changing roles of women), tight immigration policies, and medical advances and health-conscious living that have increased longevity.

Reverberations from societal aging include shrinking cities, all the more pronounced where globalization, deindustrialization, and social forces (e.g., race and class segregation) have gutted the interiors of many industrial-era cities, particularly in America's Rust Belt and Europe. Although some economically stagnant shrinking cities such as Detroit, Dresden, and Riga pose significant policy challenges, there are nonetheless untapped opportunities for urban regeneration and place-making when population is in decline. Notably, thoughtfully planned shrinking cities could support some of the transformative road contraction and land reclamation ideas discussed in chapters 4, 5, and 8 of this book. Experiences suggest such initiatives can spawn economic growth.

Certain aspects of aging societies could reduce auto-mobility and by extension favor transit-supportive growth, such as less household consumption as more and more people approach the later stages of life; residential downsizing and empty-nesting to urban cores; and a growing appreciation for walking, cycling, and other forms of "active transport" as a means to stay physically fit. On the other hand, other aspects of aging could increase mobility and car-oriented development, such as comparatively wealthy (owing in part to home price appreciation) and thus mobile older households, aging in place in car-oriented suburbs, and autonomous vehicles that offer door-to-door auto-mobility to seniors who otherwise would not be able to drive. Public policies, notably those that influence the cost of owning and using cars and that promote safe, secure mixed-use neighborhoods, will be instrumental in nudging the influences of aging in one direction or the other.

Shifting Lifestyle Preferences and the Millennials

Millennials are radically transforming the cultural landscapes of modern societies. Twenty- and thirty-somethings are far less drawn to the auto-oriented lifestyle of their parents.[15] Unlike Baby Boomers, for whom ownership of two major and costly assets—houses and automobiles—tended to be lifelong goals, Millennials are more inclined to direct their incomes to electronic gadgets, travel, eating out, going to concerts, and other life experiences.[16] According to one recent survey, 30 percent of U.S. Millennials are willing to give up owning a car even if it means paying more to travel.[17] Increasing shares of Americans aged 18 to 35 without driver's licenses further underscore dramatic lifestyle shifts that are under way.[18] Not unrelated, distances driven are falling fastest among Millennials.[19] Those in their twenties to forties are also fueling the meteoric growth in collaborative consumption, underscored by Airbnb's popularity for short-term rentals and the omnipresence of ride-hail services such as Uber and Lyft in trend-setting cities such as San Francisco and London.

Millennials are also reshaping the geomorphology of cities. Many are drawn to accessible, walkable mixed-use neighborhoods in traditional urban cores.[20] Mixed-use environments that support a live–work–shop–learn–play lifestyle are particularly popular, as is good public transit access. Over the past decade, young adults have increased as a proportion of residents in the center of nearly every U.S. city while falling as a proportion across all other areas.[21] Although in total numbers more Millennials are taking up residence in the suburbs, this is mainly because most cannot afford to live in the gentrified urban core.[22] If they could, they would. When living downtown or nearby, Millennials and their neighbors tend to own fewer cars, are less likely to drive or have a license, and are much more likely to walk, take transit, or hail an app-based ride than are residents of other parts of a city.[23]

And where Millennials go, so do employers. Over the past 5 years, America's fastest job growth has been in urban areas, reversing the past few decades of job suburbanization.[24] In the Seattle area, tech firms such as Amazon, Expedia, and Microsoft have moved offices from suburban campuses and car-oriented edge cities to downtown Seattle and surroundings to be closer to young professionals. It's no coincidence that ride-hail services such as Uber and Lyft are experiencing double-digit annual growth in Seattle.

Twenty-First-Century Employment

Structural shifts in employment, fueled by globalization, modernization, and automation, have also profoundly changed urban landscapes and how workers move about them, particularly among Millennials. Yesteryear's model of lifelong employment and rising through the ranks of vertically integrated firms is being replaced by contingent employment, marked by horizontal networks of independent contractors, consultants, free agents, freelancers, part-timers, and outsourcing. Part-time, contingent work has always risen during difficult economic times, but recent trends suggest it's here to stay, even in robust periods. Involuntary part-time work surged during the Great Recession of 2008–2010, but unlike in the past, it has remained high during the recovery.[25] Fluidity and flexibility—whether in the form of rapid job turnover, the proliferation of startups and mergers, LinkedIn networking for short-term assignments, or monthly changes in workplace locations—is the new reality of twenty-first-century urban economies.

Job fluidity coupled with trends such as shrinking household sizes will probably shape not only built environments but also future travel. Both factors work in favor of less traditional, more atomized forms of urban mobility. A recent study of app-based ride-hail services in San Francisco, for example, found most users to be college-educated professionals in their twenties who live alone or with another person.[26] Part-time, contingent work has also probably contributed to the spread of travel over hours of the day and days of week. In the United States, the share of commute trips occurring between 7 and 8 a.m. fell 5 percent from 2000 to 2011.[27] Although such trends help relieve peak-hour congestion, they also nurture mixed-use development, reflected by retail shops and "third places" such as Starbucks drawing most of their customers in the off-peak hours and on weekends.[28]

Beyond Mobility Metrics

Urban recalibration implies new metrics for gauging and assessing the performance of cities and the transportation systems that serve them. Traditionally, transportation system performance has been based primarily on vehicular speeds and delays, that is, mobility. In 1995, Reid Ewing wrote a seminal article that proposed extending and enriching performance metrics. He called for three other metrics that go beyond mobility: sustainability, accessibility, and livability.[29] We include a fourth addition: affordability.

Mobility and Sustainability

Getting the calculus right for gauging transportation system performance is critically important to recalibrating urban landscapes and creating great places. As Ewing and others have pointed out, if infill development adds traffic and increases delay, which usually is the case in the near term, denying such development simply pushes growth outward, often in a more automobile-oriented configuration. Some cities and states (notably Florida) have modified concurrency rules and impact fee programs to accept a worsening of roadway conditions in some areas as long as conditions do not deteriorate in others—called area-wide averaging of levels of service (LOS).[30]

More common in recent years have been multimodal LOS standards that support infill development by allowing roadway LOS to decline as long as LOS for other modes, including walking and cycling, improves.[31] Multimodal metrics embrace the idea of plan-ning for complete streets to accommodate all road users, regardless of vehicle speed, bulk, or weight. In recent years, a flurry of tools has surfaced, many of them available online, to assess "level and quality of service" for walking (e.g., "walk score"), cycling (e.g., "the bicycle compatibility index"), and riding transit ("transit capacity and quality of service manual"). Tools for assessing walking and cycling LOS typically reflect factors such as network connectivity and continuity, intersection designs, traffic protection, topography, cleanliness and upkeep, and wayfinding. Experiences from cities such as Zurich reveal the profound changes that can occur when introducing a multimodal framework that weighs throughputs of people versus vehicles. In Zurich's case this led to a citywide reallocation of road space and signal timings that favored trams, buses, pedestrians, and cyclists over cars.[32]

Some cities have introduced other metrics along the lines suggested by Ewing. Since the mid-1990s, Portland, Oregon, and Boulder, Colorado, have been tracking trends in VMT per capita to gauge progress in achieving citywide sustainability goals. Portland planners often boast, justifiably, that citywide VMT has steadily declined over the last two decades, owing to many years of linking transportation and land use. With the passage of Senate Bill 743, California has recently elevated VMT as the principal metric for assess-ing traffic-related environmental impacts of new development. Before its passage, envi-ronmental review had been used to block or delay environmentally meritorious projects such as the San Francisco Bicycle Plan. Across the bay, the city of Oakland has jettisoned roadway LOS altogether, replacing it with VMT per capita in all of its California Environ-mental Quality Act assessments.

Also encouraging are adjustments being introduced by the transportation engineering profession that reflect the sustainability and VMT-reducing benefits of design and com-munity reforms. New design guidelines from the American Association of State Highway and Transportation Officials contain sections on road-dieting, context-sensitive designs, and complete streets. The National Association of City Transportation Officials has like-wise issued new urban street design guidelines that embrace many of the traffic taming and active mobility ideas discussed in earlier chapters. Moreover, the latest versions of the Institute of Transportation Engineers *Trip Generation* and *Parking Generation* manuals incorporate adjustments for mixed-use projects and TOD, reflecting research that shows such developments can reduce vehicle trip rates and parking demand by more than 40 percent.[33]

Accessibility

Accessibility, a cornerstone of designing cities for people and places, has long been used by academics to study the effects of residential location on property values, employ-ment, VMT, and the like. It is also universally embraced by city planning boards, state transportation departments, and virtually all governments that have formally endorsed sustainable transportation. In the United States, a number of metropolitan planning organizations routinely track changes in access to job opportunities to guide long-range transportation planning. However, operationalizing and assigning monetary values to increased accessibility is challenging. Although willingness-to-pay estimates and land value appreciations have been used in the past to monetize accessibility benefits, such indirect measures are fraught with difficulties, often relegating accessibility to a sidebar informational item. Accessibility measures rarely enter into the benefit–cost calculus for guiding long-range transportation investment decisions.[34]

Elevating the role of accessibility in evaluating transportation system performance is critically important to achieving sustainable urban futures. Because of factors such as induced travel demand, studies have repeatedly shown that capital investments in roads and transit systems rarely measurably reduce travel times or delay; instead, they increase the number and length of trips.[35] Their chief benefit, then, is to increase opportunities to reach the places that people often want to go—that is, they increase access, not mobility.

An example of how accessibility metrics might be used to guide transportation investments comes from Fabio Casiroli's cross-city study of access via cars versus transit.[36] Casiroli examined how many residences could be reached from the main tourist hub of cities such as São Paulo (Praça da Sé) and London (Trafalgar Square) within 45 minutes during the afternoon. In the case of São Paulo, he found that more than twice as many homes could be reached from Praça da Sé within 45 minutes by car than by transit, even in one of the world's most notoriously gridlocked cities. If decarbonizing and decluttering the city are long-range goals of São Paulo's civic leaders, then reducing this two-to-one differential would be an important metric of progress. A smaller ratio would also better reflect benefits that accrue from metro rail and BRT improvements than would an estimate of travel time savings.

Elevating the role of accessibility over mobility in evaluating projects helps those living in poverty, particularly in places such as São Paulo. Travel time savings accrue mainly to motorists, yet many poor people in the developing world do not own a car. Their values of time are substantially less than for the motoring class. The ability to widen the territorial sphere for job searching, saving on food purchases, reaching medical clinics, and seeking educational opportunities is likely to benefit the poor more than saving a few minutes of time moving along an expanded roadway. Data bear this out. Studies show the poor are willing to trade travel time delays in return for lower transit fares or fuel prices; that is, they tend to be more price-sensitive and less-time sensitive than the nonpoor.[37] More social uprisings have been sparked by increases in fuel prices and bus fares than by delays in travel time.

Livability

Even more difficult to quantify and apply are measures of quality of life. Companies such as Mercer and the Economist Intelligence Unit produce annual quality-of-life rankings of global cities to guide local governments in economic development planning and corporations making employee relocation decisions. Besides quality of transportation services and traffic congestion levels, Mercer's rankings are based on factors such as political stability, crime rates, banking services, medical facilities, pollution levels, recreational offerings, climate, and housing prices. Within the United States, the livability.com Web site ranks the hundred best cities to live based on three core criteria: access to desirable things (e.g., reputable schools, good infrastructure, low-crime neighborhoods, and pleasant climates), affordability (of housing, transport, health care, and food), and diversity (not only sociodemographically but also in terms of travel alternatives and grocery options such as the presence of open-air markets).

Similar factors often weigh in when gauging livability at a finer geographic level. What is indisputable is the importance of a safe, pedestrian-friendly environment. Being able to get to everyday activities within a 5-minute walk is pretty much a prerequisite these days to being in an attractive, livable neighborhood. The Walk Score Web site reflects this: Walkability is tied to the number of amenities (i.e., shops, parks, theaters, schools and "other common destinations") that are within a quarter-mile (about 5 minutes) up to 1 mile (about 20 minutes) of one's address. Amenities within a quarter-mile receive the highest points, falling to a score of zero at a mile and beyond.

Affordability

Affordability is an important add-on to the principle of accessible cities. Even if activities or modes are close by, unless people can afford to use them, they are not accessible. For many living in the developing world, the availability of reliable and affordable bus and rail services can make the difference between being integrated into the economic and social life of a city or not. The share of marginalized city dwellers with poor access to essential facilities and services, such as public transport and clean water, is increasing worldwide.[38] As discussed in chapter 9, in Mexico City's outskirts, beyond the city's metro network, residents sometimes take two or three different *colectivos* to reach metro terminals to access day jobs in the urban core.[39] In Mexico City and elsewhere in the Global South, travel can consume 25 percent or more of daily wages, making it hard for households to own a home and build wealth.[40]

Designing cities and transport systems to increase accessibility and affordability materially helps the poor. This is particularly so for mass transportation. Priority should be given to investing in busways rather than metros to keep fares affordable. In Brazil, transit is kept affordable via national legislation, called Vale Transport, which requires employers to provide bus passes for commuting expenses that exceed 6 percent of work- ers' earnings. Through World Bank support, the Brazilian cities of Rio de Janeiro and São Paul recently introduced Bilhete Unico (single ticket), wherein free transfers can be made between private buses and public trains. Moreover, affordable housing should be sited in transit-served corridors. In Cairo tens of thousands of low-income households have been relocated to transit-accessible sites in recent years to help lower travel costs.

Helping the poor also means designing high-quality and safe walking and cycling environments. Mixed land use patterns and walking- and cycling-friendly environments allow the poor to allocate income for other urgent purposes and thus help reduce poverty. In the very poorest cities, small interventions (e.g., siting basic services such as schools, health centers, markets, and water standpipes to reduce travel distances) can make a big difference in the amount of time and energy devoted to transport. The time freed up allows women to achieve gainful employment and children to attend schools. The cardi- nal features of integrated and sustainable transport and urbanism everywhere—accessible urban activities, safe, attractive walking and cycling environs, and affordable transporta- tion—are particularly vital to the welfare of the neediest members of the world's poorest countries.

Inclusive Cities

Affordability is a key element of creating socially inclusive urban futures. Many of the ideas advanced in this book aim to create better places: better communities, better envi- ronments, and better economies, as described in chapters 2–4. However, urban betterment is often followed by higher land prices that end up pricing out the poor and often even middle-income people. In any city, there's a finite, limited supply of real estate with good access to transit, safe and walkable neighborhoods, and animated, vibrant streetscapes. Invariably, well-off segments of society outbid others for these choice areas, displacing long-time residents and the working class. A recent review referred to gentrification and displacement as "symptoms of the scarcity of quality urbanism."[41] Moving beyond mobil- ity to create cities for people and places will never gain political traction and broad-based support unless people from all walks of life and diverse backgrounds share in the benefits.

Although there's not full agreement among academics about the impacts of gentrifica- tion, it has unquestionably created tensions in cities and contributed to widening divides by class, race, and age. A recent study found a $108,000 difference in median home prices between what the American Planning Association award as Great Neighborhoods (i.e., walkable and sustainable) and census tracts immediately adjacent to them.[42] Commercial gentrification often pushes out small mom-and-pop stores, replaced by national chains such as CVS and Target.[43] The architecture of insecurity and fear, seen in fortress-style neighborhoods and gated communities, has squeezed housing markets in developed and developing cities alike. Whether Los Angeles or São Paulo, cities are increasingly segregated by ethnicity and class.[44] The sight of luxurious mansions several blocks from urban squalor is all too common in the Global South. And although flagship developments such as marketplaces, entertainment districts, and convention centers help revive urban centers, they also increase property values, displace long-time residents, and create inauthentic places.[45]

Urban reinvestments and regeneration create their fair share of problems, but some note that the alternative of disinvestment and stagnation is worse.[46] A 2014 study estimated that for every gentrified neighborhood across fifty-one U.S. metro areas, ten others remained poor, and twelve formerly stable areas became economically distressed.[47] Absent regeneration, concentrated poverty and racial divides often deepen. For instance, a recent study of Chicago's south side found that gentrification slows or stops when a neighborhood is 40 percent African American.[48]

Notwithstanding differing views about gentrification and displacement, many of the ideas advanced in this book will falter unless they are in some way socially inclusive. Broadly, actions that reduce the dominance of private cars help the poor. This includes "complete street" initiatives that direct more transportation resources away from cars and toward alternative modes (e.g., cycle tracks, streetscape enhancements for pedestrians). Also included are traffic-calming, car-free centers, and road dieting. Less inclusive are technologically driven trends such as autonomous vehicles and even app-based ride hailing: Smartphones are not ubiquitous throughout a city, nor are credit cards or bank accounts.[49]

Urban planners are well positioned to make cities more socially inclusive through their oversight of building codes and design standards. Street cross-sections and hierarchies aimed at improving circulation are giving way to more pedestrian-friendly designs across the United States. Despite liability concerns over street designs that depart from traditional standards and resistance from protective services such as fire departments, more and more cities are changing design codes to slow traffic and conserve land.[50] In 2015, Sacramento modified its zoning and development codes to include "active designs" that promote increased walking, cycling, and jogging.

Another way to encourage green mobility and inclusive development is urban infill. Notably, permitting the construction of accessory dwelling units can increase densities to the point where transit and walking become more viable in addition to increasing the stock of affordable housing. Minimum housing lot sizes also needs to be reexamined as a way to increase densities and lower costs. Downsizing living space in keeping with shifting lifestyle preferences is another option, as is the tiny house movement now under way in cities such as Portland, Oregon, and Austin, Texas.

As discussed throughout this book, TOD is often a centerpiece of sustainable growth. However, TOD has come under criticism for pricing out the poor. Too often, attractive neighborhoods around transit hubs are accompanied by rising housing prices followed by the displacement of low-income families.[51] Some areas have made impressive strides to make TOD more equitable. In the San Francisco Bay Area, the Transit-Oriented Affordable Housing (TOAH) Fund, a $50-million public–private initiative to finance affordable housing and community facilities near transit, was recently created. TOAH blends public seed capital with risk-absorbing philanthropic capital, which in turn draws private capital. As of 2016, more than $30 million in TOAH funds had gone to constructing more than nine hundred units of affordable housing near transit and ancillary commercial activities, such as child care centers and fresh-food markets.[52] Bay Area Rapid Transit (BART), the region's rail authority, recently set a target of creating twenty thousand homes, nearly half of them below market rate, on twenty-six BART-owned properties along the system's 104-mile network.

Inclusive TOD can also occur through shared prosperity. In dense cities such as Hong Kong (see chapter 7), TOD generates tremendous real estate windfalls. Redistributing some of the gains enjoyed by privileged land developers to local communities is a form of shared prosperity. Mixed-income housing trusts and below-market-rate housing mandates tied to value capture programs (such as Hong Kong's R+P, reviewed in chapter 7) are ways to share in the wealth created by transit. Affordable housing need not be some kind of alms to the needy but rather a sharing of transit's value, especially in big, congested cities.

Singapore, where some 90 percent of households own a home, is an exemplar of affordable housing amid world-class transit.[53] Of course the island-state of Singapore is unique, and its experiences are not easily transferable, but the core idea of providing families with a housing shell and bare-bone fixtures, enabling them to embellish homes as their incomes rise, has made housing more affordable. So has the practice of making it very expensive to own and use a car, freeing up income for housing. In Singapore, about twice as many households—91 percent versus 45 percent—own homes as cars.[54]

More affordable transit-oriented living can also be found in developing cities. One notable example is Metrovivienda, introduced in Bogotá, Colombia at the time the Trans-Milenio BRT system was built to make housing more affordable, principally by locating it near BRT stops so residents can economize on travel, thus freeing up income for home purchases. Metrovivienda serves a model of multisector (i.e., combined housing and transport) and accessibility planning in the Global South. (See box 11-1.)

Box 11-1

Bogotá's Metrovivienda Project: Equitable TOD[1]

In 1999, at the time Bogotá's successful TransMilenio BRT system was being built, an innovative land-banking and poverty alleviation program called Metrovivienda was launched. Under Metrovivienda, transportation and housing are treated as bundled goods. The city acquires plots when they are still used for agriculture at low prices and proceeds to plat and title the land and provide public utilities, roads, and open space. Property is sold to developers at higher prices to help cover infrastructure costs, with the proviso that average prices be kept under US$8,500 per unit and are affordable to families with incomes of US$200 per month.

A decade into the program, four Metrovivienda sites had been created near one of TransMilenio's terminuses, each between 100 and 120 hectares in size and housing some eight thousand families. At buildout, the program aims to construct 440,000 new housing units. Putting housing near stations helps the city's poor by killing two birds with one stone, providing both improved housing and public transport services. Those moving from peripheral informal settlements into transit-served Metrovivienda projects enjoy both sites and serviced housing and improved access to the urban core. The image on the next page portrays the kind of modern housing that many former residents of squatter settlements are now able to live in. It has been estimated that job accessibility levels via transit within a 1-hour travel time increased by a factor of three for those moving from informal housing to Metrovivienda projects.

An important aspect of the program is the acquisition of land in advance of BRT services. Because Metrovivienda officials serve on the board of TransMilenio, they are aware of strategic plans and timelines for extending BRT. This has enabled the organization to acquire land before prices rise in anticipation of BRT's arrival. TransMilenio also makes commuting more affordable. When living in the hillsides, most residents used two different public transit services (a feeder and a mainline), paying on average US$1.40 a day to leave and return home. With TransMilenio, feeder buses are free, resulting in an average of US$0.80 in daily travel costs. This is important because studies show that those residing near TransMilenio stations pay higher monthly rents: On average, housing prices fell between 6.8 and 9.3 percent for every 5 minutes' increase in walking time to a station.

[1] Robert Cervero, "Progressive Transport and the Poor: Bogotá's Bold Steps Forward," *Access* 27 (2005): 24–30; Daniel Rodriguez and Felipe Targa, "Value of Accessibility to Bogotá's Bus Rapid Transit System," *Transport Reviews* 24, no. 2 (2004): 587–610; Hiroaki Suzuki, Robert Cervero, and Kanako Iuchi, *Transforming Cities with Transit: Transit and Land-Use Integration for Sustainable Urban Development* (Washington, DC: World Bank, 2013).

Metrovivienda underscores the benefits of accessibility-based planning. By coupling affordable housing with affordable transport, Bogotá's leaders have improved access to jobs, shops, and services while reducing the joint costs of what often consumes two-thirds of the poor's income: housing and transport.

Box Figure 11-1. Modern Metrovevienda housing flanked by a tree-lined pedestrian promenade and bike path. (Photo by Image Bank Enterprise Renewal and Urban Development, Bogotá.)

One key feature of place-making, public space, contributes to social inclusion and cohesion. The best public spaces bring together people from all walks of life and backgrounds. Public squares gain importance in an era of increasingly privatized and commodified spaces, such as gated communities, membership-only recreational areas, and privately owned "public" spaces in malls.[55] Reclaiming streets by converting freeways to greenways and multiuser boulevards likewise improves access for all.

Lastly, social inclusion need not entail large-scale public works. Small steps can move the needle. In Durban, South Africa, local funds went to upgrade vendor stalls and widen pedestrian routes in a traditional herb market to help spur commerce and improve foot traffic circulation. A similar initiative to increase access to locally grown food and strengthen community ties through local market upgrades and urban agriculture is under way in Detroit, a partnership of Project for Public Spaces and the Kresge Foundation.[56]

Close

The best ideas for going beyond mobility will go nowhere unless there is the political will and institutional capacity to embrace and move forward with them. The ability to manage and respond to escalating demands for urban travel is particularly important in developing cities. Institutional shortcomings—such as insufficiently trained and educated civil servants or the absence of a transparent procurement process for building transport infrastructure—abound throughout the Global South. One way to bring about necessary institutional reforms in rapidly developing parts of the world is to tie loans and grants from international aid agencies to better urban planning. Institutionalizing and operationalizing accessibility-based planning is critically important, both in the United States and abroad. As more and more growth shifts to cities of the Global South, opportunities for linking land development and transport infrastructure should not be squandered.

Although integrated transport and land development can relieve congestion, cleanse the air, and conserve energy, its potential to reduce what remains the gravest problem facing the Global South—extreme and persistent poverty—is every bit as important if not more so. All that is done in the developing world must pass the litmus test of helping to alleviate poverty. Designing cities and transport systems to increase accessibility and affordability is crucial. So are initiatives that strengthen nonmotorized and public transport, keep fares affordable, and protect vulnerable populations from the hazards of motorized travel.

Some might equate the ideas advanced in this book for moving beyond mobility with social engineering. The saving grace of creating livable, more diverse, and healthier communities is that they are in keeping with shifting lifestyle preferences and choices. Because of recalcitrant building codes and planning practices of the past, one could argue that car-dependent living *is* social engineering: Most Americans and increasingly their counterparts in Europe, Canada, and Australia have few choices other than a lifestyle that compels them to drive to almost anywhere and everywhere.[57]

Shifting urban planning's focus well beyond mobility is increasingly in tune with the lifestyle preferences of city dwellers. Experiments show this. For three weeks in early 2017, two lanes of Miami's busy Biscayne Boulevard were restricted to transit, bikes, strollers, and parking while more than one hundred parking spaces in the median were converted to 75,000 square feet of community green space. Public events were held, and a playground, dog park, and nontraditional crosswalks were installed. In the words of a planner with the project's sponsor, the Miami Downtown Development Authority, "This is what happens when we prioritized people over cars and getting cars in and out as fast as possible. The response from the community was great. People asked 'why does this have to be removed?'"[58]

Notwithstanding the social engineering conspiracy theorists, what will ultimately move us beyond mobility in the planning and design of cities is to increase individual choices on where to live, work, learn, shop, and play. Our bet lies with a shifting preference for compact, mixed-use, highly walkable communities, ideally interlaced by high-quality public transit. If real estate developers know anything, it's the smell of money. If money is made in creating compact, walkable places where many day-to-day needs are nearby and community gardens, civic squares, and tot lots abound, a wider variety of living, working, and playing environments will emerge. More livable places for people stand the best chance of emerging if market forces—aided by government action that removes distortions, advance forward-looking urban planning, and ensure inclusivity and access to all—are allowed to run their course.

NOTES

CHAPTER 1

1. Michael Southworth and Eran Ben-Joseph, *Streets and the Shaping of Towns and Cities* (Washington, DC: Island Press, 2013).

2. Eran Ben-Joseph, *ReThinking a Lot: The Design and Culture of Parking* (Cambridge, MA: MIT Press, 2012).

3. Andrea Broaddus, "The Adaptable City: The Use of Transit Investment and Congestion Pricing to Influence Travel and Location Decisions in London" (PhD diss., University of California, Berkeley, 2015), 91.

4. Ibid., 102.

5. Edward L. Glaeser, *Triumph of the City: How Our Greatest Invention Makes Us Richer, Smarter, Greener, Healthier, and Happier* (New York: Penguin Press, 2011).

6. Peter Hall, *Cities in Civilization* (New York: Pantheon, 1998).

7. UN Habitat, *World Cities Report 2016* (Nairobi, Kenya: UN Habitat, 2016).

8. United Nations Population Division, "World Urbanization Prospects, the 2014 Revision," 2014, http://esa.un.org/unpd/wup/.

9. David Owen, *Green Metropolis: Why Living Smaller, Living Closer, and Driving Less Are Keys to Sustainability* (New York: Riverhead Books, 2009).

10. UN Habitat, *World Cities Report 2016.*

11. Ibid.

12. UN Population Fund, *State of World Population 2007* (New York: United Nations, 2007).

13. Judy Baker, *Urban Poverty: A Global View* (Washington, DC: The World Bank, Urban Papers Series, UP-5, 2008).

14. International Energy Agency, *World Energy Outlook* (Paris: International Energy Agency, 2016). http://www.worldenergyoutlook.org/resources/energydevelopment/energyaccessdatabase/.

15. World Health Organization, 2016. http://www.who.int/mediacentre/factsheets/fs392/en/.

16. UN Habitat, *Planning and Design for Sustainable Urban Mobility, Global Report on Human Settlements* (Nairobi, Kenya: UN Habitat, 2013).

17. Gilles Duranton and Erick Guerra, *Developing a Common Narrative on Urban Accessibility: An Urban Planning Perspective* (Washington, DC: Brookings Institution, 2017).

18. Robert W. Burchell et al., *Costs of Sprawl 2000*. TCRP Report 74 (Washington, DC: Transit Cooperative Research Program, Transportation Research Board, 2002).

19. Reid Ewing and Shima Hamidi, *Costs of Sprawl* (New York: Routledge, 2017).

20. World Health Organization, *World Health Statistics 2016: Monitoring Health for the SDGs* (Geneva, Switzerland: WHO, 2016).

21. Hall, *Cities in Civilization*.

22. Lewis Mumford, *The Highway and the City* (New York: Harcourt, Brace & World, 1963).

23. Glaeser, *Triumph of the City*.

24. Charles Kooshian and Stephen Winkelman, *Growing Wealthier: Smart Growth, Climate Change and Prosperity* (Washington, DC: Center for Clean Air Policy, 2011).

25. Lynda Schneekloth and Robert Shibley, *Placemaking: The Art and Practice of Building Communities* (New York: Wiley, 1996); Charles Bohl, "Placemaking: Developing Town Centers, Main Streets, and Urban Villages" (New York: Project for Public Space, 2002), https://www.pps.org/reference/what_is_placemaking/.

26. Jan Gehl, *Cities for People* (Washington, DC: Island Press, 2010).

27. John Whitelegg, "Time Pollution," *The Ecologist* 23, no. 4 (1993).

CHAPTER 2

1. Le Corbusier, *The City of To-morrow and Its Planning* (North Chelmsford, MA: Courier Corporation, 1987), 131.

2. Jane Jacobs, "Downtown Is for People," *The Exploding Metropolis* 168 (1958).

3. Jane Jacobs, *The Death and Life of Great American Cities* (New York: Vintage Books, 1961), 29.

4. Robert D. Putnam, *Bowling Alone: The Collapse and Revival of American Community* (New York: Simon and Schuster, 2001), 21.

5. Alejandro Portes, "Social Capital: Its Origins and Applications in Modern Sociology," in *Knowledge and Social Capital*, ed. Eric L. Lesser (Boston: Butterworth-Heinemann, 2000), 48.

6. Norman Uphoff and Chandrasekera M. Wijayaratna, "Demonstrated Benefits from Social Capital: The Productivity of Farmer Organizations in Gal Oya, Sri Lanka," *World Development* 28, no. 11 (2000): 1875–90.

7. John F. Helliwell and Robert D. Putnam, "The Social Context of Well-Being," *Philosophical Transactions: Royal Society of London Series B Biological Sciences* (2004): 1435–46.

8. Robert Putnam, "Bowling Alone: America's Declining Social Capital," *Journal of Democracy* 6, no. 1 (1995): 65–78.

9. Putnam, *Bowling Alone*.

10. David Popenoe, "Urban Sprawl: Some Neglected Sociological Considerations," *Sociology and Social Research* 63, no. 2 (1979): 255–68.

11. Raymond H. Novaco and Oscar I. Gonzalez, "Commuting and Well-Being," *Technology and Well-Being* 3 (2009): 174–205.

12. IBM Corporation, *The Globalization of Traffic Congestion: IBM 2010 Commuter Pain Survey* (Armonk, NY: IBM Corporation, 2010).

13. Herbert J. Gans, "Planning and Social Life: Friendship and Neighbor Relations in Suburban Communities," *Journal of the American Institute of Planners* 27, no. 2 (1961): 134–40.

14. David Gray, Jon Shaw, and John Farrington, "Community Transport, Social Capital and Social Exclusion in Rural Areas," *Area* 38, no. 1 (2006): 89–98.

15. Donald Appleyard, *Livable Streets* (Berkeley: University of California Press, 1981).

16. Allan Jacobs and Donald Appleyard, "Toward an Urban Design Manifesto," *Journal of the American Planning Association* 53, no. 1 (1987): 112–20.

17. Michael Southworth and Eran Ben-Joseph, *Streets and the Shaping of Towns and Cities* (Washington, DC: Island Press, 2013).

18. Eran Ben-Joseph, *ReThinking a Lot: The Design and Culture of Parking* (Cambridge, MA: MIT Press, 2012).

19. Jan Gehl, *Life Between Buildings: Using Public Space* (Washington, DC: Island Press, 2011).

20. Allan Jacobs and Donald Appleyard, "Toward an Urban Design Manifesto," *Journal of the American Planning Association* 53, no. 1 (1987): 112–20.

21. William H. Whyte, *The Social Life of Small Urban Spaces* (Naperville, IL: Conservation Foundation, 1980).

22. Ibid.

23. William H. Whyte, *City: Rediscovering the Center* (Philadelphia: University of Pennsylvania Press, 2009), 154.

24. Whyte, *The Social Life of Small Urban Spaces*, 51.

25. Robert B. Noland, Orin T. Puniello, and Stephanie DiPetrillo, *The Impact of Transit-Oriented Development on Social Capital* (San Jose, CA: Mineta National Transit Research Consortium, 2016).

26. Ben Hamilton-Baillie, "Shared Space: Reconciling People, Places and Traffic," *Built Environment* 34, no. 2 (2008): 161–81.

27. Marta Bausells, *Superblocks to the Rescue: Barcelona's Plan to Give Streets Back to Residents*, May 2016, https://www.theguardian.com/cities/2016/may/17/superblocks-rescue-barcelona-spain-plan-give-streets-back-residents.

28. Jacobs, *The Death and Life of Great American Cities*, 150.

29. Frances Bunn et al., "Area-Wide Traffic Calming for Preventing Traffic Related Injuries," *The Cochrane Library* (2003).

30. Ibid.

31. William Riggs and John Gilderbloom, "Two-Way Street Conversion Evidence of Increased Livability in Louisville," *Journal of Planning Education and Research* 36, no. 1 (2016): 105–118.

32. Ben Welle et al., *Cities Safer by Design: Guidance and Examples to Promote Traffic Safety through Urban and Street Design* (Washington, DC: World Resources Institute, 2015).

33. John Laplante and Barbara McCann, "Complete Streets: We Can Get There from Here," *Institute of Transportation Engineers. ITE Journal* 78, no. 5 (2008): 24.

34. Wenjia Zhang, "Does Compact Land Use Trigger a Rise in Crime and a Fall in Ridership? A Role for Crime in the Land Use–Travel Connection," *Urban Studies* (2015).

35. Jacobs, *The Death and Life of Great American Cities*.

36. Paul Michael Cozens, Greg Saville, and David Hillier, "Crime Prevention through Environmental Design (CPTED): A Review and Modern Bibliography," *Property Management* 23, no. 5 (2005): 328–56.

37. National Highway Traffic Safety Administration, "Fatality Analysis Reporting System," 2016, http://www.nhtsa.gov/FARS.

38. World Health Organization, *Global Status Report on Road Safety* (Geneva, Switzerland: WHO, 2009), http://whqlibdoc.who.int/publications/2009/9789241563840_eng.pdf.

39. UN Habitat, *Planning and Design for Sustainable Urban Mobility, Global Report on Human Settlements* (Nairobi, Kenya: UN Habitat, 2013).

40. Ian Roberts and Phil Edwards, *The Energy Glut: The Politics of Fatness in an Overheating World* (London: Zed Books, 2010).

41. Robert Cervero, et al., "Influences of Built Environments on Walking and Cycling: Lessons from Bogotá," *International Journal of Sustainable Transport* 3 (2009): 203–26.

42. Lawrence D. Frank, Martin A. Andresen, and Thomas L. Schmid, "Obesity Relationships with Community Design, Physical Activity, and Time Spent in Cars," *American Journal of Preventive Medicine* 27, no. 2 (2004): 87–96.

43. Ibid.

44. Michael Southworth, "Designing the Walkable City," *Journal of Urban Planning and Development* 131, no. 4 (2005): 246–57.

45. Reid Ewing and Susan Handy, "Measuring the Unmeasurable: Urban Design Qualities Related to Walkability," *Journal of Urban Design* 14, no. 1 (2009): 65–84.

46. Kevin Lynch, *The Image of the City*, Vol. 11, (Cambridge, MA: MIT Press, 1960).

47. Gordon Cullen, *The Concise Townscape* (Abingdon, UK: Routledge, 1971), 27.

48. Ewing and Handy, "Measuring the Unmeasurable: Urban Design Qualities Related to Walkability," 77.

49. Wesley E. Marshall, Daniel P. Piatkowski, and Norman W. Garrick, "Community Design, Street Networks, and Public Health," *Journal of Transport & Health* 1, no. 4 (2014): 326–40.

50. Kenneth E. Powell, Linda M. Martin, and Pranesh P. Chowdhury, "Places to Walk: Convenience and Regular Physical Activity," *American Journal of Public Health* 93, no. 9 (2003): 1519–21.

51. Eugene C. Fitzhugh, David R. Bassett, and Mary F. Evans, "Urban Trails and Physical Activity: A Natural Experiment," *American Journal of Preventive Medicine* 39, no. 3 (2010): 259–62.

52. Chris Rissel et al., "Physical Activity Associated with Public Transport Use: A Review and Modelling of Potential Benefits," *International Journal of Environmental Research and Public Health* 9, no. 7 (2012): 2454–78.

53. François Reeves, *Planet Heart: How an Unhealthy Environment Leads to Heart Disease* (Vancouver, BC: Greystone Books, 2014).

54. World Health Organization, "Global Urban Ambient Air Pollution Database (Update 2016)," http://www.who.int/phe/health_topics/outdoorair/databases/cities/en/.

55. Randall Crane and Lisa A. Scweitzer, "Transport and Sustainability: The Role of the Built Environment," *Built Environment* 29, no. 3 (2003): 238–52.

56. J. J. Lin and C. C. Gau, "A TOD Planning Model to Review the Regulation of Allowable Development Densities around Subway Stations," *Land Use Policy* 23 (2006): 353–60.

57. Janice Fanning Madden, "Why Women Work Closer to Home," *Urban Studies* 18, no. 2 (1981): 181–94.

58. Evelyn Blumenberg, "On the Way to Work: Welfare Participants and Barriers to Employment," *Economic Development Quarterly* 16, no. 4 (2002): 314–25.

59. Amy Hillier et al., "A Discrete Choice Approach to Modeling Food Store Access," *Environment and Planning B: Planning and Design* 42, no. 2 (2015): 263–78.; Amy Hillier et al., "How Far Do Low-Income Parents Travel to Shop for Food? Empirical Evidence from Two Urban Neighborhoods," *Urban Geography* 32, no. 5 (2011): 712–29.

60. Robert Doyle Bullard, Glenn Steve Johnson, and Angel O. Torres, eds., *Highway Robbery: Transportation Racism and New Routes to Equity* (Brooklyn, NY: South End Press, 2004).

61. Yang Liu, *Beyond Spatial Mismatch: Immigrant Employment in Urban America* (Ann Arbor, MI: ProQuest, 2008).

62. Evelyn Blumenberg, "On the Way to Work: Welfare Participants and Barriers to Employment," *Economic Development Quarterly* 16, no. 4 (2002): 314–25.

63. Karen Lucas, Tim Grosvenor, and Roona Simpson, *Transport, the Environment and Social Exclusion* (York, UK: York Publishing Services Limited, 2001).

64. Fengming Su and Michael G. H. Bell, "Transport for Older People: Characteristics and Solutions," *Research in Transportation Economics* 25, no. 1 (2009): 46–55.

65. Lucas, Grosvenor, and Simpson, *Transport, the Environment and Social Exclusion*, vii.

66. Charles Montgomery, *Happy City: Transforming Our Lives through Urban Design* (New York: Farrar, Straus and Giroux, 2013).

67. Warren Smit et al., "Toward a Research and Action Agenda on Urban Planning/Design and Health Equity in Cities in Low and Middle-Income Countries," *Journal of Urban Health* 88, no. 5 (2011): 875–85.

68. Ada-Helen Bayer and Leon Harper, *Fixing to Stay: A National Survey of Housing and Home Modification Issues* (Washington, DC: AARP, 2000).

69. Patsy Healey, "Collaborative Planning in Perspective," *Planning Theory* 2, no. 2 (2003): 101–23.

70. Ria S. Hutabarat Lo, "Walkability Planning in Jakarta," (PhD diss., University of California, Berkley, 2011).

71. Annette Miae Kim, *Sidewalk City: Remapping Public Space in Ho Chi Minh City.* (Chicago: University of Chicago Press, 2015).

72. Benjamin Goldfrank, "Lessons from Latin American Experience in Participatory Budgeting," *Participatory Budgeting* (2007): 91–126.

73. Ibid.

74. Greg Brown and Delene Weber, "Public Participation GIS: A New Method for National Park Planning," *Landscape and Urban Planning* 102, no. 1 (2011): 1–15.

75. Florian Steinberg, "Strategic Urban Planning in Latin America: Experiences of Building and Managing the Future," *Habitat International* 29, no. 1 (2005): 69–93; Miguel Kanai and Iliana Ortega-Alcázar, "The Prospects for Progressive Culture-Led Urban Regeneration in Latin America: Cases from Mexico City and Buenos Aires," *International Journal of Urban and Regional Research* 33, no. 2 (2009): 483–501.

CHAPTER 3

1. William Black, "Sustainable Transportation: A U.S. Perspective," *Journal of Transportation Geography* 4, no. 3 (1996): 151; Keiichi Satoh and Lawrence W. Lan, "Editorial: Development and Deployment of Sustainable Transportation," *International Journal of Sustainable Transportation* 1, no. 2 (2009): 69.

2. Keiko Hirota and Jacques Poot, "Taxes and the Environmental Impact of Private Auto Use: Evidence for 68 Cities," in *Methods and Models in Transport and Telecommunications*, ed. Aura Reggiani and Laurie Schintler (Berlin: Springer-Verlag, 2005), 311–13.

3. International Energy Agency, *World Energy Outlook 2016* (Paris: OECD/IEA, 2016).

4. Reid Ewing and Robert Cervero, "Travel and the Built Environment: A Meta-Analysis," *Journal of the American Planning Association* 76, no. 3 (2010): 265–94; David Brownstone, "Key Relationships between the Built Environment and VMT" (Special Report No. 298), in *Driving and the Built Environment: The Effects of Compact Development on Motorized Travel, Energy Use, and CO_2 Emissions* (Washington, DC, Transportation Research Board, 2008).

5. Peter Newman and Jeffrey Kenworthy, "Peak Car Use: Understanding the Demise of Automobile Dependence," *World Transport Policy and Practice* 17, no. 2 (2011): 31–42.

6. UN Habitat, *Planning and Design for Sustainable Urban Mobility: Global Report on Human Settlements 2013* (Nairobi: UN Habitat, 2013).

7. William Black, *Sustainable Transportation: Problems and Solutions* (New York: Guilford Press, 2010).

8. International Energy Agency, *World Energy Outlook* (Paris: IEA, 2011).

9. World Resources Institute, *Global Protocol for Community-Scale Greenhouse Gas Emission Inventories: An Accounting and Reporting Standard for Cities* (Washington, DC: World Resources Institute, 2014).

10. Vaclav Smil, *Making the Modern World: Materials and Dematerialization* (New York: John Wiley and Sons, 2013); also see http://www.worldcoal.org/resources/coal-statistics/coal-steel-statistics/, accessed June 23, 2015.

11. Karen Seto et al., "Human Settlements, Infrastructure and Spatial Planning," in *Climate Change 2014: Mitigation of Climate Change. Contribution of Working Group III to the Fifth Assessment Report of the Intergovernmental Panel on Climate Change*, ed. O. Edenhofer et al. (Cambridge, UK, Cambridge University Press, 2014), chapter 12.

12. UN Habitat, *Planning and Design for Sustainable Urban Mobility*.

13. International Transport Forum, *Transport Outlook: Meeting the Needs of 9 Billion People* (Paris, OECD/International Transport Forum, 2011); International Energy Agency, *Key World Energy Statistics* (Paris: IEA, 2011).

14. International Energy Agency, *World Energy Outlook*; UN Habitat, *Planning and Design for Sustainable Urban Mobility*; Ralph Sims et al., "Transport," in *Climate Change 2014: Mitigation of Climate Change. Contribution of Working Group III to the Fifth Assessment Report of the Intergovernmental Panel on Climate Change*, ed. O. Edenhofer et al. (Cambridge, UK: Cambridge University Press, 2014), chapter 12, p. 603.

15. Black, *Sustainable Transportation*.

16. IFP Energies Nouvelles, "Energy Consumption in the Transport Sector," in *Panorama 2005* (Rueil-Malmaison, France: IFPEN, 2005).

17. GTZ (The Deutsche Gesellschaft für Internationale Zusammenarbeit), *International Fuel Prices, 2009* 6 (2009), http://www.gtz.de/de/dokumente/gtz2009-en-ifp-full -version.pdf, accessed April 12, 2014; see also http://www.transport2012.org/bridging/ ressources/files/1/621,521,5F-ACC-EN.pdf.

18. UN Habitat, *Global Report on Human Settlements 2011: Cities and Climate Change* (London: Earthscan, 2011).

19. Ibid.

20. International Energy Agency, *World Energy Outlook* and *Key World Energy Statistics*.

21. Seto et al., "Human Settlements, Infrastructure and Spatial Planning."

22. Organization for Economic Development and Cooperation (OECD), *Cities and Climate Change* (Paris: OECD Publications, 2010).

23. European Commission, *Keeping Europe Moving: Sustainable Mobility for Our Continent*, Midterm review of the European Commission's 2001 Transport White Paper, COM, 314 Final (Brussels: European Commission, 2006), http://eur-lex.europa.eu /LexUriServ/LexUriServ.do?uri=COM:2006:0314:FIN:EN:PDF, accessed June 23, 2014.

24. Korea Transport Institute, *Toward an Integrated Green Transportation System in Korea* (Seoul: Korea Transport Institute, 2010).

25. A. K. Jain, *Sustainable Urban Mobility in Southern Asia* (Nairobi: UN Habitat, 2011), https://unhabitat.org/wp-content/uploads/2013/06/GRHS.2013.Regional.South- ern.Asia_.pdf, accessed May 11, 2015.

26. International Energy Agency, *World Energy Outlook*.

27. David Banister, "The Sustainability Mobility Paradigm," *Transport Policy* 15 (2008): 73–80.

28. Arnulf Grubler et al., "Urban Energy Systems," in *Global Energy Assessment: Toward a Sustainable Future* (Cambridge, UK: Cambridge University Press, 2012), 1307– 1400.

29. World Health Organization, *Ambient Air Pollution: A Global Assessment of Exposure and Burden of Disease* (Geneva, Switzerland: World Health Organization, 2016).

30. World Health Organization, Global Urban Ambient Air Pollution Database (Update 2016) (Geneva, Switzerland: WHO, 2016), http://www.who.int/phe/health_topics /outdoorair/databases/cities/en/.

31. Yi-Chi Chen, Lu-Yen Chen, and Fu-Tien Jeng, "Analysis of Motorcycle Exhaust Regular Testing Data: A Case Study of Taipei City," *Journal of the Air & Waste Management Association* 59, no. 6 (2009): 757–62; Michael Greenstone et al., "Lower Pollution, Longer Lives Life Expectancy Gains if India Reduced Particulate Matter Pollution," *Economics and Political Weekly* 50, no. 8 (2015): 40–46.

32. United Nations Development Programme (UNDP), *China Human Development Report 2005* (Beijing: UNDP China and China Institute for Reform and Development, 2008), http://www undp.org.cn/downloads/nhdr2005/NHDR2005_complete.pdf, accessed June 19, 2013.

33. Wojciech Suchorzewski, *Sustainable Urban Mobility in Transitional Economies* (Nairobi: UN Habitat, 2011), https://unhabitat.org/wp-content/uploads/2013/06/GRHS .2013.Regional.Transitional.Countries.pdf, accessed April 12, 2017.

34. John Pucher et al., "Urban Transport Trends and Policies in China and India: Impacts of Rapid Economic Growth," *Transport Reviews* 27, no. 4 (2007): 379–410; Jain, *Sustainable Urban Mobility in Southern Asia.*

35. Gordon Pirie, *Sustainable Urban Mobility in "Anglophone" Sub-Saharan Africa* (Nairobi: UN Habitat, 2011), https://unhabitat.org/wp-content/uploads/2013/06/GRHS .2013.Regional.Anglophone.Africa.pdf, accessed January 9, 2015.

36. European Commission–Environment, *TREMOVE: An EU-Wide Model* (Brussels: European Commission, 2011), http://ec.europa.eu/environment/air/pollutants/models /tremove.htm, accessed July 17, 2011.

37. Suchorzewski, *Sustainable Urban Mobility in Transitional Economies.*

38. World Health Organization, *Burden of Disease from Environmental Noise* (Copenhagen, World Health Organization Regional Office for Europe, 2011).

39. Seto et al., "Human Settlements, Infrastructure and Spatial Planning."

40. Tom Daniels, *When City and Country Collide: Managing Growth in the Metropolitan Fringe* (Washington, DC: Island Press, 1998).

41. Yvonne Rydin, et al., "Shaping Cities for Health: Complexity and the Planning of Urban Environments in the 21st century," *The Lancet* 379, no. 9831 (2012): 2079–2108.

42. Steve Hankley and Julian D. Marshall, "Impacts of Urban Form on Future US Passenger-Vehicle Greenhouse Gas Emissions," *Energy Policy* 38 (2010): 4880–87.

43. Zhan Guo, Asha Weinstein Agrawal, and Jennifer Dill, "Are Land Use Planning and Congestion Pricing Mutually Supportive?," *Journal of the American Planning Association* 77, no. 3 (2011): 232–50.

44. Organisation for Economic Co-operation and Development (OECD), *Cities and Climate Change* (Paris: OECD Publishing, 2010).

45. UN Habitat, *Planning and Design for Sustainable Urban Mobility.*

CHAPTER 4

1. Peter Kresl and Balwant Singh, "Urban Competitiveness and US Metropolitan Centres," *Urban Studies* 49, no. 2 (2012): 239–54.

2. Siemens AG, "Megacities Report," 2007, http://www.citymayors.com/development /megacities.html.

3. The Economist Intelligence Unit, "Liveanomics: Urban Liveability and Economic Growth," September 2010, https://www.eiuperspectives.economist.com/sites/default/files/LON%20-%20IS%20-%20Philips%20liveable%20cities%20Report%2002%20WEB.pdf.

4. Katherine Levine Einstein and David M. Glick, "Mayoral Policy-Making: Results from the 21st Century Mayor Leadership Survey" (Boston: Boston University, Initiative on Cities, October 2014).

5. Katherine Einstein, David Glick, and Conor Le Banc, "2016 Menino Survey of Mayors" (Boston: Boston University Initiative on Cities, 2017).

6. World Bank, *Tanzania Economic Update 2014*, 5th ed., 2013, http://documents.worldbank.org/curated/en/393381468122079213/pdf/PRIORITY00000005th0Issue01900602014.pdf.

7. Peter Hall, *Cities of Tomorrow: An Intellectual History of Urban Planning and Design in the Twentieth Century*, 3rd ed. (Oxford, UK: Blackwell, 2002); Peter Hall, *Good Cities, Better Lives: How Europe Discovered the Lost Art of Urbanism* (London: Routledge, 2014); Robert J. Rogerson, "Quality of Life and Competitiveness," *Urban Studies* 36, no. 5–6 (1999): 969–85; Tim Whitehead, David Simmonds, and John Preston, "The Effect of Urban Quality Improvements on Economic Activity," *Journal of Environmental Management* 80, no. 1 (2006): 1–12.

8. Peter Hall, *Cities in Civilization: Culture, Technology, and Urban Order* (London, Weidenfeld & Nicolson, 1998).

9. Geoffrey Booth, *Transforming Suburban Business Districts* (Washington, DC: Urban Land Institute, 2001).

10. Ann Markusen and Greg Schrock, "The Distinctive City: Divergent Patterns in Growth, Hierarchy and Specialization," *Urban Studies* 43, no. 8 (2006): 1301–23.

11. Richard Florida, *The Rise of the Creative Class: And How It's Transforming Work, Leisure, Community, and Everyday Life* (New York: Basic Books, 2002).

12. Michael Storpher and Michael Manville, "Behaviour, Preferences and Cities: Urban Theory and Urban Resurgence," *Urban Studies* 43, no. 8 (2006): 1247–48; Edward Glaeser and Joshua D. Gottlieb, "The Economics of Place Making Policies," *Brookings Papers on Economic Activity* 39, no. 1 (2008): 155–253.

13. Ronald D. Brunner, et al., "Improving Data Utilization: The Case-Wise Alternative," *Policy Sciences* 20, no. 4 (1987): 365–94.

14. Brad Broberg, "The New Norm: The Real Estate World Has a New Look as the Economy Recovers," *On Common Ground* (Summer 2011): 4–9.

15. National Association of Realtors, *2011 NAR Community Preference Survey* (Washington, DC: National Association of Realtors, 2011).

16. Broberg, "The New Norm," 6.

17. Ania Wiekowski, "Back to the City," *Harvard Business Review*, May 2010, http://hbr.org/2010/05/back-to-the-city/ar/1, accessed April 12, 2017.

18. James F. Sallis, et al., "An Ecological Approach to Creating Active Living Communities," *Annual Review of Public Health* 27 (2006): 297–322.

19. Daniel Kahneman, et al., "A Survey Method for Characterizing Daily Life Experience: The Day Reconstruction Method," *Science* 306, no. 5702 (2004): 1776–80.

20. Bruno S. Frey and Alois Stutzer, *Happiness and Economics. How the Economy and Institutions Affect Well-Being* (Princeton, NJ: Princeton University Press, 2002).

21. Frontier Group, "Transportation and the New Generation: Why Young People Are Driving Less and What It Means for Transportation Policy" (Washington, DC: Frontier Group, 2012).

22. Brian A. Clark, "What Makes a Community Walkable," *On Common Ground* (Winter 2017): 12–17.

23. Lisa Rayle et al., "App-Based, On-Demand Ride Services; Comparing Taxi and Ridesourcing Trips and User Characteristics in San Francisco" (Berkeley: University of California Transportation Center), UCTC-FR-2014-08, http://www.uctc.net/research/papers/UCTC-FR-2014-08.pdf, accessed January 7, 2015.

24. National Association of Realtors, *2013 Community Preference Survey* (Washington, DC; NAR, 2013), https://www.nar.realtor/sites/default/files/reports/2013/2013-community-preference-press-release.pdf; Brad Broberg, "The Walkable Demand," *On Common Ground* (Winter 2017): 4–11.

25. Broberg, "The Walkable Demand."

26. National Association of Realtors, *2015 Community Preference Survey* (Washington, DC: NAR, 2015), https://www.nar.realtor/sites/default/files/reports/2015/nar-psu-2015-poll-press-release.pdf.

27. Christopher Leinberger and Michael Rodriguez, "Foot Traffic Ahead: Ranking Walkable Urbanism in America's Largest Metros" (Washington, DC: Smart Growth America, 2016).

28. Christopher Leinberger, "DC: The WalkUP Wake-Up Call" (Washington, DC: The George Washington School of Business, 2012).

29. John Renne, "The TOD Index," December 2016, http://www.TODIndex.com.

30. John Renne, "Changing Preferences for Transportation and Transit-Oriented Communities Signal a Gradual Move to a Post-Oil Based Society," *The European Financial Review* (August–September 2016): 65–68.

31. Broberg, "The Walkable Demand"; Leinberger and Rodgriguez, "Foot Traffic Ahead."

32. Brad Broberg, "Where Are The New Jobs Going?" *On Common Ground* (Summer 2016): 4–6.

33. Jeffrey R. Kenworthy and Felix B. Laube, *An International Sourcebook of Automobile Dependence in Cities: 1960–1990* (Boulder: University Press of Colorado, 1999).

34. Ibid., 632.

35. Jeffrey Kenworthy, "Decoupling Urban Car Use and Metropolitan GDP Growth," *World Transport Policy and Practice* 19, no. 4 (2013): 8–21.

36. Chuck Kooshian and Steve Winkelman, "Growing Wealthier: Smart Growth, Climate Change and Prosperity" (Washington, DC: Center for Clean Air Policy, 2011).

37. Peter Newman and Jeffrey Kenworthy, *The End of Automobile Dependence: How Cities Are Moving Beyond Car-Based Planning* (Washington, DC: Island Press, 2015).

38. QuantEcon, "Driving the Economy: Automotive Travel, Economic Growth, and the Risks of Global Warming Regulations" (Portland, OR: Cascade Policy Institute, 2009).

39. Remy Prud'homme and Chang-Woon Lee, "Sprawl, Speed and the Efficiency of Cities," *Urban Studies* 36, no. 11 (1999): 1849–58; Robert Cervero, "Efficient Urbanisation: Economic Performance and the Shape of the Metropolis," *Urban Studies* 38, no. 10 (2001): 1651–71.

40. The 2014 Mercer Quality of Life Worldwide City Report ranked Zurich number two, behind Vienna; see http://www.mercer.com/newsroom/2014-quality-of-living-survey.html, accessed January 6, 2015.

41. Robert Cervero, *The Transit Metropolis: A Global Inquiry* (Washington, DC: Island Press, 1998).

42. David Ashauer, "Highway Capacity and Economic Growth," *Economic Perspectives* (September 1990): 14–24; Marlon Boarnet, "Highways and Economic Productivity: Interpreting Recent Evidence," *Journal of Planning Literature* 11, no. 4 (1997): 476–86.

43. Boarnet, "Highways and Economic Productivity"; Saurav Dev Bhatta and Matthew P. Drennan, "The Economic Benefits of Public Investment in Transportation: A Review of Recent Literature," *Journal of Planning Education and Research* 22, no. 3 (2003): 288–96.

44. Cambridge Systematics, Robert Cervero, and David Aschuer, *Economic Impact Analysis of Transit Investments: Guidebook for Practitioners* (Washington, DC: National Academy Press, Transit Cooperative Research Program, Report 35, National Research Council, 1998).

45. Genevieve Giuliano, "Land Use Impacts of Transportation Investments: Highways and Transit," in *The Geography of Urban Transportation*, ed. Susan Hanson and Genevieve Giuliano (New York: Guilford, 2004) pp. 237–73.

46. Robert Cervero, "Transport Infrastructure and Global Competitiveness: Balancing Mobility and Livability," *Annals, AAPSS* 626 (November 2009): 210–25.

47. Marlon G. Boarnet and Andrew F. Haughwout, "Do Highways Matter: Evidence and Policy Implications of Highway's Influences on Metropolitan Development" (Washington, DC: Brookings Institution Center on Urban and Metropolitan Policy, 2000).

48. Richard Voith, "Changing Capitalization of CBD-Oriented Transportation Systems: Evidence from Philadelphia, 1970–1988," *Journal of Urban Economics* 33, no. 3 (1993): 361–76.

49. Robert Cervero, "Effects of Light and Commuter Rail Transit on Land Prices: Experiences in San Diego County," *Journal of the Transportation Research Forum* 43, no. 1 (2004): 121–38.

50. Carol Atkinson-Palombo, "Comparing the Capitalization Benefits of Light-Rail Transit and Overlay Zoning for Single-Family Houses and Condos by Neighborhood Type in Metropolitan Phoenix, Arizona," *Urban Studies* 47, no. 11 (2010): 2409–26; Michael Duncan, "Comparing Rail Transit Capitalization Benefits for Single-Family and Condominium Units in San Diego, California," *Transportation Research Record* 2067 (2008): 120–30.

51. Saksith Chalermpong and Kaiwan Wattana, "Rent Capitalization of Access to Rail Transit Stations; Spatial Hedonic Models of Office Rent in Bangkok," *Journal of the Eastern Asia Society for Transportation Studies* 8 (2009): 926–40.

52. Robert Cervero and Jin Murakami, "Rail + Property Development in Hong Kong: Experiences and Extensions," *Urban Studies* 46, no. 10 (2009): 2019–43.

53. Foster Vivien and Cecilia Briceño-Garmendia, "Africa's Infrastructure: A Time for Transformation" (Washington, DC: World Bank, 2010).

54. Kenneth Gwilliam, *Cities on the Move: A World Bank Urban Transport Strategy Review* (Washington, DC: World Bank Publications, 2002).

55. Robert Cervero and Mark Hansen, "Induced Travel Demand and Induced Road Investment: A Simultaneous Equation Analysis," *Journal of Transport Economics and Policy* 36, no. 3 (2002): 469–90; Gilles Duranton and Matthew A. Turner, "The Fundamental Law of Road Congestion: Evidence from US Cities," *The American Economic Review* 101, no. 6 (October 1, 2011): 2616–52.

56. Hiroaki Suzuki, Robert Cervero, and Kanako Iuchi, *Transforming Cities with Transit* (Washington, DC: The World Bank, 2013).

57. David Banister, "The Sustainable Mobility Paradigm," *Transport Policy* 15 (2008): 74; Hall, *Good Cities, Better Lives*.

58. D. Gordon Bagby, "The Effects of Traffic Flow on Residential Property Values," *Journal of the American Planning Association* 46, no. 1 (1980): 88–94.

59. Kenneth Button, *Transport Economics,* 3rd ed. (Cheltenham, UK: Edward Elgar, 2010).

60. Carmen Hass-Klau, "Impact of Pedestrianization and Traffic Calming," *Transport Policy* 1, no. 1 (1993): 21–31.

61. Sally Cairns, Stephen Atkins, and Phil Goodwin, "Disappearing Traffic? The Story So Far," *Municipal Engineer* 151, no. 1 (2002): 13–22.

62. Robert Cervero, "Urban Reclamation and Regeneration in Seoul, South Korea," in *Physical Infrastructure Development: Balancing the Growth, Equity and Environmental Imperatives*, ed. William Ascher and Corinne Krupp (New York, Palgrave Macmillan, 2010), chapter 7.

63. Chang-Deok Kang and Robert Cervero, "From Elevated Freeway to Urban Greenway: Land Value Impacts of Seoul, Korea's CGC Project," *Urban Studies* 46, no. 13 (2009): 2771–94.

64. Robert Cervero and Chang-Deok Kang, "Bus Rapid Transit Impacts on Land Uses and Land Values in Seoul, Korea," *Transport Policy* 18, no. 1 (2011): 102–16.

65. Kang and Cervero, "From Elevated Freeway to Urban Greenway."

66. Myungjun Jang and Chang-Deok Kang, "The Effects of Urban Greenways on the Geography of Office Sectors and Employment Density in Seoul, Korea," *Urban Studies* 53, no. 5 (2016): 1022–41.

67. Robert Cervero, Junhee Kang, and Kevin Shively, "From Elevated Freeways to Surface Boulevards: Neighborhood and Housing Price Impacts in San Francisco," *Journal of Urbanism* 2, no. 1 (2009): 31–50.

68. Whitehead, Simmonds, and Preston, "The Effect of Urban Quality Improvements on Economic Activity."

69. Richard Florida, *Cities and the Creative Class* (New York: Routledge, 2005); Dionysia Lambiri, Bianca Biagi, and Vincente Royuela, "Quality of Life in the Economic and Urban Economic Literature," *Social Indicators Research* 84, no. 1 (2007): 1–25; Janet Kelly, et al., "Placemaking as an Economic Development Strategy for Small and Midsized Cities," *Urban Affairs Review* 53, no. 3 (2017): 435–62.

70. John Kain and John Quigley, "Measuring the Value of Housing Quality," *Journal of the American Statistical Association* 65, no. 330 (1970): 532–48; Paul Chesire and Stephen Sheppard, "On the Price of Land and the Value of Amenities," *Economica* 62, no. 246 (1995): 247–67.

71. Paul K. Asabere, George Hachey, and Steven Grubaugh, "Architecture, Historic Zone, and the Value of Homes," *Journal of Real Estate Finance and Economics* 2, no. 3 (1989): 181–95; Kerry D. Vandell and Jonathan S. Lane, "The Economics of Architecture and Urban Design: Some Preliminary Findings," *Real Estate Economics* 17, no. 2 (1989): 235–60.

72. Harry Frech and Ronald N. Lafferty, "The Effect of the California Coastal Commission on Housing Prices," *Journal of Urban Economics* 16, no. 1 (1984): 105–23.

73. Janet E. Kohlhase, "The Impact of Toxic Waste Sites on Housing Values," *Journal of Urban Economics* 30, no. 1 (1991): 1–26.

74. A. Mitchell Polinsky and Steven Shavell, "Amenities and Property Values in a Model of an Urban Area," *Journal of Public Economics* 5, no. 1–2 (1976): 119–29.

75. Molly Epsey and Kuame Owusu-Edusei, "Neighborhood Parks and Residential Property Values in Greenville, South Carolina," *Journal of Agricultural and Applied Economics* 33, no. 3 (1002): 487–92.

76. Margot Lutzenhiser and Noelwah R. Netusil, "The Effect of Open Spaces on a Home's Sales Price," *Contemporary Economic Policy* 19, no. 3 (2001): 291–98.

77. Benjamin Bolitzer and Noelwah Netusil, "The Impact of Open Spaces on Property Values in Portland, Oregon," *Journal of Environmental Management* 59, no. 3 (2000): 185–93.

78. Soren T. Anderson and Sarah E. West, "Open Space, Residential Property Values, and Spatial Context," *Regional Science and Urban Economics* 36, no. 6 (2006): 773–89; Carolyn Dehring and Neil Dunse, "Housing Density and the Effect of Proximity to Public Open Space on Aberdeen, Scotland," *Real Estate Economics* 34, no. 4 (2006): 553–66.

79. Edward L. Glaeser, Jed Kolko, and Albert Saiz, "Consumer City," *Journal of Economic Geography* 1, no. 1 (2001): 27–50.

80. Rena Sivitanidou, "Urban Spatial Variation in Office-Commercial Rents: The Role of Spatial Amenities and Commercial Zoning," *Journal of Urban Economics* 38, no. 1 (1995): 23–49.

81. Mark Eppli and Charles Tu, *Valuing the New Urbanism* (Washington, DC: Urban Land Institute, 1999); Christopher Leinberger, *The Option of Urbanism: Investing in a New American Dream* (Washington, DC: Island Press, 2007); Keith Bartholomew and Reid Ewing, "Hedonic Price Effects of Pedestrian- and Transit-Designed Development," *Journal of Planning Literature* 26, no. 1 (2011): 18–34.

82. Mark Eppli and Charles Tu, "An Empirical Examination of Traditional Neighborhood Development," *Real Estate Economics* 29, no. 3 (2001): 485–50; Pnina O. Plaut and Marlon G. Boarnet, "New Urbanism and the Value of Neighborhood Design," *Journal of Architectural and Planning Research* 20, no. 3 (2003): 254–65.

83. Honogwei Dong, "Were Home Prices in New Urbanist Neighborhoods More Resilient in the Recent Housing Downturn?," *Journal of Planning Education and Research* 35, no. 1 (2015): 5–18.

84. Harrison Fraker, *The Hidden Potential of Sustainable Neighborhoods: Lessons from Low-Carbon Communities* (Washington, DC: Island Press, 2013).

85. Reid Ewing and Otto Clemente, *Measuring Urban Design: Metrics for Livable* (Washington, DC: Island Press, 2013).

86. Hugh F. Kelly and Andrew Warren, *Emerging Trends in Real Estate 2015* (Washington, DC: Urban Land Institute, 2015).

87. David A. Goldberg, "A Prescription for Fiscal Fitness? Smart Growth and the Municipal Bottom Line," *On Common Ground* (Summer 2011): 34–38.

88. Robert R. Burchell, et al., "The Cost of Sprawl 2000," TCRP Report 74 (Washington, DC: Transit Cooperative Research Program, 2002).

89. Pamela Blais, The *Economics of Urban Form* (Toronto: Greater Toronto Area Task Force, 1996).

90. The Global Commission on the Economy and Climate, "The Sustainable Infrastructure Imperative: Financing for Better Growth and Development," The 2016 New Climate Economy Report (Washington, DC: New Climate Economy, 2016).

CHAPTER 5

1. Michael Parkinson, "The Thatcher Government's Urban Policy: A Review," *Town Planning Review* 60, no. 4 (1989): 421.

2. Ian Colquhoun, *Urban Regeneration: An International Perspective* (London: B.T. Batsford, 1995).

3. Paul Hardin Kapp, "The Artisan Economy and Post-industrial Regeneration in the US," *Journal of Urban Design* 22, no. 4 (2017): 477–93.

4. Markus Moos, "From Gentrification to Youthification? The Increasing Importance of Young Age in Delineating High-Density Living," *Urban Studies* 53, no. 14 (2016): 2903–20.

5. Luke J. Juday, "The Changing Shape of American Cities" (Charlottesville: Weldon Cooper Center Demographics Research Group, University of Virginia, 2015), 6–7.

6. Joe Cortright, "The Young and Restless and the Nation's Cities," *City Observatory* 8 (2014).

7. Matthew Wansborough and Andrea Mageean, "The Role of Urban Design in Cultural Regeneration," *Journal of Urban Design* 5, no. 2 (2000): 181–197.

8. National Trust for Historic Preservation, "Older, Smaller, Better: Measuring How the Character of Buildings and Blocks Influences Urban Vitality" (Washington, DC: National Trust for Historic Preservation, May 2014).

9. Kevin Lynch, *The Image of the City*, vol. 11. (Cambridge, MA: MIT Press, 1960).

10. Peter Hall, *Good Cities, Better Lives: How Europe Discovered the Lost Art of Urbanism* (London: Routledge, 2014).

11. DETR, "The Condition of London Docklands in 1981: Regeneration Research Report" (London: Office of the Deputy Prime Minister, 1997).

12. Peter Hall, *Urban & Regional Planning*, 3rd ed. (London and New York: Routledge, 1992).

13. Harvey S. Perloff, "New Towns Intown," *Journal of the American Institute of Planners* 32 (May 1966): 155–61.

14. Local Government, Planning & Land Act of 1980 (Section 136), http://www.legislation .gov.uk/ukpga/1980/65/section/136.

15. Matthew Carmona, "The Isle of Dogs: Four Development Waves, Five Planning Models, Twelve Plans, Thirty-Five Years, and a Renaissance . . . of Sorts," *Progress in Planning* 71, no. 3 (2009): 104.

16. LDDC 1998 Regeneration Statement (London: LDDC, 1998).

17. Brian C. Edwards, *London Docklands: Urban Design in an Age of Deregulation* (Amsterdam: Elsevier, 2013), 35–36.

18. Department of Transportation, "Light Rail and Tram Statistics: England 2014/15," https://www.gov.uk/government/uploads/system/uploads/attachment_data /file/433286/light-rail-and-tram-statistics-2014-15.pdf.

19. Carmona, "The Isle of Dogs."

20. Ibid., 123.

21. Marco van Hoek, "Regeneration in European Cities: Making Connections," Case study of Kop van Zuid, Rotterdam (York, UK: Joseph Rowntree Foundation, 2007), 57.

22. Ibid., 50.

23. Ibid., 59.

24. Robert Shibley, Bradshaw Hovey, and R. Teaman, "Buffalo Case Study," in *Remaking Post-Industrial Cities: Lessons from North America and Europe*, ed. Donald K. Carter (New York: Routledge, 2016), 25–45.

25. Bay Area Economics, "Charlotte Streetcar Economic Development Study," City of Charlotte, April 2009.

26. Joe Huxley, *Value Capture Finance: Making Development Pay Its Way* (London: ULI Europe, 2015).

27. Andrea C. Ferster, "Rails-to-Trails Conversions: A Review of Legal Issues," *Planning & Environmental Law* 58, no. 9 (2006): 4; James Lilly, "Rail-to-Trail Conversions: How Communities Are Railroading Their Way out of Recession towards Healthy Living," *University of Baltimore Journal of Land and Development* 2, no. 2 (2013): 167.

28. Lilly, "Rail-to-Trail Conversions," 167.

29. Eugene C. Fitzhugh, David R. Bassett, and Mary F. Evans, "Urban Trails and Physical Activity: A Natural Experiment," *American Journal of Preventive Medicine* 39, no. 3 (2010): 259–62; Ross C. Brownson, et al. "Promoting Physical Activity in Rural Communities: Walking Trail Access, Use, and Effects," *American Journal of Preventive Medicine* 18, no. 3 (2000): 235–41.

30. Rails-to-Trails Conservancy, "Virginia's Washington & Old Dominion Railroad Regional Park," 2008, http://www.railstotrails.org/trailblog/2008/december/01/virginias -washington-old-dominion-railroad-regional-park/

31. Kate Ascher and Sabina Uffer, "The High Line Effect," CTBUH Research paper, 2015, 227.

32. Ibid, 226.

33. Ibid, 227–28.

34. Patrick McGeehan, "The High Line Isn't Just a Sight to See; It's Also an Economic Dynamo," *The New York Times* 5 (2011).

35. Michael Levere, "The Highline Park and Timing of Capitalization of Public Goods," *Working Paper* (2014).

36. Kevin Loughran, "Parks for Profit: The High Line, Growth Machines, and the Uneven Development of Urban Public Spaces," *City & Community* 13, no. 1 (2014): 49–68.

37. Kristina Shevory, "Cities See Another Side to Old Tracks," *The New York Times*, August 2, 2011.

38. "Atlanta BeltLine Overview," The Atlanta Beltline Web site, https://beltline.org /about/the-atlanta-beltline-project/atlanta-beltline-overview/.

39. "A Catalyst for Urban Growth and Renewal," The Atlanta Beltline Web site, http://beltline.org/progress/progress/economic-development-progress/.

40. Dan Immergluck, "Large Redevelopment Initiatives, Housing Values and Gentrification: The Case of the Atlanta Beltline," *Urban Studies* 46, no. 8 (2009): 1723–45.

41. Great Allegheny Passage Web site, https://gaptrail.org/.

42. Caompos, Inc. "The Great Allegheny Passage Economic Impact Study (2007–2008)," 2009.

43. See "creative clusters" in Michael Keane, *Creative Industries in China: Art, Design and Media* (New York: John Wiley & Sons, 2013).

CHAPTER 6

1. Robert Cervero, *America's Suburban Centers: The Transportation–Land Use Link* (Boston: Unwin-Hyman, 1989).

2. Robert Cervero, *Suburban Gridlock* (New Brunswick, NJ: Rutgers Press, 1986); *Suburban Gridlock II* (Piscataway, NJ: Transaction Press, 2013).

3. Cervero, *America's Suburban Centers*.

4. Joel Garreau, *Edge City: Life on the New Frontier* (New York: Anchor, 1992).

5. Robert Lang, *Edgeless Cities: Exploring the Elusive Metropolis* (Washington, DC: Urban Land Institute, 2003).

6. Cervero, *America's Suburban Centers*.

7. Elizabeth Kneebone, "Jobs Revisited: The Changing Geography of Metropolitan Employment" (Washington DC, Brookings Institution, Metropolitan Policy Program, 2009).

8. Ellen Dunham-Jones and June Williamson, *Retrofitting Suburbia: Urban Design Solutions for Redesigning Suburbs* (Hoboken, NJ: John Wiley & Sons Inc., 2009).

9. Urban Land Institute, "Housing in the Evolving American Suburb" (Washington, DC: Urban Land Institute, 2016).

10. Joe Cortright, "Surging Center City Job Growth," *City Observatory* (February 2015).

11. Urban Land Institute, "Housing in the Evolving American Suburb."

12. Kneebone, "Jobs Revisited."

13. Brad Broberg, "The Walkable Demand," *On Common Ground* (Winter 2017): 4–11.

14. Chris Leinberger and Patrick Lynch, "Foot Traffic Ahead: Ranking Walkable Urbanism in America's Largest Metros" (Washington, DC: Smart Growth America, 2016).

15. Dong W. Sohn and Anne Vernez Moudon, "The Economic Value of Office Clusters: An Analysis of Assessed Property Values, Regional Form, and Land Use Mix in King County, Washington," *Journal of Planning Education and Research* 28, no. 1 (2008): 86–99.

16. Louis H. Masotti and Jeffrey K. Haden, *The Urbanization of the Suburbs* (Beverly Hills: Sage Publications, 1973).

17. Dunham-Jones and Williamson, *Retrofitting Suburbia*.

18. Robert Burchell and Sahan Mukherji, "Conventional Development versus Managed Growth: the Cost of Sprawl," *American Journal of Preventive Medicine* 93, no. 9 (2003): 1534–40.

19. Howard Frumkin, Lawrence Frank, and Richard Jackson, *Urban Sprawl and Public Health: Designing, Planning, and Building for Healthy Communities* (Washington, DC: Island Press, 2004).

20. DPZ, "Retrofit-Infill: Suburban Retrofit Infill: A Lexicon of Advanced Techniques," Miami, Florida, 2008, https://transect.org/docs/SuburbanRetrofitBoards.pdf, accessed February 12, 2016. In "Retrofit-Infill," DPZ define the S7 "business park" as: homogeneous, auto-dependent, with limited connectivity, and lacking a relationship between buildings and street; a random, train-wreck pattern of building placement; front lawns; one-to-multistory buildings; and a civic space consisting largely of indoor lunch cafeterias. The urban center (T5), on the other hand, has a mix of houses, commercial activity, offices, workplaces, and civic buildings; predominantly attached buildings; buildings oriented to streets forming a street wall; 3- to 5-story buildings; and civic spaces made up of parks, plazas, and median landscaping.

21. Galina Tachieva, *Sprawl Repair Manual* (Washington, DC: Island Press, 2010).

22. Paul Lukez, *Suburban Transformations* (Princeton, NJ: Princeton Architectural Press, 2007).

23. Dunham-Jones and Williamson, *Retrofitting Suburbia*.

24. James Braswell, "Reinventing the Office Park," *Planetizen* July 29, 2014, http://www.planetizen.com/node/70529, accessed August 14, 2016.

25. Jay Fitzgerald, "Developers Take Steps to Reinvest Suburban Office Parks," *Boston Globe*, July 27, 2014, http://www.bostonglobe.com/business/2014/07/26/suburban-office-parks-turning-live-work-play-development-compete-with-cities/kYJHwumXiLKU2bFvCvhBeM/story.html?hootPostID=cc6a261a6d1864b314b832e2aa1822bb.

26. Ibid.

27. Reid Ewing et al., "Traffic Generated by Mixed-Use Developments: Six-Region Study Using Consistent Built Environmental Measures," *Journal of Urban Planning and Development* 137, no. 3 (2011): 248–61.

28. Robert Cervero, "Land-Use Mixing and Suburban Mobility," *Transportation Quarterly* 42, no. 3 (1988): 429–46.

29. Ibid., 435–36.

30. Robert Dunphy, "The Suburban Office Parking Conundrum," *Development Magazine*, Fall 2016, http://www.naiop.org/en/Magazine/2016/Fall-2016/Development-Ownership/The-Suburban-Office-Parking-Conundrum.aspx.

31. Ibid.

32. Fee and Munson, Inc., *Hacienda Business Park: Design Guidelines* (San Francisco, CA: Fee and Munson, Inc., 1983).

33. Robert Cervero and Bruce Griesenbeck, "Factors Influencing Commuting Choices in Suburban Labor Markets: A Case Analysis of Pleasanton, California," *Transportation Research A* 22, no. 3 (1988): 151–61.

34. Kathleen McCormick, "Cottle Transit Village: Dense Mixed Use in San Jose," *Urban Land* 74, no. 9/10 (2015): 94–98.

35. Ibid., 97.

36. Cervero, *Suburban Gridlock* and *America's Suburban Centers*; Garreau, *Edge City*.

37. Luke Mullens, "The Audacious Plan to Turn a Sprawling DC Suburb into a Big City," *The Washingtonian*, Open House Blog, Development, March 29, 2015, http://www.washingtonian.com/blogs/openhouse/development/the-audacious-plan-to-turn-a-sprawling-dc-suburb-into-a-big-city.php.

38. Ibid.

39. Robert Cervero et al., *Transit Oriented Development in America: Experiences, Challenges, and Prospects,* Report 102 (Washington, DC: Transit Cooperative Research Program, 2004), 94–98.

40. Mullens, "The Audacious Plan."

41. Lisa Rein and Kafia Hosh, "Transformed Tysons Corner Still Years Away in Fairfax," *Washington Post*, June 23, 2010.

42. Hiroaki Suzuki, Robert Cervero, and Kanako Iuchi, *Transforming Cities with Transit* (Washington, DC, The World Bank, 2013).

43. Lisa Selin Davis, "Luxury Living on the Mall Parking Lot," *The Wall Street Journal*, December 11, 2015, http://www.wsj.com/articles/luxury-living-on-the-mall-parking-lot-1418313891.

44. Ron Heckman, "Infill Retail Not without Its Challenges," *Urban Land*, November 13, 2013, http://urbanland.uli.org/news/infill-retail-not-without-challenges/.

45. See http://thorntonplaceliving.com/apartments/, accessed March 27, 2015.

46. Urban Land Institute, *Shifting Suburbs: Reinventing Infrastructure for Compact Development* (Washington, DC: Urban Land Institute, 2012).

47. Ellen Dunham-Jones and June Williamson, "Mass Transit Systems Are Expanding into the Suburbs," in *Urban Transportation Innovations Worldwide: A Handbook of Best Practices*, ed. Roger Kemp and Carl J. Stephani (Jefferson, NC: McFarland, 2015).

48. G. M. Filisko, "The Suburbs Were Made for Walking," *On Common Ground* (Winter 2017): 24–29.

49. Urban Land Institute, *Shifting Suburbs*.

CHAPTER 7

1. By *public transport* we mean high-capacity, shared passenger services available to the general public, such as conventional buses, metros (e.g., heavy-rail transit), light-rail transit, streetcars (or tramways), commuter trains, and paratransit (e.g., microbuses and minibuses). The term *public transport* is more universally used, but in the United States *transit* or *public transit* is favored. The terms are synonymous and are used interchangeably here. Of note, *transit* is the *T* in *TOD*, the focus of this chapter.

2. Peter Calthorpe, *The New American Metropolis: Ecology, Community, and the American Dream* (New York: Princeton Architectural Press, 1993); Robert Cervero, Christopher Ferrell, and Stephen Murphy, "Transit-Oriented Development and Joint Development in the United States: A Literature Review," *Research Results Digest Number 52*, Transit Cooperative Research Program, October 2002, http://gulliver.trb.org/publications/tcrp/tcrp_rrd_52.pdf; Carey Curtis, John L Renne, and Luca Bertolini, *Transit Oriented Development: Making It Happen* (Surrey, UK: Ashgate, 2009).

3. Michael Bernick and Robert Cervero, *Transit Villages for the 21st Century* (New York: McGraw-Hill, 1997).

4. Ibid.; Luca Bertolini and Tejo Spit, *Cities on Rails: The Redevelopment of Railway Station Areas* (London: E & FN Spon, 1998).

5. Brad Bromberg, "Where Are the New Jobs Going?," *On Common Ground* (Summer 2015): 4–11.

6. Dan Costello, et al., *The Returning City: Historic Presentation and Transit in the Age of Civic Revival* (Washington, DC: Federal Transit Administration, National Trust for Historic Preservation, 2003), 10.

7. Anthony Venables, "Evaluating Urban Transport Improvements: Cost–Benefit Analysis in the Presence of Agglomeration and Income Taxation," *Journal of Transport Economics and Policy* 41, no. 2 (2007): 173–88.

8. Bertolini and Spit, *Cities on Rails*; Hank Dittmar and Gloria Ohland, eds., *The New Transit Town: Best Practices in Transit-Oriented Development* (Washington, DC: Island Press, 2004).

9. Michael Marks, "People Near Transit: Improving Accessibility and Rapid Transit Coverage in Large Cities" (New York: Institute for Transportation Development and Policy, 2016).

10. Peter Hall, *Cities of Tomorrow: An Intellectual History of Urban Planning and Design in the Twentieth Century* (Oxford, UK: Blackwell Publishing, 1988).

11. Robert Cervero, *The Transit Metropolis: A Global Inquiry* (Washington, DC: Island Press, 1998).

12. Bertolini and Spit, *Cities on Rails*.

13. Bernick and Cervero, *Transit Villages for the 21st Century*, 5.

14. Center for Transit-Oriented Development, "Transit-Oriented Development Strategic Plan/Metro TOD Program" (Washington, DC: Center for Transit-Oriented Development, undated).

15. Reconnecting America and the Center for Transit-Oriented Development, "TOD 202: Station Area Planning," 2008, http://www.reconnectingamerica.org/resource-center/books-and-reports/2008/tod-202-station-area-planning/.

16. Portland Sustainable Transport Lab, "2012 Portland Metropolitan Regional Transportation System Performance Report," Portland State University, 2013; Center for Transit-Oriented Development, "Transit-Oriented Development Strategic Plan."

17. Robert Cervero, "Transit-Supportive Development in the United States: Experiences and Prospects" (Washington, DC: U.S. Department of Transportation, Federal Transit Administration, 1993).

18. Reid Ewing and Keith Bartholomew, *Pedestrian and Transit-Oriented Design* (Washington, DC: Urban Land Institute and American Planning Association, 2013), Appendix E.

19. Edward Beimborm, and Harvey Rabinowitz, "Guidelines for Transit-Sensitive Suburban Land Use Design" (Washington, DC: U.S. Department of Transportation, Urban Mass Transportation Administration, 1991); Cervero, "Transit-Supportive Development in the United States: Experiences and Prospects"; Reid Ewing, "Pedestrian and Transit-Friendly Design" (Tallahassee: Florida Department of Transportation, 1996); and Ewing and Bartholomew, *Pedestrian and Transit-Oriented Design*.

20. Ewing and Bartholomew, *Pedestrian and Transit-Oriented Design*.

21. Cervero, "Transit-Supportive Development in the United States."

22. Pace, "Transit Supportive Guidelines," undated, http://www.pacebus.com/guidelines/index.asp.

23. Robert Cervero and John Landis, "Twenty Years of BART: Land Use and Development Impacts," *Transportation Research A* 31, no. 4 (1997): 309–33; Bernick and Cervero, *Transit Villages for the 21st Century*.

24. Bernick and Cervero, *Transit Villages for the 21st Century*; Federal Highway Administration, "The Fruitvale Transit Village Project" (Washington, DC: FHA, n.d.), http://www.fhwa.dot.gov/environment/environmental_justice/case_studies/case6.cfm, accessed February 21, 2015.

25. Calthorpe, *The New American Metropolis*; Robert Cervero et al., "Transit Oriented Development in America: Experiences, Challenges, and Prospects," Report 102 (Washington, DC: Transit Cooperative Research Program, 2004).

26. Robert Cervero, Ben Caldwell, and Jesus Cuellar, "Bike-and-Ride: Build It and They Will Come," *Journal of Public Transportation* 16, no. 4 (2013): 83–105.

27. Robert Cervero, "Light Rail and Urban Development," *Journal of the American Planning Association* 50, no. 2 (1984): 133–47; Gloria Ohland and Shellie Poticha, *Street Smart: Streetcars and Cities in the Twenty-First Century* (Washington, DC: Reconnecting America, 2006).

28. Reconnecting America, "TOD 101: Why Transit-Oriented Development and Why Now?" (Oakland, CA: Reconnecting America and the Center for Transit-Oriented Development, 2007), 6.

29. Ibid.

30. Population Count Census Tract 51 in Multnomah County, U.S. Decennial Census 1990, 2010.

31. Reconnecting America, *Encouraging Transit Oriented Development*: *Cases That Work* (Washington, DC: Reconnecting America, 2012).

32. Ian Carleton and Robert Cervero, "Developing and Implementing the City of Los Angeles' Transit Corridors Strategy: Coordinated Action toward a Transit-Oriented Metropolis," City of Los Angeles, Office of the Mayor, 2012.

33. William H. K. Lam and Michael G. H. Bell, *Advanced Modeling for Transit Operations and Service Planning* (Oxford, England: Elsevier, 2003); Robert Cervero and Jin Murakami, "Rail + Property Development in Hong Kong: Experiences and Extensions," *Urban Studies* 46, no. 10 (2009): 2019–43.

34. Cervero and Murakami, "Rail + Property Development." The urban design audits were qualitative assessments of three to five primary walking corridors from 500 meters away to station entrances of sampled MTR stations. R+P projects were judged to have transit-oriented designs if they included mixed land uses (notably

convenience stores) and high-quality walking environments (reflected by high connectivity and physical integration, well-designed skywalks that provided grade separation from motorized traffic, good signage, and the presence of parks, open space, and other civic amenities).

35. Ibid.

36. Ibid.

37. Robert Cervero and Cathleen Sullivan, "Green TODs: Marrying Transit-Oriented Development and Green Urbanism," *International Journal of Sustainable Development & World Ecology* 18, no. 3 (2011), 210–18.

38. Timothy Beatley, *Green Urbanism: Learning from European Cities* (Washington, DC: Island Press, 2000); Peter Newman, Timothy Beatley, and Heather Boyer, *Resilient Cities: Responding to Peak Oil and Climate Change* (Washington, DC: Island Press, 2009).

39. Cervero and Sullivan, "Green TODs."

40. Harrison Fraker, *The Hidden Potential of Sustainable Neighborhoods: Lessons from Low-Carbon Communities* (Washington, DC: Island Press, 2013).

41. Between 1997 and 2002, a full environmental impact profile of Hammarby Sjöstad was commissioned by the City of Stockholm. For drawing comparative insights, a reference level was defined: "The reference level used to measure the anticipated reduction in environmental impact in Hammarby Sjöstad is the technology level current in the early 1990s, when planning work on the city district began." This reference level can be viewed as conventional new development in the Stockholm region at the time. Hammarby Sjöstad is far more built out today, so the results from nearly a decade ago could very well have changed (probably in the direction of even larger differentials relative to the reference level as the project has matured and expanded). At the time the assessment was conducted, approximately five thousand apartment units had been constructed, less than half of the total development today. This was a full life-cycle evaluation that included energy expenditures and waste tied to site clearance, construction, and operation phases of the development. Grontmij AB, *Report Summary: Follow Up of Environmental Impact in Hammarby Sjöstad* (Stockholm: Grontmij AB, 2008).

42. Ibid.

43. Nicole Foletta and Simon Field, "Europe's Vibrant Low Car(bon) Communities" (New York: Institute for Transportation Development and Policy, 2011).

44. Cervero and Sullivan, "Green TODs."

45. Robert Cervero and Cathleen Sullivan, "TODs for Tots," *Planning* (February 2011): 27–31.

46. "GWI Terrain: An Eco Area," undated, http://gwl-terrein.nl/bezoekers/gwl-terrain-an-urban-eco-area/, accessed September 25, 2016.

47. Andrea Broaddus, "A Tale of Two Eco-Suburbs in Freiburg, Germany: Parking Provision and Car Use," *Transportation Research Record* 2187 (2010): 114–22.

48. Robert Cervero, et al., *Transit Oriented Development in America: Experiences, Challenges, and Prospects* (Washington, DC: Transit Cooperative Research Program, Report 102, 2004).

49. Ibid.

50. Ruth Knack, "Great Places: Year Nine," *Planning* 81, no. 11 (2015): 13–24.

51. Hyungun Sung and Ju-Taek Oh, "Transit-Oriented Development in a High-Density City: Identifying Its Association with Transit Ridership in Seoul, Korea," *Cities* 28, no. 1 (2011): 70–82.

CHAPTER 8

1. David Banister, *Unsustainable Transport: City Transport in the New Century* (London: Routledge, 2005, 2008); Gabriel Dupuy, *Towards Sustainable Transport: The Challenge of Car Dependence* (Montrouge, France: John Libbey Eurotext, 2011).

2. Kenneth Button, *Transportation Economics* (Cheltenham, UK: Edward Elgar, 2010), 270.

3. Timothy Beatley, *Green Urbanism: Learning from European Cities* (Washington, DC: Island Press, 2000).

4. Beatley, *Green Urbanism*; Nicole Foletta and Simon Field, "Europe's Vibrant New Low Car(bon) Communities" (New York: ITDP Publications, 2011).

5. Wikipedia, The Free Encyclopedia, "List of Car-Free Places," undated, http://en.wikipedia.org/wiki/List_of_car-free_places, accessed February 20, 2015.

6. Andrea Broaddus, "Tale of Two Eco-Suburbs in Freiburg, Germany: Encouraging Transit and Bicycle Use by Restricting Parking Provisions," *Transportation Research Record: Journal of the Transportation Research Board* 2187 (2010): 114–22; Robert Cervero and Cathleen Sullivan, "Green TODs: Marrying Transit-Oriented Development and Green Urbanism," *International Journal of Sustainable Development & World Ecology* 18, no. 3 (2011): 210–18.

7. Sustainability Office, City of Freiburg, "Freiburg: Green City," http://www.fwtm.freiburg.de/servlet/PB/show/1199617l2/GreenCity E.pdf, accessed May 14, 2015.

8. City of Barcelona, poster display of "Superblocks," Smart City Expo and World Congress, Barcelona, Spain, November 14–16, 2016.

9. Carmen Hass-Klau, *The Pedestrian and City Traffic* (London: Belhaven Press, 1990); Carmen Hass-Klau, "Impact of Pedestrianisation and Traffic Calming on Retailing," *Transport Policy* 1, no, 1 (1993): 21–31.

10. Phil Goodwin, Carmen Haas-Klau, and Stephen Cairns, "Evidence on the Effects of Road Capacity Reduction on Traffic Levels," *Journal of Transportation Engineering + Control* 39, no. 6 (1998): 348–54.

11. Will Reisman, "Road Diets Used as Tool for Reclaiming Neighborhoods in San Francisco," *San Francisco Examiner,* August 24, 2012.

12. Matthew Roth, "San Francisco Planners Proud of Long List of Road Diets," *Streetsblog San Francisco,* March 31, 2010.

13. Herman Huang, J. Richard Stewart, and Charles Zegeer, "Evaluation of Lane Reduction 'Road Diet' Measures and Their Effects on Crashes and Injuries" (Washington, DC: U.S. Department of Transportation, Highway Safety Information System, 2002).

14. Congress for the New Urbanism, https://www.cnu.org/highways/chattanooga, accessed May 4, 2015.

15. Federal Highway Administration, "Street Designs: Part 2, Sustainable Roads," http://www.fhwa.dot.gov/publications/publicroads/11marapr/02.cfm, accessed May 4, 2015.

16. Robert Cervero, "Green Connectors: Off Shore Examples," *Planning* (May 2003): 25–29.

17. Steffen Lehmann, "Low Carbon Cities; More Than Just Buildings," in *Low Carbon Cities: Transforming Urban Systems,* ed. S. Lehmann (London: Routledge, 2015), chapter 1, 1–55.

18. Congress for the New Urbanism, "Freeways without Futures," undated, https://www.cnu.org/highways-boulevards/freeways-without-futures/2017, accessed April 13, 2017.

19. Robert Cervero, "Urban Reclamation and Regeneration in Seoul, South Korea," in *Physical Infrastructure Development: Balancing the Growth, Equity and Environmental Imperatives*, ed. William Ascher and Corinne Krupp (New York: Palgrave Macmillan, 2010), chapter 7, 187–201.

20. Seoul Metropolitan Government, Cheonggyecheon Restoration Project, Seoul, Korea, 2003, http://www.metro.seoul/kr/kor2000/chungaehome/.

21. Cheong Gye Cheon, which means "clear valley stream," had long been a source of fresh water and "heart and soul" of urban life in Seoul, going back to the fourteenth century. During the Chosun dynasty (1392–1910), city dwellers did their laundry in the stream and often socialized on its banks. After the Korean War (1950–1953), the stream's character quickly changed when temporary refugee housing was built along its banks. Untreated waste was dumped directly into the waterway, turning it into a veritable cesspool and eventually prompting city officials to cover the stream with an elevated freeway.

22. The CGC freeway, 50–80 meters in width and 6 kilometers in length, opened in 1971 in the heart of central Seoul. Below the road were the running stream and a sewer trunk line. The CGC freeway quickly became an important conduit for movement to and within central-city Seoul, gaining importance as new towns began to populate the region's periphery in the 1980s and 1990s. However, time quickly took its toll on the facility. A 1992 study by the Korean Society of Civil Engineers found that more than 20 percent of the freeway's steel beams were seriously corroded and in need of urgent repair. The Seoul Metropolitan Government immediately began repairing the road's understructure; however, because of concerns about the road's long-term safety and stability, this was seen as a stopgap to either reconstructing the freeway or tearing it down. See Robert Cervero, "Urban Reclamation and Regeneration in Seoul, Republic of Korea," *Low Carbon Cities: Transforming Urban Systems*, ed. S. Lehmann (London: Routledge, 2015), 224–34.

23. The CGC project was not without controversy. Besides concerns over possible increases in traffic congestion, many small shopkeepers and merchants opposed the project for fear of losing business. Alongside the former elevated freeway was an assembly of small-scale shops and markets selling shoes, apparel, tools, electronic goods, and appliances. In 2000, more than 200,000 merchants and 60,000 shops were within 2 kilometers of the freeway. To some, the freeway-to-greenway conversion threatened to alter the existing tradeshed and disrupt the flow of customers

and logistics. Moreover, informal vendors would lose their spots under the freeway, in the past an unwanted place where they, and they alone, could ply their trade rent-free. After intensive negotiations, the Seoul Metropolitan Government was able to head off opposition by financially compensating merchants and relocating a number of shops to a newly constructed market center south of the Han River that was easily accessible by highways and public transit.

24. "The 15 Coolest Neighborhoods in the World in 2016," *How I Travel* blog, http://www.howitravel.co/the-15-coolest-neighborhoods-in-the-world-in-2016, accessed December 15, 2016.

25. John Pucher, et al., "Public Transport Reforms in Seoul: Innovations Motivated by Funding Crisis," *Journal of Public Transportation* 8, no. 5 (2005): 41–62.

26. Cervero, "Urban Reclamation and Regeneration in Seoul."

27. Seoul Development Institute, *Monitoring on Bus Operation and Level of Service* (Seoul: Seoul Development Institute, 2005).

28. Seoul Development Institute, *Study on Urban Structure and Form in CGC Project* (Seoul: Seoul Development Institute, 2006).

29. Ibid.

30. Chang-Deok Kang and Robert Cervero, "From Elevated Freeway to Urban Greenway: Land Value Impacts of Seoul, Korea's CGC Project," *Urban Studies* 46, no. 13 (2009): 2771–94.

31. Robert Cervero and Chang-Deok Kang, "From Elevated Freeway to Linear Park: Land Price Impacts of Seoul, Korea's CGC Project," VWP-2008-7 (Berkeley: Institute of Transportation Studies, UC Berkeley Center for Future Urban Transportation, 2008); Chang-Deok Kang, "Land Market Impacts and Firm Geography in a Green and Transit-Oriented City: The Case of Seoul, Korea" (PhD diss. D09-003, Berkeley: Fischer Center for Real Estate and Urban Economics, University of California, 2009); Myungjun Jang and Chang-Deok Kang, "The Effects of Urban Greenways on the Geography of Office Sectors and Employment Densities in Seoul, Korea," *Urban Studies* 53, no. 5 (2016): 1022–41.

32. A location quotient (LQ) measures an area's industrial or occupational specialization relative to a larger geographic unit, in our case the proportion of total workers in creative class industries for distance bands of up to 1,000 meters from the greenway entrances or motorway on-ramps relative to all workers in the Seoul region located beyond the 1,000-meter buffer; see http://www.bea.gov/faq/index.cfm?faq_id=478#sthash.6MJf6wZW.dpuf.

33. Seoul Development Institute, *Monitoring on Bus Operation and Level of Service.*

34. Kee Yeon Hwang, "Cheong Gye Cheon Restoration & City Regeneration: Cheong Gye Cheon: Urban Revitalization and Future Vision" (Seoul: Seoul Metropolitan Government, 2006).

35. William Lathrop, "San Francisco Freeway Revolt," *Transportation Engineering Journal* 97 (1971): 133–44.

36. Evan Rose, "Changing Spaces," *Urban Land* 62, no. 3 (2003): 85.

37. Rose, "Changing Spaces," 84–89; Bonnie Fisher, "Close Up: the Embarcadero," *Planning* 71, no. 1 (2005): 16–17.

38. Elizabeth Macdonald, "Building a Boulevard," *Access* 28 (2006): 2–9.

39. Robert Cervero, Junhee Kang, and Kevin Shively, "From Elevated Freeways to Surface Boulevards: Neighborhood and Housing Price Impacts in San Francisco," *Journal of Urbanism* 2, no. 1 (2009): 31–50.

40. Rose, "Changing Spaces."

41. Rose, "Changing Spaces," 87.

42. San Francisco Planning and Urban Research Association (SPUR), "Cutting through Transportation Tangles: Two Issues," Report 265 (San Francisco: SPUR, 1990).

43. Surface Transportation Policy Project (STPP), "Dangerous by Design: Pedestrian Safety in California" (San Francisco: STPP, 2000).

44. Cervero et al., "From Elevated Freeways to Surface Boulevards."

45. Systan, Inc., "Central Freeway Evaluation Report, San Francisco" (San Francisco: City and County of San Francisco Department of Planning, 1997).

46. San Francisco Department of Park and Traffic, "Octavia Boulevard Operation, Six Month Report," San Francisco, unpublished report, 2006.

47. Macdonald, "Building a Boulevard."

48. Lehmann, "Low Carbon Cities."

CHAPTER 9

1. United Nations Population Division, "World Urbanization Prospects, the 2014 Revision," 2014, http://esa.un.org/unpd/wup/.

2. WardsAuto Web site, 2012, http://wardsauto.com/.

3. "China Overtakes US as World's Biggest Car Market," *The Guardian*, January 8, 2010, http://www.guardian.co.uk/business/2010/jan/08/china-us-car-sales-overtakes.

4. Boris Pushkarev, Jeffrey Zupan, and Robert Cumella, *Urban Rail in America: An Exploration of Criteria for Fixed-Guideway Transit* (Bloomington: Indiana University Press, 1982); Peter Newman and Jeffrey Kenworthy, "Urban Design to Reduce Automobile Dependence," *Opolis* 2, no. 1 (2006): 35–52; Erick Guerra and Robert Cervero, "Cost of a Ride: The Effects of Densities on Fixed-Guideway Transit Ridership and Costs," *Journal of the American Planning Association* 77, no. 3 (2011): 267–90, doi:10.1080/01944363.2011.589767.

5. Somik Vinay Lall, J. Vernon Henderson, and Anthony J. Venables, *Africa's Cities* (Washington, DC: World Bank, 2017), https://openknowledge.worldbank.org/handle/10986/25896.

6. INEGI, "Encuesta Intercensal 2015," 2015, http://www.inegi.org.mx/est/contenidos/Proyectos/encuestas/hogares/especiales/ei2015/.

7. Roger Behrens, Dorothy McCormick, and David Mfinanga, eds., *Paratransit in African Cities: Operations, Regulation and Reform* (London and New York: Routledge, 2016), 11.

8. UN Habitat, *Planning and Design for Sustainable Urban Mobility: Global Report on Human Settlements* (Nairobi, Kenya: UN Habitat, 2013).

9. Ibid.

10. Secretaría Distrital de Movilidad de Bogotá, "Informe de Indicadores. Encuesta de Movilidad de Bogotá 2011" (Bogotá: Alcaldía Mayor de Bogotá (DC), 2013).

11. Hua Zhang, Susan A. Shaheen, and Xingpeng Chen, "Bicycle Evolution in China: From the 1900s to the Present," *International Journal of Sustainable Transportation* 8, no. 5 (2014): 317–35, doi:10.1080/15568318.2012.699999.

12. John Pucher and Ralph Buehler, "Making Cycling Irresistible: Lessons from the Netherlands, Denmark and Germany," *Transport Reviews* 28, no. 4 (2008): 495–528, doi:10.1080/01441640701806612.

13. Deike Peters, "Gender and Sustainable Urban Mobility," *Thematic Study Prepared for Sustainable Urban Mobility: Global Report on Human Settlements*, 2013, http://civitas -initiative.eu/sites/default/files/unhabitat_gender_surbanmobilitlity_0.pdf.

14. International Transport Forum, "Improving Safety for Motorcycle, Scooter and Moped Riders," ITF Research Reports (Paris: OECD Publishing, 2015).

15. "Dinas Pendapatan Dan Pengelolaan Aset Daerah Provinsi Jawa Tengah," 2015, http://dppad.jatengprov.go.id.

16. Teik Hua Law, Hussain Hamid, and Chia Ning Goh, "The Motorcycle to Passenger Car Ownership Ratio and Economic Growth: A Cross-Country Analysis," *Journal of Transport Geography* 46 (2015): 122–28, doi:10.1016/j.jtrangeo.2015.06.007.

17. Shuhei Nishitateno and Paul J. Burke, "The Motorcycle Kuznets Curve," *Journal of Transport Geography* 36 (2014): 116–23, doi:10.1016/j.jtrangeo.2014.03.008.

18. Shlomo Angel et al., "The Dimensions of Global Urban Expansion: Estimates and Projections for All Countries, 2000–2050," *Progress in Planning* 75, no. 2 (2011): 53–107, doi:10.1016/j.progress.2011.04.001; Shlomo Angel, Stephen C. Sheppard, and Daniel L. Civco, "The Dynamics of Global Urban Expansion" (Washington, DC: The World Bank, Transport and Urban Development Department, 2005), https: //www.citiesalliance.org/ca/sites/citiesalliance.org/files/CA_Docs/resources/upgrad-ing/urban-expansion/1.pdf.

19. Erick Guerra, "The Geography of Car Ownership in Mexico City: A Joint Model of Households' Residential Location and Car Ownership Decisions," *Journal of Transport Geography* 43 (2015): 171–80, doi:10.1016/j.jtrangeo.2015.01.014.

20. James E. Rosenbaum, "Changing the Geography of Opportunity by Expanding Residential Choice: Lessons from the Gautreaux Program," *Housing Policy Debate* 6, no. 1 (1995): 231–69, doi:10.1080/10511482.1995.9521186; Sako Musterd and Roger Andersson, "Housing Mix, Social Mix, and Social Opportunities," *Urban Affairs Review* 40, no. 6 (2005): 761–90, doi:10.1177/1078087405276006; George Galster et al., "Does Neighborhood Income Mix Affect Earnings of Adults? New Evidence from Sweden," *Journal of Urban Economics* 63, no. 3 (2008): 858–70, doi:10.1016/j .jue.2007.07.002; Tama Leventhal and Jeanne Brooks-Gunn, "Moving to Opportunity: An Experimental Study of Neighborhood Effects on Mental Health," *American Journal of Public Health* 93, no. 9 (2003): 1576–82; Anne C. Case and Lawrence F. Katz, "The Company You Keep: The Effects of Family and Neighborhood on Disadvantaged Youths," Working Paper (National Bureau of Economic Research, 1991), http://www.nber.org/papers/w3705.

21. Board of Governors of the Federal Reserve System, "Mortgage Debt Outstanding, June 2016," 2016, https://www.federalreserve.gov/econresdata/releases/mortout

stand/current.htm; U.S. Census Bureau, "American Community Survey (ACS)," 2015, http://www.census.gov/programs-surveys/acs/.

22. Gilles Duranton and Erick Guerra, "Developing a Common Narrative on Urban Accessibility: An Urban Planning Perspective" (Washington, DC: Brookings Institution, 2017).

23. Figures vary somewhat by *favela* definition and by source.

24. Shack/Slum Dwellers International, "SDI's Practices for Change," 2015, http://sdinet .org/about-us/sdis-practices-for-change/.

25. Jose Brakarz and Wanda Aduan, "Favela-Bairro: Scaled-Up Urban Development in Brazil" (Washington, DC: Inter-American Development Bank, 2004), http://web .worldbank.org/archive/website00819C/WEB/PDF/BRAZIL_F.PDF.

26. Ayse Pamuk and Paulo Fernando A Cavalieri, "Alleviating Urban Poverty in a Global City: New Trends in Upgrading Rio-de-Janeiro's Favelas," *Habitat International* 22, no. 4 (1998): 449–62, doi:10.1016/S0197-3975(98)00022-8; Elizabeth Riley, Jorge Fiori, and Ronaldo Ramirez, "Favela Bairro and a New Generation of Housing Programmes for the Urban Poor," *Geoforum, Urban Brazil*, 32, no. 4 (2001): 521–31, doi:10.1016/S0016-7185(01)00016-1; Brakarz and Aduan, "Favela-Bairro"; Roberto Segre, "Formal–Informal Connections in the Favelas of Rio de Janeiro: The Favela-Bairro Programme," in *Rethinking the Informal City: Critical Perspectives from Latin America*, ed. Felipe Hernandez, Peter Kellet, and Lea K. Allen, Remapping Cultural History 11 (New York: Berghahn Books, 2009), 163; Inter-American Development Bank, "Development Effectiveness Overview 2010" (Washington, DC: Inter-American Development Bank, 2010), https://publications.iadb.org /bitstream/handle/11319/2133/Development%20Effectiveness%20Overview%20 2010.pdf?sequence=1; Fernando Luiz Lara, "Favela Upgrade in Brazil: A Reverse of Participatory Processes," *Journal of Urban Design* 18, no. 4 (2013): 553–64, doi:10 .1080/13574809.2013.824363.

27. World Bank, "Vietnam: Urban Upgrading Project" (Washington, DC: World Bank, 2004), http://documents.worldbank.org/curated/en/105001468762926749/Vietnam -Urban-Upgrading-Project; IEG Review Team, "Vietnam: Urban Upgrading Project" (Washington, DC: World Bank, 2016), http://documents.worldbank.org/curated /en/850671467056929965/Vietnam-Urban-Upgrading-Project.

28. Inter-American Development Bank, "Development Effectiveness Overview 2010. pdf," 99–102.

29. David Gouverneur, *Planning and Design for Future Informal Settlements: Shaping the Self-Constructed City* (New York: Routledge, 2015); Shlomo Angel, *Planet of Cities* (Cambridge, MA: Lincoln Institute of Land Policy, 2012), http://wagner.nyu.edu /files/faculty/publications/PlanetofCities_Shlomo_Web_Chapter.pdf.

30. Peter Land, *The Experimental Housing Project (PREVI), Lima: Design and Technology in a New Neighborhood* (Bogotá: Universidad de Los Andes, 2015); Gouverneur, *Planning and Design for Future Informal Settlements*.

31. Cedric Pugh, "Housing Policy Development in Developing Countries," *Cities* 11, no. 3 (1994): 159–80, doi:10.1016/0264-2751(94)90057-4.

32. Michael Cohen, "Aid, Density, and Urban Form: Anticipating Dakar," *Built Environment* 33, no. 2 (May 31, 2007): 145–56, doi:10.2148/benv.33.2.145; The World

Bank, "Senegal: Sites and Services Project. Project Completion Report" (Washington, DC: The World Bank, 1983), http://documents.worldbank.org/curated/en/525191468777917949/Senegal-Sites-and-Services-Project.

33. Cohen, "Aid, Density, and Urban Form."

34. Ministère de l'Urbanisme et de l'Aménagement du Territoire, "Plan Directeur d'Urbanisme de la Région de Dakar, Horizon 2025-Bilan du PDU de Dakar 2001" (Dakar: Ministère de l'Urbanisme et de l'Aménagement du Territoire, 2001).

35. McGuirk, Justin, "PREVI: The Metabolist Utopia," *Domus Magazine*, April 21, 2011, http://www.domusweb.it/en/architecture/2011/04/21/previ-the-metabolist-utopia.html; Gouverneur, *Planning and Design for Future Informal Settlements*.

36. Ministère de l'Urbanisme et de l'Aménagement du Territoire, "Plan Directeur d'Urbanisme de la Région de Dakar."

37. The World Bank, "Housing: Enabling Markets to Work" (Washington, DC: The World Bank, April 30, 1993), http://documents.worldbank.org/curated/en/387041468345854972/Housing-enabling-markets-to-work; Cedric Pugh, "Urbanization in Developing Countries: An Overview of the Economic and Policy Issues in the 1990s," *Cities* 12, no. 6 (1995): 381–98, doi:10.1016/0264-2751(95)00083-X; Cecilia Zanetta, "The Evolution of the World Bank's Urban Lending in Latin America: From Sites and Services to Municipal Reform and Beyond," *Habitat International* 25, no. 4 (2001): 513–33, doi:10.1016/S0197-3975(01)00022-4.

38. The World Bank, "Senegal: Sites and Services Project"; The World Bank, "Senegal: Municipal and Housing Development Project" (Washington, DC: The World Bank, 1997), http://documents.worldbank.org/curated/en/309091468760177120/Senegal-Municipal-and-Housing-Development-Project.

39. Maguemati Wabgou, "Governance of Migration in Senegal: The Role of Government in Formulating Migration Policies," in *International Migration and National Development in Sub-Saharan Africa*, ed. Aderanti Adepojou, Ton Van Naerssen, and Annalies Zoomers (Boston: Brill, 2007), 141–60; Mona Serageldin and Erick Guerra, "Migration, Remittances and Investment in Sub-Saharan Africa" (Cambridge, MA: Institute for International Urban Development, 2008).

40. Paavo Monkkonen, "The Housing Transition in Mexico Expanding Access to Housing Finance," *Urban Affairs Review* 47, no. 5 (2011): 672–95, doi:10.1177/1078087411400381; Paavo Monkkonen, "Housing Finance Reform and Increasing Socioeconomic Segregation in Mexico," *International Journal of Urban and Regional Research* 36, no. 4 (2011): 757–72, doi:10.1111/j.1468-2427.2011.01085.x; María del Carmen Pardo and Ernesto Velasco Sánchez, *El Proceso de Modernización en el Infonavit 2001–2006: Estrategia, Redes y Liderazgo* (México, D.F.: Colegio de México, 2006).

41. Monkkonen, "The Housing Transition in Mexico Expanding Access to Housing Finance."

42. Ibid.; Monkkonen, "Housing Finance Reform and Increasing Socioeconomic Segregation in Mexico."

43. Ibid.

44. Erick Guerra, "Has Mexico City's Shift to Commercially Produced Housing Increased Car Ownership and Car Use?," *Journal of Transport and Land Use* 8, no. 2 (2015): 171–89.

45. Beatriz García Peralta and Andreas Hofer, "Housing for the Working Class on the Periphery of Mexico City: A New Version of Gated Communities," *Social Justice* 33, no. 3 (January 1, 2006): 129–41.

46. World Resources Institute, *Statement: Development Banks Announce "Game Changer" for Sustainable Transport at Rio+20*, 2012, http://www.wri.org/news/2012/06/statement-development-banks-announce-game-changer-sustainable-transport-rio20.

47. Hiroaki Suzuki, Robert Cervero, and Kanako Iuchi, *Transforming Cities with Transit: Transit and Land-Use Integration for Sustainable Urban Development* (World Bank Publications, 2013).

48. Robert Cervero, *The Transit Metropolis: A Global Inquiry* (Washington, DC: Island Press, 1998).

49. Robert Cervero, "Linking Urban Transport and Land Use in Developing Countries," *Journal of Transport and Land Use* 6, no. 1 (2013): 7–24.

50. Robert Cervero and Jennifer Day, "Suburbanization and Transit-Oriented Development in China," *Transport Policy* 15, no. 5 (2008): 315–23, doi:10.1016/j.tranpol.2008.12.011.

51. Cervero, "Linking Urban Transport and Land Use in Developing Countries."

52. Ming Zhang, "Chinese Edition of Transit-Oriented Development," *Transportation Research Record: Journal of the Transportation Research Board* 2038 (2007): 120–27, doi:10.3141/2038-16; Cervero and Day, "Suburbanization and Transit-Oriented Development in China."

53. Georges Darido, Mariana Torres-Montoya, and Shomik Mehndiratta, "Urban Transport and CO_2 Emissions: Some Evidence from Chinese Cities" (Washington, DC: World Bank, 2009).

54. Ming Zhang, "Chinese Edition of Transit-Oriented Development," *Transportation Research Record: Journal of the Transportation Research Board* 2038 (2007): 120–27, doi:10.3141/2038-16.

55. Jinling Liu and Yong Zhang, "Analysis to Passenger Volume Effect of Land Use along Urban Rail Transit," *Urban Transport of China* 2 (2004): 54–57.

56. Zhang, "Chinese Edition of Transit-Oriented Development."

57. Robert Cervero and Jin Murakami, "Rail and Property Development in Hong Kong: Experiences and Extensions," *Urban Studies* 46, no. 10 (2009): 2019–43, doi:10.1177/0042098009339431.

58. Wen-ling Li and Jing Huang, "The Conception of Transit Metropolis in Guangzhou," in *2010 International Conference on Mechanic Automation and Control Engineering*, 2010, 20, doi:10.1109/MACE.2010.5535305.

59. Hiroaki Suzuki et al., *Financing Transit-Oriented Development with Land Values: Adapting Land Value Capture in Developing Countries* (Washington, DC: World Bank Publications, 2015).

60. Herbert Levinson et al., "Bus Rapid Transit: Synthesis of Case Studies," *Transportation Research Record* 1841 (2003): 1–11, doi:10.3141/1841-01; Dario Hidalgo, "TransMilenio: El Sistema de Transporte Masivo en Bogotá," in *Urban Mobility for All*, Tenth International CODATU Conference (Lome, Togo: Coopération pour le Développement et l'Amélioration des Transport Urbains et Périurbains, 2002).

61. Dario Hidalgo and Luis Gutiérrez, "BRT and BHLS around the World: Explosive Growth, Large Positive Impacts and Many Issues Outstanding," *Research in Transportation Economics* 39, no. 1 (2013): 8–13, doi:10.1016/j.retrec.2012.05.018; Robert Cervero, "Bus Rapid Transit (BRT): An Efficient and Competitive Mode of Public Transport," 20th ACEA, Scientific Advisory Group Report (Brussels, 2013), http://escholarship.org/uc/item/4sn2f5wc.pdf.

62. Suzuki, et al., *Transforming Cities with Transit.*

63. Robert L. Knight and Lisa L. Trygg, "Evidence of Land Use Impacts of Rapid Transit Systems," *Transportation* 6, no. 3 (1977): 231–47; Samuel Seskin, Robert Cervero, and Parsons, Brinckerhoff, Quade & Douglas, "Transit and Urban Form. Volume 1, Part 1: Transit, Urban Form and the Built Environment: A Summary of Knowledge," 1996, http://pubsindex.trb.org/view.aspx?id=467996; Robert Cervero and John Landis, "Twenty Years of the Bay Area Rapid Transit System: Land Use and Development Impacts," *Transportation Research Part A: Policy and Practice* 31, no. 4 (1997): 309–33, doi:10.1016/S0965-8564(96)00027-4.

64. Robert Cervero and Danielle Dai, "BRT TOD: Leveraging Transit Oriented Development with Bus Rapid Transit Investments," *Transport Policy* 36 (2014): 127–38, doi:10.1016/j.tranpol.2014.08.001.

65. Suzuki et al., *Transforming Cities with Transit.*

66. Institute for Transportation and Development Policy, "Improving Access for Guangzhou's Urban Villages," *Institute for Transportation and Development Policy*, August 24, 2015, https://www.itdp.org/improving-access-for-guangzhous-urban-villages/.

67. Hidalgo and Gutiérrez, "BRT and BHLS around the World."

68. Ibid.

69. Manish Shirgaokar, "Expanding Cities and Vehicle Use in India: Differing Impacts of Built Environment Factors on Scooter and Car Use in Mumbai," *Urban Studies* 53, no. 15 (2016): 3296–3316.

70. Erick Guerra, "Mexico City's Suburban Land Use and Transit Connection: The Effects of the Line B Metro Expansion," *Transport Policy* 32 (2014): 105–14, doi:10.1016/j.tranpol.2013.12.011.

71. Sistema de Transporte Colectivo, "Metro de La Ciudad de México," 2016, http://www.metro.cdmx.gob.mx/operacion/afluencia.html.

72. Juan Pablo Bocarejo et al., "An Innovative Transit System and Its Impact on Low Income Users: The Case of the Metrocable in Medellín," *Journal of Transport Geography* 39 (July 2014): 49–61, doi:10.1016/j.jtrangeo.2014.06.018; Peter Brand and Julio D. Dávila, "Mobility Innovation at the Urban Margins: Medellín's Metrocables," *City* 15, no. 6 (2011): 647–661.

73. Dirk Heinrichs and Judith S. Bernet, "Public Transport and Accessibility in Informal Settlements: Aerial Cable Cars in Medellín, Colombia," *Transportation Research Procedia* 4 (2014): 55–67, doi:10.1016/j.trpro.2014.11.005.

74. Brand and Dávila, "Mobility Innovation at the Urban Margins"; Heinrichs and Bernet, "Public Transport and Accessibility in Informal Settlements."

75. Heinrichs and Bernet, "Public Transport and Accessibility in Informal Settlements."

76. Christine Zhen-Wei Qiang, "Telecommunications and Economic Growth," unpublished paper, World Bank, Washington, DC, 2009.

CHAPTER 10

1. Lisa Rayle et al., "Just a Better Taxi? A Survey-Based Comparison of Taxis, Transit, and Ridesourcing Services in San Francisco," *Transport Policy* 45 (2016): 168–78, doi:10.1016/j.tranpol.2015.10.004.

2. A. Hawkins, "Uber and Lyft Just Got a Big Boost from the Public Transportation World," *The Verge*, March 16, 2016, http://www.theverge.com/2016/3/16/11248412 /uber-lyft-APTA-public-transportation-study-last-mile, accessed October 4, 2016.

3. Robert Cervero, "Electric Station Cars in the San Francisco Bay Area," *Transportation Quarterly* 51, no. 2 (1997): 51–61.

4. Hawkins, "Uber and Lyft Just Got a Big Boost from the Public Transportation World."

5. Erick Guerra, "Planning for Cars That Drive Themselves: Metropolitan Planning Organizations, Regional Transportation Plans, and Autonomous Vehicles," *Journal of Planning Education and Research* 36, no. 2 (2016): 210–24, doi:10 .1177/0739456X15613591.

6. U.S. Department of Transportation, "National Transportation Statistics," 2013, http://www.rita.dot.gov/bts/sites/rita.dot.gov.bts/files/publications/national_trans- portation_statistics/index.html.

7. Sven Beiker, "History and Status of Automated Driving in the United States," in *Road Vehicle Automation*, ed. Gereon Meyer and Sven Beiker, Lecture Notes in Mobility (Basel, Switzerland: Springer International Publishing, 2014); Steven Shladover, "Why We Should Develop a Truly Automated Highway System," *Transportation Research Record: Journal of the Transportation Research Board* 1651 (1998): 66–73, doi:10.3141/1651-10.

8. Ford Media Center, "Ford Targets Fully Autonomous Vehicle for Ride Sharing in 2021; Invests in New Tech Companies, Doubles Silicon Valley Team," https://media .ford.com/content/fordmedia/fna/us/en/news/2016/08/16/ford-targets-fully -autonomous-vehicle-for-ride-sharing-in-2021.html, accessed January 30, 2017.

9. John Markoff, "Google's Next Phase in Driverless Cars: No Steering Wheel or Brake Pedals," *The New York Times*, May 27, 2014, http://www.nytimes.com/2014/05/28 /technology/googles-next-phase-in-driverless-cars-no-brakes-or-steering-wheel. html; Tim Higgins, "Google's Self-Driving Car Program Odometer Reaches 2 Million Miles," *Wall Street Journal*, October 5, 2016, sec. Tech, http://www.wsj.com/articles /googles-self-driving-car-program-odometer-reaches-2-million-miles-1475683321.

10. Alex Davies, "How Daimler Built the World's First Self-Driving Semi," *WIRED*, May 11, 2015, http://www.wired.com/2015/05/daimler-built-worlds-first-self-driving-semi/.

11. Burford Furman et al., "Automated Transit Networks (ATN): A Review of the State of the Industry and Prospects for the Future," Mineta Transportation Institute Report, September 2014, http://trid.trb.org/view/2014/M/1323833.

12. CityMobil2, "Cities Demonstrating Automated Road Passenger Transport," accessed June 2, 2015, http://www.citymobil2.eu/en/; "Easymile | Shared Driverless Vehicles | Driverless Transportation," *EasyMile*, accessed January 30, 2017, http://easymile .com/; "Delphi Selected by Singapore Land Transport Authority for Autonomous Vehicle Mobility-on-Demand Program," http://investor.delphi.com/investors /press-releases/press-release-details/2016/Delphi-Selected-by-Singapore-Land

-Transport-Authority-for-Autonomous-Vehicle-Mobility-on-Demand-Program /default.aspx, accessed January 30, 2017.

13. Steven Shladover, "What If Cars Could Drive Themselves?," *ACCESS Magazine* 1, no. 16 (2000), http://escholarship.org/uc/item/0v70n7p2; Sebastian Thrun, "Toward Robotic Cars," *Communications of the ACM* 53, no. 4 (April 1, 2010): 99–106, doi:10.1145/1721654.1721679; Daniel Fagnant and Kara Kockelman, "The Travel and Environmental Implications of Shared Autonomous Vehicles, Using Agent-Based Model Scenarios," *Transportation Research Part C: Emerging Technologies* 40 (2014): 1–13, doi:10.1016/j.trc.2013.12.001; James Anderson et al., "Autonomous Vehicle Technology: A Guide for Policymakers" (Washington, DC: RAND Corporation, 2014); Clifford Winston and Fred Mannering, "Implementing Technology to Improve Public Highway Performance: A Leapfrog Technology from the Private Sector Is Going to Be Necessary," *Economics of Transportation* 3, no. 2 (2014): 158–65, doi:10.1016/j.ecotra.2013.12.004.

14. Adam Millard-Ball, "Pedestrians, Autonomous Vehicles, and Cities," *Journal of Planning Education and Research*, October 27, 2016, doi:10.1177/0739456X16675674.

15. National Association of City Transportation Officials, "NACTO Releases Policy Recommendations for the Future of Automated Vehicles," June 23, 2016, http://nacto .org/2016/06/23/nacto-releases-policy-recommendations-for-automated-vehicles/.

16. Furman et al., "Automated Transit Networks (ATN)"; CityMobil2, "Cities Demonstrating Automated Road Passenger Transport."

17. Guerra, "Planning for Cars That Drive Themselves."

18. Donald Shoup, *The High Cost of Free Parking* (Chicago: Planners Press, American Planning Association, 2005).

19. Mikhail Chester, Arpad Horvath, and Samer Madanat, "Parking Infrastructure: Energy, Emissions, and Automobile Life-Cycle Environmental Accounting," *Environmental Research Letters* 5, no. 3 (2010): 034001, doi:10.1088/1748-9326/5/3/034001.

20. Ibid.; Michael Manville and Donald Shoup, "Parking, People, and Cities," *Journal of Urban Planning and Development* 131, no. 4 (2005): 233–45, doi:10.1061 /(ASCE)0733-9488(2005)131:4(233).

21. Manville and Shoup, "Parking, People, and Cities"; Chester et al., "Parking Infrastructure."

22. Shoup, *The High Cost of Free Parking*.

23. Timothy Sider et al., "Smog and Socioeconomics: An Evaluation of Equity in Traffic-Related Air Pollution Generation and Exposure," *Environment and Planning B: Planning and Design* 42, no. 5 (2015): 870–87, doi:10.1068/b130140p.

24. Melvin M. Webber, *The Urban Place and the Nonplace Urban Realm*, 1964.

25. Tim Althoff, Ryen W. White, and Eric Horvitz, "Influence of Pokémon Go on Physical Activity: Study and Implications," *arXiv:1610.02085 [Cs]*, October 6, 2016, http://arxiv.org/abs/1610.02085.

26. David Jones, *Mass Motorization and Mass Transit: An American History and Policy Analysis* (Bloomington: Indiana University Press, 2008).

27. "The Head of CMU's Robotics Lab Says Self-Driving Cars Are 'Not Even Close,'" *Motherboard*, https://motherboard.vice.com/en_us/article/robotics-lab-uber-gutted -says-driving-cars-are-not-even-close-carnegie-mellon-nrec, accessed February 1, 2017.

CHAPTER 11

1. Robert Cervero, "Why Go Anywhere?" *Scientific American* 273, no. 3 (1995): 92–93.

2. Peter Newman and Jeffrey Kenworthy, *Cities and Automobile Dependence: A Sourcebook* (Aldershot, England: Grower, 1989); Reid Ewing and Robert Cervero, "Travel and the Built Environment," *Journal of the American Planning Association* 76 (2010): 262–94.

3. Ewing and Cervero, "Travel and the Built Environment," 276.

4. Zhan Guo, Asha W. Agrawal, and Jennifer Dill, "Are Land Use Planning and Congestion Pricing Mutually Supportive? Evidence from a Pilot Mileage Fee Program in Portland, OR,," *Journal of the American Planning Association* 77, no. 3 (2011): 232–50.

5. See TomTom Traffic Index on worldwide traffic congestion: http://www.tomtom .com/en_gb/trafficindex/list.

6. Wendall Cox, "New Zealand Has Worst Traffic Congestion: International Data," *New Geography*, November 13, 2013; see www.negeography.com/content/004048 -new-zealand-has-worst-traffic-international-data, accessed February 15, 2017.

7. The exponential decay relationship between VMT per capita and urban densities holds at multiple geographic scales, regardless of whether data observations are cities, districts, or neighborhoods. See Newman and Kenworthy, *Cities and Automobile Dependence*; Ewing and Cervero, "Travel and the Built Environment," 87–114.

8. Hiroaki Suzuki, Robert Cervero, and Kanako Iuchi, "Transforming Cities with Transit," (Washington, DC: World Bank, 2013).

9. Eric Eidler, "The Worst of All World: Los Angeles, California, and the Emerging Reality of Dense Sprawl," *Transportation Research Record: Journal of the Transportation Research Board* 1902 (2005): 1–9.

10. Robert Cervero, *The Transit Metropolis: A Global Inquiry* (Washington, DC: Island Press, 1998).

11. Steven Fader, *Density by Design: New Directions in Residential Development* (Washington, DC: Urban Land Institute, 2000).

12. Robert Cervero and Peter Bosselmann, "Transit Villages: Assessing the Market Potential through Visual Simulation," *Journal of Architecture and Planning Research* 15, no. 3 (1998): 181–96; Reid Ewing and Keith Bartholomew, *Pedestrian- and Transit-Oriented Design* (Washington, DC: Urban Land Institute and American Planning Association, 2013).

13. Erick Guerra and Robert Cervero, "Cost of a Ride: The Effects of Densities on Fixed-Guideway Transit Ridership and Costs," *Journal of the American Planning Association* 77, no. 3 (2011): 27–290.

14. UN Habitat, *Urbanization and Development: Emerging Futures* (Nairobi: UN Habitat, World Cities Report, 2016).

15. Brian Taylor, et al., "Typecasting Neighborhoods and Travelers: Analyzing the Geography of Travel Behavior Among Teens and Young Adults in the US" (Los Angeles: UCLA Luskin School of Public Affairs, Institute of Transportation Studies, 2015), http: //www.lewis.ucla.edu/wp-content/uploads/sites/2/2015/10/Geography-of-Youth -Travel_Final-Report.pdf?mc_cid=68d255b9a1&mc_eid=cc6e1ea4c7.

16. Todd Litman, "The Future Isn't What It Used to Be: Changing Trends and Their Implications for Transportation Planning" (Victoria, BC: Victoria Transport Policy

Institute, 2015), 1–44, http://www.vtpi.org/future.pdf, accessed November 15, 2016.

17. Tony Dutzik, Jeff Inglis, and Phineas Baxandall, "Millennials in Motion: Changing Travel Habits of Young Americans and Implications for Public Policy" (Washington, DC: US PIRG Education Fund, 2014).

18. Michael Sivak and Brandon Schoettle, "Recent Decreases in the Proportion of Persons with a Driver's License across All Age Groups," University of Michigan Transportation Research Institute, UMTRI-2016-5, 2016, http://www.umich.edu/~umtriswt/PDF/UMTRI-2016-4.pdf, accessed January 24, 2017.

19. Ibid.; Michael Sivak, "Has Motorization in the U.S. Peaked? Vehicle Ownership and Distance Drive, 1984 to 2015," University of Michigan Transportation Research Institute, Report no. SWT-2017-4, http://www.umich.edu/~umtriswt/PDF/SWT-2017-4.pdf, accessed February 14, 2017.

20. Luke J. Juday, "The Changing Shape of American Cities" (Charlottesville: Demographics Research Group, Weldon Cooper Center for Public Service, University of Virginia, 2015), http://www.coopercenter.org/sites/default/files/node/13/ChangingShape-AmericanCities_UVACooperCenter_March2015.pdf, accessed September 23, 2016.

21. Ibid.

22. Taylor et al., "Typecasting Neighborhoods and Travelers"; Juday, "The Changing Shape of American Cities."

23. Taylor et al., "Typecasting Neighborhoods and Travelers"; Lisa Rayle, et al., "Just a Better Taxi? A Survey-Based Comparison of Taxis, Transit, and Ridesourcing Services in San Francisco," *Transport Policy* 45 (2016): 168–78.

24. Brad Broberg, "Where Are the New Jobs Going?" *On Common Ground*, Summer 2016, 4–6.

25. Rob Valletta and Catherine van der List, "Involuntary Part-Time Work: Here to Stay?" San Francisco, Federal Reserve Bank of San Francisco, June 2015, http://www.frbsf.org/economic-research/files/el2015-19.pdf, accessed January 11, 2017.

26. Rayle et al., "Just a Better Taxi?"

27. American Association of State Highway and Transportation Officials (AASHTO), "Commuting in America: The National Report on Commuting Patterns and Trends" (Washington, DC: AASHTO, 2015).

28. Robert Cervero, "Land-Use Mixing and Suburban Mobility," *Transportation Quarterly* 42, no. 3 (1988): 429–46.

29. Reid Ewing, "Measuring Transportation Performance," *Transportation Quarterly* 49, no. 1 (1995): 91–104; Reid Ewing, "Beyond Speed: The Next Generation of Transportation Performance Measures," in *Transportation & Land Use Innovations: When You Can't Pave Your Way out of Traffic Congestion* (Chicago: Planners Press, 1996).

30. The state of Florida, which in 1993 set concurrency standards to ensure that adequate supplies of roads and other infrastructure were in place to accommodate new growth, later introduced areawide averaging of LOS. In fast-growing cities such as Orlando, infill development was allowed even if conditions at some intersections and along some segments deteriorated as long as the overall system was working fairly well. See Ewing, "Beyond Speed."

31. Todd Littman, "Multi-modal Level-of-Service Indicators: Tools for Evaluating the Quality of Transportation Services and Facilities," in *TDM Encyclopedia* (Victoria, BC: Victoria Transport Policy Institute, 2015), www.vtpi.org/tdm/tdm129.htm, accessed February 14, 2017.

32. Cervero, *The Transit Metropolis.*

33. Reid Ewing, et al., "Traffic Generated by Mixed-Use Developments: A Six-Region Study Using Consistent Built Environmental Measures," *Journal of Urban Planning and Development* 137, no. 3 (2011): 248–61; Hollie Lund, Robert Cervero, and Richard Willson, "A Re-evaluation of Travel Behavior in California TODs," *Journal of Architecture and Planning Research* 23, no. 3 (2006): 247–63; Robert Cervero and G. Arrington, "Vehicle Trip Reduction Impacts of Transit-Oriented Housing," *Journal of Public Transportation* 11, no. 3 (2008): 1–17; Robert Cervero, Arlie Adkins, and Catherine Sullivan, "Are Suburban TODs Over-Parked?," *Journal of Public Transportation* 13, no. 2 (2010): 47–70.

34. Robert Cervero, "Going Beyond Travel-Time Savings: An Expanded Framework for Evaluating Urban Transport Projects" (Washington, DC: The International Bank for Reconstruction and Development/The World Bank, Department for International Development, Transport Research Support Program, 2011), http://siteresources.worldbank.org/INTTRANSPORT/Resources /336291-1239112757744/5997693-1294344242332/Traveltimesaving.pdf.

35. David Metz, "The Myth of Travel Time Savings," *Transport Reviews* 28, no. 3 (2008): 321–36; Cervero, "Going Beyond Travel-Time Savings."

36. Fabio Casiroli, "The Mobility DNA of Cities," *Urban Age* (December 2009): 1–3.

37. Cervero, "Going Beyond Travel-Time Savings."

38. UN Habitat, "Global Report on Human Settlements: Planning and Design for Sustainable Urban Mobility" (Nairobi: UN Habitat, 2013).

39. Cervero, *The Transit Metropolis*; Erick Guerra, "Mexico City's Suburban Land Use and Transit Connection: The Effects of the Line B Metro Expansion," *Transport Policy* 32 (2014): 105–14.

40. Eduardo Vasconcellos, *Urban Transport, Environment and Equity: The Case for Developing Countries* (London: Earthscan, 2001); Robin Carruthers, Malise Dick, and Anuja Saurkar, "Affordability of Public Transport in Developing Countries," World Bank Transport Paper TP-3 (Washington, DC: World Bank, 2005).

41. Miriam Zuk, et al., "Gentrification, Displacement and the Role of Public Investment: A Literature Review," Working Paper 2015-05 (San Francisco: Federal Research Bank of San Francisco, August 2015), http://www.frbsf.org/community-development/.

42. Emily Talen, Sunny Menozzi, and Chloe Schaefer, "What Is a 'Great Neighborhood'? An Analysis of APA's Top-Rated Places," *Journal of the American Planning Association* 81, no. 2 (2015): 121–41.

43. Sharon Zukin, *Naked City: The Death and Life of Authentic Urban Places* (New York: Oxford University Press, 2009); Zuk et al., "Gentrification, Displacement and the Role of Public Investment."

44. Teresa Caldeira, *City of Walls: Crime, Segregation and Citizenship in São Paulo* (Berkeley: University of California Press, 2001).

45. Susan Fainstein, *The Just City* (Ithaca, NY: Cornell University Press, 2011); Zuk et al., "Gentrification, Displacement and the Role of Public Investment."

46. Richard Florida, *The Rise of the Creative Class: And How It's Transforming Work, Leisure, Community and Everyday Life* (New York: Basic Books, 2002); Lance Freeman and Frank Braconi, "Gentrification and Displacement New York City in the 1990s," *Journal of the American Planning Association* 70, no. 1 (2004): 39–52.

47. Joseph Cortright and Dillon Mahmoudi, "Neighborhood Change, 1970 to 2010 Transition and Growth in Urban High Poverty Neighborhoods," Impresa Consulting, http://impresaconsulting.com/sites/all/les/Cortright_Neighborhood_Change _2014.pdf, accessed January 26, 2017.

48. Jackelyn Hwanga and Robert J. Sampson, "Divergent Pathways of Gentrification: Racial Inequality and the Social Order of Renewal in Chicago Neighborhoods," *American Sociological Review* 79, no. 4 (2014): 726–51.

49. Greg Lindsay, "Now Arriving: A Connected Mobility Roadmap for Public Transport" (Montreal: New Cities Foundation, 2016).

50. Michael Southworth and Erin Ben-Joseph, *Streets and the Shaping of Towns and Cities* (Washington, DC: Island Press, 2003).

51. Gerritt J. Knaap, Chengr Ding, and Lewis Hopkins, "Do Plans Matter? The Effects of Light Rail Plans on Land Values in Station Areas," *Journal of Planning Education and Research* 21, no. 1 (2001): 32–39; Zuk et al., "Gentrification, Displacement and the Role of Public Investment."

52. Nancy Andrews and Audrey Choi, "Equitable Transit-Oriented Development: A New Paradigm for Inclusive Growth in Metropolitan America" (San Francisco: Morgan Stanley, 2016), http://www.liifund.org/justgoodcapital/2016/10/11/equitable -transit-oriented-development-new-paradigm-inclusive-growth-metropolitan- america/, accessed December 15, 2016.

53. Cervero, *The Transit Metropolis.*

54. See http://www.singstat.gov.sg/statistics, accessed March 24, 2017.

55. Michael Sorkin, ed., *Variations on a Theme Park: The New American City and the End of Public Space* (New York: Macmillan, 1992); Stefan Al, ed., *Mall City: Hong Kong's Dreamworlds of Consumption* (Honolulu: University of Hawaii Press, 2016).

56. Project for Public Space, "Placemaking & the Future of Cities" (New York: Project for Public Space, 2015).

57. Kenneth T. Jackson, *Crabgrass Frontier: The Suburbanization of the United States* (New York: Oxford University Press, 1985).

58. Susannah Nesmith, "Miami Street Experiment Prioritizes People," *Planning* (March 2017): 10.

SELECTED BIBLIOGRAPHY

Angel, Shlomo. *Planet of Cities*. Cambridge, MA: Lincoln Institute of Land Policy, 2012.

Appleyard, Don. *Liveable Streets*. Berkeley, CA: University of California Press, 1981.

Banister, David. *Unsustainable Transport: City Transport in the 21st Century*. London: Routledge, 2005.

Beatley, Timothy. *Green Urbanism: Learning from European Cities*, Washington, DC: Island Press, 2000.

Bernick, Michael, and Robert Cervero. *Transit Villages for the 21st Century*. New York: McGraw-Hill, 1997.

Black, William. *Sustainable Transportation: Problems and Solutions*. New York: Guilford Press, 2010.

Calthorpe, Peter. *The New American Metropolis: Ecology, Community, and the American Dream*. New York: Princeton Architectural Press, 1993.

Calthorpe, Peter. *Urbanism in the Age of Climate Change*. Washington, DC: Island Press, 2011.

Cervero, Robert. *The Transit Metropolis: A Global Inquiry*. Washington, DC: Island Press, 1998.

Dunham-Jones, Ellen, and June Williamson. *Retrofitting Suburbia: Urban Design Solutions for Redesigning Suburbs*. New York: John Wiley & Sons, 2009.

Duranton, Gilles, and Erick Guerra. *Developing a Common Narrative on Urban Accessibility: An Urban Planning Perspective*. Washington, DC: Brookings Institution, 2017.

Ewing, Reid, and Keith Bartholomew. *Pedestrian- & Transit-Oriented Design*. Washington, DC: Urban Land Institute and the American Planning Association, 2013.

Ewing, Reid, and Shima Hamidi. *Costs of Sprawl*. New York: Routledge, 2017.

Fainstein, Susan. *The Just City*. Ithaca, NY: Cornell University Press, 2011.

Florida, Richard. *The Rise of the Creative Class: And How It's Transforming Work, Leisure, Community and Everyday Life*. New York: Basic Books, 2002.

Fraker, Harrison. *The Hidden Potential of Sustainable Neighborhoods: Lessons from Low-Carbon Communities*. Washington DC: Island Press, 2013.

Gehl, Jan. *Cities for People*. Washington, DC: Island Press, 2010.

Givoni, Moshe, and David Banister. *Moving towards Low Carbon Mobility*. Cheltenham, UK: Edward Elgar, 2013.

Glaeser, Edward L. *Triumph of the City: How Our Greatest Invention Makes Us Richer, Smarter, Greener, Healthier, and Happier*. New York: Penguin, 2011.

Gomez-Ibanez, Jose, William B. Tye, and Clifford Winston, eds. *Transportation Economics and Policy Handbook*. Washington, DC: Brookings Institution Press, 1999.

Hall, Peter. *Cities of Tomorrow: An Intellectual History of Urban Planning and Design in the Twentieth Century*. Oxford, UK: Blackwell, 2002.

Hall, Peter. *Good Cities, Better Lives: How Europe Discovered the Lost Art of Urbanism*. London: Routledge, 2014.

Hanson, Susan, and Genevieve Giuliano, eds. *The Geography of Urban Transportation*, 3rd ed. New York: The Guilford Press, 2004.

Hickman, Robin, Moshe Givoni, David Bonilla, and David Banister, eds. *Handbook on Transport and Development*. Cheltenham, UK: Edward Elgar, 2015.

Jacobs, Allan. *Great Streets*. Cambridge, MA: MIT Press, 1993.

Kaufmann, Vincent. *Re-thinking Mobility: Contemporary Sociology*. Aldershot, UK: Ashgate, 2002.

Newman, Peter, Timothy Beatley, and Heather Boyer. *Resilient Cities: Responding to Peak Oil and Climate Change*. Washington, DC: Island Press, 2009.

Newman, Peter, and Jeffrey Kenworthy. *The End of Automobile Dependency: How Cities Are Moving Beyond Car-Based Planning*. Washington, DC: Island Press, 2015.

Putnam, Robert. *Bowling Alone: The Collapse and Revival of American Community*. New York: Simon & Schuster, 2000.

Southworth, Michael, and Eran Ben-Joseph. *Streets and the Shaping of Towns and Cities*. Washington, DC: Island Press, 2013.

Suzuki, Hiroaki, Robert Cervero, and Kanako Iuchi. 2013. *Transforming Cities with Transit: Transit and Land-Use Integration for Sustainable Urban Development*. Washington, DC: World Bank Publications, 2013.

Vasconcellos, Eduardo. *Urban Transport, Environment and Equity: The Case for Developing Countries*. London: Earthscan, 2001.

Whyte, William Hollingsworth. *The Social Life of Small Urban Spaces*. Washington, DC: The Conservation Foundation, 1980.

INDEX

Page numbers followed by "f" indicate drawings and photographs and page numbers followed by "t" indicate tables.